OXFORD SHAKESPEARE CONCORDANCES

OXFORD SHAKESPEARE CONCORDANCES

THE COMEDY OF ERRORS

A CONCORDANCE TO THE TEXT
OF THE FIRST FOLIO

OXFORD
AT THE CLARENDON PRESS
1969

Oxford University Press, Ely House, London W.1

GLASGOW NEW YORK TORONTO MELBOURNE WELLINGTON
CAPE TOWN SALISBURY IBADAN NAIROBI LUSAKA ADDIS ABABA
BOMBAY CALCUTTA MADRAS KARACHI LAHORE DACCA
KUALA LUMPUR SINGAPORE HONG KONG TOKYO

FILMSET BY COMPUTAPRINT LIMITED
AND PRINTED IN GREAT BRITAIN
AT THE UNIVERSITY PRESS, OXFORD
BY VIVIAN RIDLER
PRINTER TO THE UNIVERSITY

THE COMEDY OF ERRORS

The Lee facsimile of the First Folio (Oxford, 1902) from which the concordance to *Err.* was made demonstrates the corrected variant of H2^v, recorded by Professor Hinman (*Printing and Proof-Reading*, Oxford, 1963, v. 1, p. 257). His order of printing (v. 2, p. 514) for this section of F runs:

D D	D? B	D B	D? D	D? B	D? B	Ax A*x
H3^v:4	H3:4^v	H2^v:5	H2:5^v	H1^v:6	H1:6^v	I3^v:4

				A*x	
By A*x	By A*x	By A*x	By A*x	By By	
I3:4^v	I1^v:6	I2:5^v	I1:6^v	I2^v:5	

TABLE OF LINE AND ACT/SCENE NUMBERS

Page	Col.	Comp.	F line nos.	Globe act/scene nos.
H1	a	D?	1–49	1.1.1–1.1.46
	b	D?m	50–99	1.1.96
H1^v	a	D?	100–64	1.2.2
	b	D?	165–229	1.2.64
H2	a	D?	230–88	2.1.14
	b	D?	289–353	2.1.77
H2^v	a	D	354–419	2.2.24
	b	D	420–85	2.2.92
H3	a	D?	486–549	2.2.156
	b	D?	550–615	2.2.221
H3^v	a	D	616–76	3.1.46
	b	D	677–742	3.1.81
H4	a	D	743–808	3.2.22
	b	D	809–74	3.2.83
H4^v	a	B	875–940	3.2.155
	b	B	941–97	4.1.15
H5	a	B	998–1063	4.1.75
	b	B	1064–1127	4.2.21
H5^v	a	D	1128–90	4.3.7
	b	D	1191–1254	4.3.72
H6	a	B	1125–1317	4.3.139
	b	B	1318–81	4.4.96
H6^v	a	B	1382–1445	4.4.149
	b	B	1446–1503	5.1.37
I1	a	B	1504–67	5.1.98
	b	B	1568–1630	5.1.158

Page	Col.	Comp.	F line nos.	Globe act/scene nos.
I1ᵛ	a	B	1631–94	5.1.217
	b	B	1695–1760	5.1.281
I2	a	B	1761–1822	5.1.337
	b	B	1823–88	5.1.398
I2ᵛ	a	B	1889–1903	5.1.411
	b	B	1904–20	5.1.426

The following misprints, etc. have been corrected in the text:

H2	314	bereft , (the mark after t removed)
H4	743	afether,
H6	1366	crontraries?

June 1968

T. H. H.

PREFACE

ALTHOUGH responsibility for the text and arrangement of the concordances is solely that of the editor, their preparation has entailed the laborious collaboration of many individuals and organizations, to whom the Press and the editor are very grateful. The texts were prepared at the English Electric Computers Ltd. Data Processing Bureau, London, under the supervision of Mr. David Lyon; Mrs. Elizabeth Lyon undertook the first proof-reading of the uncorrected texts. The main concordance programmes were written and tested by Miss Patricia Fell of the Bureau Support Group, English Electric Computers, Ltd., Kidsgrove, Staffs., and were run on the KDF9 computer at the Oxford University Computing Laboratory, Oxford. Without the continued and valued co-operation of the Director, staff, and (particularly) operators at the Laboratory, this project would have come to nothing. The magnetic tapes were prepared for publication by filmsetting by Computaprint, Ltd., London. The editor is greatly obliged to the secretarial staff of the Clarendon Press, who encouraged him to undertake this work and who continually supported him through all the vicissitudes of its preparation. What good lies in these concordances must be credited, after Shakespeare, to these people and others too numerous to mention.

T. H. HOWARD-HILL

'*Trevenny*'
Noke, Oxford

GENERAL INTRODUCTION

IN this series of Oxford Shakespeare Concordances, a separate volume is devoted to each of the plays. The text for each concordance is the one chosen as copy-text by Dr. Alice Walker for the Oxford Old Spelling Shakespeare now in preparation.

Each concordance takes account of every word in the text, and represents their occurrence by frequency counts, line numbers, and reference lines, or a selection of these according to the interest of the particular word. The number of words which have frequency counts only has been kept as low as possible. The introduction to each volume records the facsimile copy of the text from which the concordance was prepared, a table of Folio through line numbers and Globe edition act and scene numbers, a list of the misprints corrected in the text, and an account of the order of printing, and the proof-reading, abstracted from Professor Charlton Hinman's *The Printing and Proof-Reading of the First Folio of Shakespeare* (Oxford, 1963).

The following notes on the main features of the concordances may be helpful.[1]

A. *The Text*

The most obvious misprints have been corrected, on conservative principles, and have been listed for each play in the introduction to the corresponding concordance. Wrong-fount letters have been silently corrected.

Obvious irregularities on the part of the original compositor—for example the anomalous absence of full stops after speech prefixes—have been normalized and noted. Colons, semicolons, exclamation and interrogation marks after italicized words have been modernized to roman fount after current practice, since this aspect of

---

[1] An account of the principles and methods by which the concordances were edited appears in *Studies in Bibliography*, vol. 22, 1969.

compositorial practice would not normally be studied from a concordance. The spacing of words in the original printed texts, particularly in 'justified' lines, is extremely variable; spacing has been normalized on the basis of the compositor's practice as revealed in the particular column or page.

For ease of reference, the contractions *S.*, *L.*, *M.*, and forms such as *Mist.* and tildes, have been expanded when the compositor's own preferred practice is clear, and the expansion has been noted in the text. For M^r, the superior character has been lowered silently. Superior characters like the circumflex in *baâ* and those in $\overset{t}{y}$, $\overset{e}{y}$, $\overset{u}{y}$, and $\overset{c}{w}$, have been ignored. The reader should find little difficulty in distinguishing the original form of the pronominal contractions when they are encountered in the text. They are listed under Y and W respectively.

B. *Arrangement of entries*

The words in the text are arranged alphabetically, with numerals and & and &c listed at the end. Words starting with I and J, and U and V, will be found together under I and V respectively. The reader should note that the use of U for the medial V (and I for J) leads in some cases to an unfamiliar order of entry. For example, ADUISED is listed before ADULTERY. The reader will usually find the word he wants if he starts his inquiry at the modern spelling, for when the old spelling differs considerably from the modern spelling, a reference such as 'ENFORCE *see* inforce' will direct the reader to the entry in the concordance.

In hyphenated compounds where the hyphen is the second or third character of the heading-word (as in A-BOORD), the hyphenated form may be listed some distance from other occurrences of the same word in un-hyphenated form. In significant cases, references are given to alert the user.

Under the heading-word, the line numbers or lines of context are in the order of the text. The heading-word is followed by a frequency count of the words in short and long (that is, marked with an asterisk) lines, and the reference lines. When a word has been treated as one to have a frequency count only, or a list of the line numbers and count, any further count which follows will refer to the reference lines listed under the same heading. Where there are two counts but no reference lines (as with AN), the first count refers to the speech prefix.

C. *Special Forms*

(*a*) The following words have not been given context lines and line references but are dealt with only by the counting of their frequency:

A AM AND ARE AT BE BY HE I IN IS IT OF ON SHE THE THEY TO WAS WE WITH YOU

These forms occur so often in most texts that the reader can locate them more easily by examining the text of the play than he could by referring to an extensive listing in the concordance.

Homographs of these words (for example I = *ay*) have been listed in full and are given separate counts under the same heading-word.

(*b*) A larger number of words, consisting mainly of variant spellings, have been given line references as well as frequency counts.

These words are: ACTUS AN AR ART ATT AU BEE BEEING BEEN BEENE BEING BENE BIN BUT CAN CANST CE COULD COULDST DE DECIMA DES DID DIDD DIDDEST DIDDST DO DOE DOES DOEST DOETH DONE DOO DOOE DOOES DOOEST DOOING DOON DOONE DOOS DOOST DOOTH DOS DOST DOTH DU E EN EST ET ETC FINIS FOR FROM HA HAD HADST HAH HAS HAST HATH HAUE HEE HEEL HEELE HEL HELL HER HIM HIR HIS IE IF IL ILL ILLE INTO LA LE LES MA MAIE MAIEST MAIST MAY ME MEE MIGHT MIGHTEST MIGHTST MINE MOI MOY MY NE NO NOE NON NONA NOR NOT O OCTAUA OFF OH OR OU OUR OUT PRIMA PRIMUS QUARTA QUARTUS QUE QUINTA QUINTUS SCAENA SCENA SCOENA SECUNDA SECUNDUS SEPTIMA SEPTIMUS SEXTA SHAL SHALL SHALT SHEE SHOLD SHOLDE SHOLDST SHOULD SHOULDE SHOULDST SIR SO SOE TE TERTIA TERTIUS THAT THEE THEIR THEIRE THEM THEN THER THERE THESE THEYR THIS THOSE THOU THY TIS TU VN VNE VOS VOSTRE VOUS VS WAST WEE WER WERE WERT WHAT WHEN WHER WHERE WHICH WHO WHOM WHOME WHY WIL WILL WILT WILTE WOLD WOLDE WOLDST WOULD WOULDE WOULDEST WOULDST YE YEE YF YOUE YOUR YT & &c 1 2 3 4.

Homographs of words on this list (e.g. *bee* = n.) have been listed in full, and also have separate counts.

(*c*) All speech prefixes, other than *All.*, *Both.*, and those which represent the names of actors, have been treated as count-only words. In some cases, however, where a speech prefix corresponds to a form already on the count-only list (e.g. *Is.*), a full entry has been given. In some other cases, when two counts are given for the same heading-word for no apparent reason, the count which does not correspond to the following full references or to the list of line references is that of the speech prefix form (for example AN in *The Tempest*).

(*d*) Hyphenated compounds such as *all-building-law* have been listed under the full form, and also under each main constituent after the first. In this example there are entries under ALL-BUILDING-LAW, BUILDING, and LAW. When, however, one of the constituents of the compound is a word on the count- or location-only list ((*a*) or (*b*) above), it is dealt with in whichever of these two lists applies. References such as 'AT *see also* bemock't-at-stabs' are given to assist the reader in such cases.

Simple or non-hyphenated compounds such as *o'th'King* have been listed only under the constituent parts—in this example under OTH and KING.

(*e*) 'Justified' lines where the spellings *may* have been affected by the compositor's need to fit the text to his measure are distinguished by an asterisk at the beginning of the reference line. If only location is being given, the asterisk occurs before the line reference. If only frequency counts are being given, the number *after* the asterisk records the frequency of forms occurring in 'justified' lines. Lines which do not extend to the full width of the compositor's measure have not been distinguished as 'justified' lines, even though in many cases the shorter line may have affected the spelling.

D. *Line Numbers*

The lines in each text have been numbered from the first *Actus Primus* or stage direction and thereafter in normal reading order, including all stage directions and act and scene divisions. Each typographical line has been counted as a unit when it contains matter for inclusion in the concordance. Catchwords are not included in the count. The only general exception is that turn-overs are regarded as belonging to their base-lines; where a turn-over occurs on a line by itself, it has been reckoned as part of the base-line, and the line containing only the turn-over has not been counted as a separate line. Turn-overs may readily be distinguished by vertical stroke and single bracket after the last word of the base-line; for example *brought with* | (*child*,.

When two or more lines have been joined in order to provide a fuller context, the line-endings are indicated by a vertical stroke |, and the line reference applies to that part of the line before the vertical stroke. For the true line-numbers of words in the following part of the context line, the stated line-number should be increased by one each time a vertical stroke occurs, save when the next word is a turn-over.

The numbering of the quarto texts has been fitted to that of the corresponding Folio texts; lines in the Quarto which do not occur in the Folio are prefixed by +. The line references are similarly specified. The line references of these concordances therefore provide a consistent permanent numbering of each typographical line of text, based on the First Folio.

THE COMEDY OF ERRORS

1

ABOORD = 5
Vnwilling I agreed, alas, too soone wee came aboord.   64
That staies but till her Owner comes aboord,   1075
I haue conuei'd aboord, and I haue bought   1077
I long that we were safe and sound aboord.   1453
Therefore away, to get our stuffe aboord. *Exeunt*   1461
ABOUE = 1
Husband Ile dine aboue with you to day,   ·   603
ABOUT = 4*3
What will you walke with me about the towne,   185
And about euening come your selfe alone,   757
*markes I had about mee, as the marke of my shoulder,   931
Gold. Well sir, I will? Haue you the Chaine about | you?   1027
Gold. 'Tis so: and that selfe chaine about his necke,   1474
That he is borne about inuisible,   1662
These people saw the Chaine about his necke.   1735
ABSENCE = 1
From whom my absence was not six moneths olde,   48
ABUSED = 1
That hath abused and dishonored me,   1675
ACCIDENTALLY = 1
Which accidentally are met together.   1837
ACCORDING = 1
According to the statute of the towne,   168
ACCORDS = 1
Then let your will attend on their accords.   299
ACHE *see* ake
ACKNOWLEDGE = 1
Thou sham'st to acknowledge me in miserie.   1803
ACQUAINTED = 3
Be secret false: what need she be acquainted?   801
As if I were their well acquainted friend,   1185
Belike his wife acquainted with his fits,   1273
ACTUS *l*.1 272 616 980 1462 = 5
AD = *2
ADAM = 1*3
haue you got the picture of old *Adam* new apparel'd?   1197
Ant. What gold is this? What *Adam* do'st thou | meane?   1198
S.Dro. Not that *Adam* that kept the Paradise: but   1200
*that *Adam* that keepes the prison; hee that goes in the   1201
ADDITION = 1
And take vnmingled thence that drop againe | Without addition or
diminishing,   522
ADIUDGED = 1
But though thou art adiudged to the death,   149
ADMIT = 1
To admit no trafficke to our aduerse townes: 19
ADR = 41*21
ADRI = 10*4, 1
Exeunt. Manet Offic. Adri. Luci. Courtizan   1426
ADRIA = 1
ADRIANA see also Ad., Adr., Adri., Adria. = 8*1
Enter Adriana, wife to Antipholis Sereptus, with | Luciana her Sister.   273
Enter Adriana and Luciana.   504
I am not *Adriana*, nor thy wife.   507
Enter Adriana.   ·   706
To *Adriana* Villaine hie thee straight: 1091

ADRIANA cont.

S.Dromio. To Adriana, that is where we din'd,	1098
Enter Adriana and Luciana.	1103
Enter Adriana, Luciana, Courtizan, and a Schoole- |master, call'd Pinch.	1321
*They draw. Enter Adriana, Luciana, Courtezan, & others.	1497

ADUENTURES = 1

And in this mist at all aduentures go.	612

ADUERSE = 1

To admit no trafficke to our aduerse townes:	19

ADUERSITIE = 1*1

A wretched soule bruis'd with aduersitie,	308
*E.Dro. Nay 'tis for me to be patient, I am in aduer- |sitie.	1301

ADUISDE = 1

Sleeping or waking, mad or well aduisde:	609

ADUISED = 1

E.Ant. My Liege, I am aduised what I say,	1691

ADULTERATE = 1

I am possest with an adulterate blot,	535

ADUOCATE = 1

My soule should sue as aduocate for thee:	148

AEMILIA = 3

That hadst a wife once call'd Aemilia,	1828
And speake vnto the same Aemilia.	1831
Fa. If I dreame not, thou art Aemilia,	1838

AFFECTION = 1

Stray'd his affection in vnlawfull loue,	1518

AFFECTIONS = 1

Doe their gay vestments his affections baite?	370

AFFORDS = *1

*Bal. Good meat sir is co(m)mon that euery churle affords.	643

AFFRAID = 1

S.Ant. I see these Witches are affraid of swords.	1448

AFTER = 4

After his brother; and importun'd me	129
Straight after did I meete him with a Chaine.	1436
After you first forswore it on the Mart,	1738
After so long greefe such Natiuitie.	1896

AFTERNOONE = 1

But till this afternoone his passion | Ne're brake into extremity of rage.	1514

AFTERWARD = 1

And afterward consort you till bed time:	191

AGAINE = 16*2

Againe, if any Siracusian borne | Come to the Bay of Ephesus, he dies:	22
If I should pay your worship those againe,	250
Luc. Till he come home againe, I would forbeare.	305
*Adri. Go back againe, thou slaue, & fetch him home.	351
Dro. Goe backe againe, and be new beaten home?	352
As you loue stroakes, so iest with me againe:	403
And take vnmingled thence that drop againe | Without addition or diminishing,	522
*S.Dro. Nor to day here you must not come againe | when you may.	667
Then gentle brother get you in againe;	811
Establish him in his true sence againe.	1331
Luc. God for thy mercy, they are loose againe.	1442
Let's call more helpe to haue them bound againe. | Runne all out.	1444
Enter Antipholus and Dromio againe.	1473
Till I haue brought him to his wits againe,	1565

AGAINE *cont.*

To make of him a formall man againe:	1574
Duke. Yet once againe proclaime it publikely,	1602
Met vs againe, and madly bent on vs	1624
We came againe to binde them: then they fled	1626

AGAINST = 13*2

Now trust me, were it not against our Lawes,	145
Against my Crowne, my oath, my dignity,	146
Heerein you warre against your reputation,	747
Why at this time the dores are made against you.	754
Against your yet vngalled estimation,	763
Against my soules pure truth, why labour you,	824
Dro. In her forhead, arm'd and reuerted, making | warre against her heire.	914
Ile stop mine eares against the Mermaids song.	954
Thither I must, although against my will:	1101
Of his owne doores being shut against his entrance.	1272
On purpose shut the doores against his way:	1274
Against thee presently, if thou dar'st stand:	1495
Against the Lawes and Statutes of this Towne,	1595
Adr. Iustice most sacred Duke against the Abbesse.	1605
E.Ant. Iustice (sweet Prince) against y Woman there:	1673

AGE = 2

Hath homelie age th'alluring beauty tooke	365
I see thy age and dangers make thee dote.	1810

AGREED = 1

Vnwilling I agreed, alas, too soone wee came aboord.	64

AGREES = 1

Adri. How ill agrees it with your grauitie,	562

AH = 3

Ah doe not teare away thy selfe from me;	519
Adr. Ah *Luciana,* did he tempt thee so?	1104
Adr. Ah but I thinke him better then I say:	1131

AIDE = 1

Chac'd vs away: till raising of more aide	1625

AIME = 1

My foode, my fortune, and my sweet hopes aime;	852

AKE = 1

Luce. Let him knocke till it ake.	701

AL = *1

Dro. Marry sir, she's the Kitchin wench, & al grease,	886

ALAS = 4

Vnwilling I agreed, alas, too soone wee came aboord.	64
Alas poore women, make vs not beleeue	807
Luc. Alas how fiery, and how sharpe he lookes.	1333
Adr. Alas, I sent you Monie to redeeme you,	1371

ALBEIT = 1

Albeit my wrongs might make one wiser mad.	1694

ALIKE = 2

Of such a burthen Male, twins both alike:	59
Fortune had left to both of vs alike,	108

ALL = 39*5

*And by the doome of death end woes and all.	6
Excludes all pitty from our threatning lookes:	14
Could all my trauells warrant me they liue.	142
Try all the friends thou hast in *Ephesus,*	155
The villaine is ore-wrought of all my monie.	262

ALL *cont.*
Man more diuine, the Master of all these,	294
Ant. Well sir, learne to iest in good time, there's a | time for all things.	458
An. You would all this time haue prou'd, there is no | time for all things.	494
Who euery word by all my wit being scan'd,	545
Wants wit in all, one word to vnderstand.	546
S.Dro. I neuer spake with her in all my life.	559
Who all for want of pruning, with intrusion,	573
Or sleepe I now, and thinke I heare all this?	578
And in this mist at all aduentures go.	612
E.Anti. Good signior *Angelo* you must excuse vs all,	619
Luce. What needs all that, and a paire of stocks in the | towne?	704
Adr. Who is that at the doore y keeps all this noise?	707
And let vs to the Tyger all to dinner,	756
Luc. All this my sister is, or else should be.	854
Ant. Where *America*, the *Indies*? | *Dro.* Oh sir, vpon her nose, all ore embellished with	922
As all the mettall in your shop will answer.	1070
Blowes faire from land: they stay for nought at all,	1080
A Wolfe, nay worse, a fellow all in buffe:	1145
Thou art, as you are all a sorceresse:	1249
E.Dro. Here's that I warrant you will pay them all.	1291
I coniure thee by all the Saints in heauen.	1341
Ant. Dissembling harlot, thou art false in all,	1389
Cur. When as your husband all in rage to day	1433
Let's call more helpe to haue them bound againe. | *Runne all out.*	1444
Ant. I will not stay to night for all the Towne,	1460
Who I made Lord of me, and all I had,	1609
With him his bondman, all as mad as he,	1613
To do him all the grace and good I could.	1636
I thinke you all haue drunke of *Circes* cup:	1747
I thinke you are all mated, or starke mad.	1760
And all the Conduits of my blood froze vp:	1794
All these old witnesses, I cannot erre.	1798
Ant. The Duke, and all that know me in the City,	1804
All gather to see them.	1815
And the twin *Dromio*, all were taken vp;	1842
And heare at large discoursed all our fortunes,	1885
And all that are assembled in this place:	1886
Duke. With all my heart, Ile Gossip at this feast.	1897

ALLIES = 1
The passages of allies, creekes, and narrow lands:	1147

ALLURING = 1
Hath homelie age th'alluring beauty tooke	365

ALMANACKE = 1
Here comes the almanacke of my true date:	206

ALMOST = 3
Before her selfe (almost at fainting vnder	49
Hath almost made me Traitor to my selfe:	952
I haue not breath'd almost since I did see it.	1654

ALONE = 3
Would that alone, a loue he would detaine,	383
And about euening come your selfe alone,	757
Alone, it was the subiect of my Theame:	1534

ALONG = 1 *1
Ant. Come goe along, my wife is comming yon-|der.	1323

5

ALONG *cont.*
   *By'th'way, we met my wife, her sister, and a rabble more | Of vilde
   Confederates: Along with them   1712
ALTERD = 1
   How now sir, is your merrie humor alter'd?   402
ALTHOUGH = 1
   Thither I must, although against my will: 1101
ALTOGETHER = 1
   Cries out, I was possest. Then altogether   1722
ALWAIES = 1*1
   Before the alwaies winde-obeying deepe   66
   *thinkes a man alwaies going to bed, and saies, God giue | you good
   rest.   1215
AM *see also* I'me = 44*14
AMAINE = 1
   Two shippes from farre, making amaine to vs: 95
AMAZD = *1
   *that I amaz'd ranne from her as a witch. And I thinke, if   933
AMENDS = *1
   **Ant.* Ile make you amends next, to giue you nothing   448
AMERICA = 1
   Ant. Where *America,* the *Indies?* | *Dro.* Oh sir, vpon her nose, all ore
   embellished with   922
AMISSE = 1
   What error driues our eies and eares amisse?   579
AMONG = 1
   Among my wife, and their confederates,   999
AMOUNT = 2
   Cannot amount vnto a hundred Markes,   28
   Which doth amount to three odde Duckets more   1013
AMPLE = 1
   Ran hether to your Grace, whom I beseech | To giue me ample
   satisfaction   1728
AN *l.**409 472 535 568 593 595 597 633 637 677 745 806 825 *868 *901
   975 981 1051 *1119 1142 1177 *1203 1212 *1219 *1238 1308 *1310 1707
   1746 = 5*4 = 21*8
ANATOMIE = 1
   A meere Anatomie, a Mountebanke,   1715
AND = 366*73, 2*2
   Nay, and you will not sir, Ile take my heeles.   259
   *I had rather haue it a head, and you vse these blows   431
   Ant. And if I haue not sir, I hope you haue: 1029
   *be wise, and if you giue it her, the diuell will shake | her Chaine, and
   fright vs with it.   1257
ANG = 4*2
ANGEL = *1
   *came behinde you sir, like an euill angel, and bid you for- | sake your
   libertie.   1203
ANGELO see also Ang. = *1, 2*2
   **Enter Antipholus of Ephesus, his man Dromio, Angelo the | Goldsmith,*
   and Balthaser the Merchant.   617
   **E.Anti.* Good signior *Angelo* you must excuse vs all,   619
   Enter Angelo with the Chaine.   955
   Off. One *Angelo* a Goldsmith, do you know him?   1427
ANGELS = *2
   *Delay: Here are the angels that you sent for to deliuer | you. 1222
   *they appeare to men like angels of light, light is an   1238

ANIE = *1
*S.Dro. Was there euer anie man thus beaten out of   442
ANON = 3
Anon I'me sure the Duke himselfe in person   1588
Anon I wot not, by what strong escape   1620
Come go with vs, wee'l looke to that anon,   1904
ANOTHER = 4*2
At length another ship had seiz'd on vs,   115
That in the Ocean seekes another drop,   200
*S.Dro. Lest it make you choilericke, and purchase me | another drie
basting.   456
*S.Dro. Yes, to pay a fine for a perewig, and recouer | the lost haire of
another man.   469
*Luce. Haue at you with another, that's when? can | you tell?   688
*And now let's go hand in hand, not one before another. | Exeunt.   1918
ANSWER = 7*2
Ant. Now as I am a Christian answer me,   242
S.Dro. What answer sir? when spake I such a word?   408
*May answer my good will, and your good welcom here.   639
Good sir say, whe'r you'l answer me, or no: 1046
Ant. I answer you? What should I answer you.   1048
As all the mettall in your shop will answer.   1070
*any man to answer it that breakes his Band: one that   1214
Why beare you these rebukes, and answer not?   1558
ANSWERD = *1
*S.Dro. If thy name be cailed Luce, Luce thou hast an-|swer'd him
well.   690
ANSWERE = 1
That thus so madlie thou did didst answere me?   407
ANSWERST = *1
*Luc. Why prat'st thou to thy selfe, and answer'st not?   588
ANT = 68*31
ANTI = 25*13
ANTIP = *1
ANTIPH = 1
ANTIPHOLIS = 3
Enter Antipholis Erotes, a Marchant, and Dromio.   162
Enter Adriana, wife to Antipholis Sereptus, with | Luciana her Sister.   273
Enter Antipholis Errotis.   394
ANTIPHOLUS see also An., Anti., Antip., Antiph., E.An., E.Ant.,
Eph.Ant., S.Ant., S.Anti. = 22*2
Adri. I, I, Antipholus, looke strange and frowne,   505
Luc. Come, come, Antipholus, we dine to late.   615
*Enter Antipholus of Ephesus, his man Dromio, Angelo the | Goldsmith,
and Balthaser the Merchant.   617
Enter Iuliana, with Antipholus of Siracusia.   786
Iulia. And may it be that you haue quite forgot | A husbands office?
shall Antipholus   787
Ang. Mr Antipholus. | Anti. I that's my name.   956
Is growing to me by Antipholus,   989
Enter Antipholus Ephes.Dromio from the Courtizans.   995
Enter Antipholus Siracusia.   1183
Cur. Well met, well met, Master Antipholus: 1228
Cur. Now out of doubt Antipholus is mad,   1264
Enter Antipholus Ephes. with a Iailor.   1280
Enter Antipholus Siracusia with his Rapier drawne, | and Dromio Sirac.   1440
Enter Antipholus and Dromio againe.   1473

7

ANTIPHOLUS cont.

Signior *Antipholus*, I wonder much | That you would put me to this shame and trouble,	1477
*Adr. May it please your Grace, *Antipholus* my husba(n)d,	1608
Enter Antipholus, and E.Dromio of Ephesus.	1665
*Mar.Fat. Vnlesse the feare of death doth make me | dote, I see my sonne *Antipholus* and *Dromio.*	1671
Fath. Is not your name sir call'd *Antipholus*?	1766
Tell me, thou art my sonne *Antipholus.*	1799
Haue I bin Patron to *Antipholus,*	1808
Enter the Abbesse with Antipholus Siracusa, | and Dromio Sir.	1811
These two *Antipholus*, these two so like,	1833
Duke. Antipholus thou cam'st from *Corinth* first.	1848

ANY = 13*4

Nay more, if any borne at *Ephesus* | Be seene at any *Siracusian* Marts and Fayres:	20
Againe, if any *Siracusian* borne | Come to the Bay of *Ephesus*, he dies:	22
Gaue any Tragicke Instance of our harme:	67
Or that, or any place that harbours men:	139
Sirra, if any aske you for your Master,	605
*S.Dro. Breake any breaking here, and Ile breake your | knaues pate.	730
And if the winde blow any way from shore,	938
If any Barke put forth, come to the Mart,	940
If any ship put out, then straight away. *Exit.*	979
*S.Dro. Oh yes, if any houre meete a Serieant, a turnes | backe for verie feare.	1168
**any man to answer it that breakes his Band: one that	1214
**Is there any ships puts forth to night? may we be gone?	1218
His word might beare my wealth at any time.	1471
To walke where any honest men resort.	1492
If any friend will pay the summe for him,	1603
Rings, Iewels, any thing his rage did like.	1616

ANYTHING *see* thing

APART = *1

*Duke. Stay, stand apart, I know not which is which.	1850

APE = 1

Ant. Thou hast thine owne forme. | *S.Dro.* No, I am an Ape.	593

APPARANTLY = 1

If he should scorne me so apparantly.	1066

APPARELD = 1

haue you got the picture of old *Adam* new apparel'd?	1197

APPARELL = 1

Apparell vice like vertues harbenger:	798

APPEARE = 1*1

E.Ant. I thinke thou art an asse. | *E.Dro.* Marry so it doth appeare	633
**they appeare to men like angels of light, light is an	1238

APPREHENDED = 1

This very day a *Syracusian* Marchant | Is apprehended for a riuall here,	165

APPROACHT = *1

*E.Dro. Return'd so soone, rather approacht too late:	208

APPROOUED = 1

Till I haue vs'd the approoued meanes I haue,	1572

AQUA-VITAE = 1

The Oyle, the *Balsamum*, and Aqua-vitae.	1078

ARE *see also* y'are = 34*11

ARESTED = 1*1

*S.Dro. I know not at whose suite he is arested well;	1154

ARESTED *cont.*
Tell me, was he arested on a band? 1161
ARMADOES = *1
    *to the hot breath of Spaine, who sent whole Ar-|madoes of Carrects to
be ballast at her nose. 925
ARMD = *1
    *Dro. In her forhead, arm'd and reuerted, making | warre against her
heire. 914
ARME = 1*1
    Though others haue the arme, shew vs the sleeue: 809
    *the Mole in my necke, the great Wart on my left arme, 932
AROSE = 1
    And thereupon these errors are arose. 1877
ARRANT = *1
    *no wife, no mistresse: so that my arrant due vnto my 348
ARREST = 5*1
    Mar. Well Officer, arrest him at my suite. 1056
    Arrest me foolish fellow if thou dar'st. 1063
    Gold. Heere is thy fee, arrest him Officer. 1064
    Offic. I do arrest you sir, you heare the suite. 1067
    *Ant. Thou hast subborn'd the Goldsmith to arrest | mee. 1369
    He did arrest me with an Officer. 1707
ARRESTED = 4
    Tell her, I am arrested in the streete, 1095
    Adr. What is he arrested? tell me at whose suite? 1153
    Say now, whose suite is he arrested at? 1425
    E.Ant. And you sir for this Chaine arrested me. 1868
ARRIUED = 1
    And soone, and safe, arriued where I was: 52
ART *l.*29 149 157 207 515 568 591 595 633 *669 *866 1249 *1308 1389
    1390 1493 1799 1822 1838 1839 = 17*5
AS = 43*15
    As could not be distinguish'd but by names. 56
    Such as sea-faring men prouide for stormes: 83
    Was carried towards *Corinth*, as we thought. 90
    Her part, poore soule, seeming as burdened 110
    By Fishermen of *Corinth*, as we thought. 114
    My soule should sue as aduocate for thee: 148
    E.Dro. I pray you iest sir as you sit at dinner: 227
    Ant. Now as I am a Christian answer me, 242
    As nimble Iuglers that deceiue the eie: 264
    As much, or more, we should our selues complaine: 311
    Dro. Am I so round with you, as you with me, 358
    As you loue stroakes, so iest with me againe: 403
    S.Dro. Marry sir, by a rule as plaine as the plaine bald | pate of Father
time himselfe. 463
    Ant. Why, is Time such a niggard of haire, being (as 471
    For know my loue: as easie maist thou fall 520
    As take from me thy selfe, and not me too. 524
    As strange vnto your towne, as to your talke, 544
    But I should know her as well as she knowes me. 598
    Ile say as they say, and perseuer so: 611
    *It would make a man mad as a Bucke to be so bought | and sold. 727
    And as a bud Ile take thee, and there lie: 836
    Ant. As good to winke sweet loue, as looke on night. 846
    Dro. Marry sir, such claime as you would lay to your 876
    *horse, and she would haue me as a beast, not that I bee-|ing 877

AS *cont.*

*Dro. A very reuerent body: I such a one, as a man	881
*markes I had about mee, as the marke of my shoulder,	931
*that I amaz'd ranne from her as a witch. And I thinke, if	933
Dro. As from a Beare a man would run for life,	944
Perchance I will be there as soone as you.	1022
But sirrah, you shall buy this sport as deere,	1069
As all the mettall in your shop will answer.	1070
S.Dro. You sent me for a ropes end as soone,	1087
*Adri. As if time were in debt: how fondly do'st thou | reason?	1170
As if I were their well acquainted friend,	1185
*as much to say, God make me a light wench: It is writ-|ten,	1237
Thou art, as you are all a sorceresse:	1249
Ile giue thee ere I leaue thee so much money | To warrant thee as I am rested for.	1282
*I beare it on my shoulders, as a begger woont her brat:	1318
Cur. When as your husband all in rage to day	1433
Off. Away, they'l kill vs. | *Exeunt omnes, as fast as may be, frighted.*	1446
*Mar. Speake softly, yonder as I thinke he walkes.	1472
Adr. As roughly as my modestie would let me.	1527
With him his bondman, all as mad as he,	1613
And euer as it blaz'd, they threw on him	1645
As this is false he burthens me withall.	1686
Forsooth tooke on him as a Coniurer:	1719
And with no-face (as 'twere) out-facing me,	1721
Curt. As sure (my Liege) as I do see your Grace.	1757
For lately we were bound as you are now.	1773

ASIA = 1

Roming cleane through the bounds of *Asia*,	136

ASKD = 1

He ask'd me for a hundred markes in gold:	338

ASKE = 1*1

Sirra, if any aske you for your Master,	605
*S.Dro. Some diuels aske but the parings of ones naile,	1254

ASKT = 1

Luce. I thought to haue askt you. | *S.Dro.* And you said no.	694

ASPECT = 1*1

If you will iest with me, know my aspect,	427
**Rubies, Carbuncles, Saphires, declining their rich As-|pect	924

ASPECTS = 1

Some other Mistresse hath thy sweet aspects:	506

ASSAYING = 1

Or loose my labour in assaying it.	1566

ASSE = 6*2

Luc. If thou art chang'd to ought, 'tis to an Asse.	595
'Tis so, I am an Asse, else it could neuer be,	597
E.Ant. I thinke thou art an asse. | *E.Dro.* Marry so it doth appeare	633
You would keepe from my heeles, and beware of an asse.	637
*Thou wouldst haue chang'd thy face for a name, or thy | name for an asse.	677
*Dro. I am an asse, I am a womans man, and besides | my selfe.	868
*Anti. Thou art sensible in nothing but blowes, and | so is an Asse.	1308
*E.Dro. I am an Asse indeede, you may prooue it by	1310

ASSEMBLED = 1

And all that are assembled in this place:	1886

ASSEMBLIES = 1

Ab. Haply in priuate. | *Adr.* And in assemblies too.	1528

ASSES = 1
  Adr. There's none but asses will be bridled so.   288
ASSURD = *1
  Dromio, swore I was assur'd to her, told me what priuie   930
AT = 62*16
ATTACH = 2
  Or Ile attach you by this Officer.   987
  Either consent to pay this sum for me, | Or I attach you by this Officer.   1060
ATTACHD = 1
  That I should be attach'd in *Ephesus*,   1286
ATTAINE = 1
  What simple thiefe brags of his owne attaine?   802
ATTEND = 3
  I bought, and brought vp to attend my sonnes.   61
  Then let your will attend on their accords.   299
  Adr. I will attend my husband, be his nurse,   1567
ATTENDANT = 2
  That his attendant, so his case was like,   130
  And with his mad attendant and himselfe,   1622
ATTENDANTS = 1
  *Enter the Duke of Ephesus, with the Merchant of Siracusa, | Iaylor, and
  other attendants.*   2
ATTURNEY = 1
  And will haue no atturney but my selfe,   1569
AUANT = 1
  Ant. Auant thou witch: Come *Dromio* let vs go.   1261
AUGHT *see* ought
AUOID = *1
  Ant. Auoid then fiend, what tel'st thou me of sup-|(ping?   1248
AUOIDE = 1
  Ant. Sathan auoide, I charge thee tempt me not.   1231
AUSTEERELY = 1
  Might'st thou perceiue austeerely in his eie,   1105
AWAY = 14
  For with long trauaile I am stiffe and wearie. | Get thee away.   177
  Ile weepe (what's left away) and weeping die.   391
  Ah doe not teare away thy selfe from me;   519
  If any ship put out, then straight away. *Exit*.   979
  And then sir she beares away. Our fraughtage sir,   1076
  Farre from her nest the Lapwing cries away;   1133
  My Ring away. This course I fittest choose,   1278
  An. Feare me not man, I will not breake away,   1281
  Came to my house, and tooke away my Ring,   1434
  Off. Away, they'l kill vs. | *Exeunt omnes, as fast as may be, frighted*.   1446
  Therefore away, to get our stuffe aboord. *Exeunt*   1461
  Some get within him, take his sword away: 1499
  Chac'd vs away: till raising of more aide   1625
  S.Dromio. I Sir am *Dromio*, command him away.   1820
AY *see also* I = 1
  Adr. Ay me, it is my husband: witnesse you,   1661
AYE = *1
  Luc. Aye me poore man, how pale and wan he looks.   1399
A-CROSSE = *1
  Adri. Backe slaue, or I will breake thy pate a-crosse.   354
A-ROW = 1
  Beaten the Maids a-row, and bound the Doctor,   1643

BABES = 1
And pitteous playnings of the prettie babes 75
BACK = *2
*Adri. Go back againe, thou slaue, & fetch him home. 351
*A back friend, a shoulder-clapper, one that counterma(n)ds 1146
BACKE = 5*1
Had not their backe beene very slow of saile; 119
Dro. Goe backe againe, and be new beaten home? 352
*Adri. Backe slaue, or I will breake thy pate a-crosse. 354
Adr. The houres come backe, that did I neuer here. 1167
*S.Dro. Oh yes, if any houre meete a Serieant, a turnes | backe for verie feare. 1168
Hath he not reason to turne backe an houre in a day? 1177
BAD = 2
And by me; had not our hap beene bad: 42
Still did I tell him, it was vilde and bad. 1536
BAGGAGE = 1
Anti. Thou baggage let me in. 698
BAGGE = 1
And why dost thou denie the bagge of gold? 1384
BAILE = 3
Ant. I do obey thee, till I giue thee baile. 1068
And that shall baile me: hie thee slaue, be gone, 1096
Adr. I sent you monie sir to be your baile 1870
BAITE = 1
Doe their gay vestments his affections baite? 370
BAL = *3
BALD = 2*3
*S.Dro. Marry sir, by a rule as plaine as the plaine bald | pate of Father time himselfe. 463
*S.Dro. There's no time for a man to recouer his haire | that growes bald by nature. 466
*S.Dro. Thus I mend it: Time himselfe is bald, and 500
therefore to the worlds end, will haue bald followers. 501
*An. I knew 'twould be a bald conclusion: but soft, | who wafts vs yonder. 502
BALL = 1
That like a foot-ball you doe spurne me thus: 359
BALLAST = *1
*to the hot breath of Spaine, who sent whole Ar-|madoes of Carrects to be ballast at her nose. 925
BALSAMUM = 1
The Oyle, the *Balsamum*, and Aqua-vitae. 1078
BALTH = 1
BALTHASAR = 1
Where *Balthasar* and I did dine together. 1700
BALTHASER = 1
*Enter Antipholus of Ephesus, his man Dromio, Angelo the | Goldsmith, and Balthaser the Merchant. 617
BALTHAZAR see also Bal., Balth., Baltz. = 1*1
*E.An. Y'are sad signior *Balthazar*, pray God our cheer 638
E.An. Oh signior *Balthazar*, either at flesh or fish, 641
BALTZ = *1
BAND = 2*2
Tell me, was he arested on a band? 1161
S.Dro. Not on a band, but on a stronger thing: 1162
*S.Dro. I sir, the Serieant of the Band: he that brings 1213

BAND *cont.*
   *any man to answer it that breakes his Band: one that   1214
BANKEROUT = *1
   S.Dro. Time is a verie bankerout, and owes more then | he's worth to
   season.   1172
BANKRUPT *see* bankerout
BARE = 2*1
   *tongue, I thanke him, I bare home vpon my shoulders: 349
   bare head, with the Headsman, & other | Officers.   1600
   A thred-bare Iugler, and a Fortune-teller,   1716
BARGAINE = 1
   Vpon what bargaine do you giue it me?   420
BARKE = 3*1
   If any Barke put forth, come to the Mart,   940
   Dro. Master, there's a Barke of *Epidamium,*   1074
   You sent me to the Bay sir, for a Barke.   1088
   *that the Barke *Expedition* put forth to night, and then   1220
BARRD = 1
   Sweet recreation barr'd, what doth ensue | But moodie and dull
   melancholly,   1547
BARREN = 1
   Are my discourses dull? Barren my wit,   367
BARRENNESSE = *1
   Dro. I found it by the barrennesse, hard in the palme | of the hand.   911
BASE-VIOLE = *1
   *a Base-Viole in a case of leather; the man sir, that when   1207
BASTARD = 1
   Shame hath a bastard fame, well managed,   805
BASTING = 2
   Ant. In good time sir: what's that? | *S.Dro.* Basting.   451
   S.Dro. Lest it make you chollericke, and purchase me | another drie
   basting.   456
BATTERING = *1
   S.Dro. Sconce call you it? so you would leaue batte-|ring,   430
BAY = 4
   Againe, if any *Siracusian* borne | Come to the Bay of *Ephesus,* he dies: 22
   Enter Dromio Sira. from the Bay.   1073
   You sent me to the Bay sir, for a Barke.   1088
   Who put vnluckily into this Bay   1594
BE = 70*14
BEADS = 1
   S.Dro. Oh for my beads, I crosse me for a sinner.   583
BEAMES = 1*1
   But creepe in crannies, when he hides his beames: 426
   Ant. For gazing on your beames faire sun being by.   843
BEAR = *1
   Adr. But were you wedded, you wold bear some sway   302
BEARD = 1
   Whose beard they haue sindg'd off with brands of fire,   1644
BEARE = 16*3
   The pleasing punishment that women beare)   50
   Might beare him company in the quest of him: 132
   To beare the extremitie of dire mishap: 144
   Ant. Goe beare it to the Centaure, where we host,   171
   Perchance you will not beare them patiently.   251
   By the wrongs I suffer, and the blowes I beare,   635
   Beare a faire presence, though your heart be tainted,   799

BEARE *cont.*

Dro. As from a Beare a man would run for life,	944
Anti. No beare it with you, least I come not time e-|nough.	1025
Adr. Go *Dromio*, there's the monie, beare it straight,	1179
*I beare it on my shoulders, as a begger woont her brat:	1318
Dro. God and the Rope-maker beare me witnesse,	1378
Beare me forthwith vnto his Creditor,	1412
Adr. Go beare him hence, sister go you with me:	1424
His word might beare my wealth at any time.	1471
Binde *Dromio* too, and beare them to my house.	1500
And beare him home for his recouerie.	1508
Why beare you these rebukes, and answer not?	1558
Nor send him forth, that we may beare him hence.	1630

BEARES = 2*1

Anti. Then she beares some bredth?	903
And then sir she beares away. Our fraughtage sir,	1076
Dro. In veritie you did, my bones beares witnesse,	1364

BEARING = 1

By rushing in their houses: bearing thence	1615

BEAST = 1*2

*horse, and she would haue me as a beast, not that I bee-|ing	877
*a beast she would haue me, but that she being a ve-|rie beastly creature layes claime to me.	878
To be disturb'd, would mad or man, or beast:	1553

BEASTLY = *1

*a beast she would haue me, but that she being a ve-|rie beastly creature layes claime to me.	878

BEASTS = 1*1

The beasts, the fishes, and the winged fowles	292
*beasts, and what he hath scanted them in haire, hee hath | giuen them in wit.	474

BEAT = 4*2

for in conclusion, he did beat me there.	350
Luci. Selfe-harming Iealousie; fie beat it hence.	378
Or I will beat this method in your sconce.	429
He met me on the Mart, and that I beat him,	625
*That you beat me at the Mart I haue your hand to show;	630
Anti. You'll crie for this minion, if I beat the doore | downe.	702

BEATEN = 4*1

Dro. Goe backe againe, and be new beaten home?	352
*to, or else I shall seek my wit in my shoulders, but I pray | sir, why am I beaten?	433
Ant. Dost thou not know? | *S.Dro.* Nothing sir, but that I am beaten.	435
S.Dro. Was there euer anie man thus beaten out of	442
Beaten the Maids a-row, and bound the Doctor,	1643

BEATING = *3

Dro. And he will blesse y crosse with other beating:	355
*me with beating: when I am warme, he cooles me with	1314
*beating: I am wak'd with it when I sleepe, rais'd with	1315

BEATS = 1*1

*Thinkst y I iest? hold, take thou that, & that. *Beats Dro.*	418
Anti. Wilt thou still talke? *Beats Dro.*	1327

BEAUTIE = 3

I see the Iewell best enamaled | Will loose his beautie: yet the gold bides still	385
Since that my beautie cannot please his eie,	390
First, he did praise my beautie, then my speech.	1120

14

BEAUTY = 1
    Hath homelie age th'alluring beauty tooke   365
BECAME = 3
    There had she not beene long, but she became   53
    At eighteene yeeres became inquisitiue   128
    What then became of them, I cannot tell: 1846
BECAUSE = 5*1
    She is so hot because the meate is colde: 212
    The meate is colde, because you come not home: 213
    You come not home, because you haue no stomacke: 214
    Luc. Because their businesse still lies out adore.   285
    Antiph. Because that I familiarlie sometimes   421
    S.Dro. Because it is a blessing that hee bestowes on   473
BECOME = 1
    Looke sweet, speake faire, become disloyaltie: 797
BED = 8*1
    And afterward consort you till bed time: 191
    Luci. Not this, but troubles of the marriage bed.   301
    So he would keepe faire quarter with his bed: 384
    Keepe then faire league and truce with thy true bed,   540
    'Tis double wrong to truant with your bed,   803
    Nor to her bed no homage doe I owe: 830
    *thinkes a man alwaies going to bed, and saies, God giue | you good
    rest.   1215
    In bed he slept not for my vrging it,   1532
    When thou didst make him Master of thy bed,   1635
BEEING *l.*877 = *1
BEENE *see also* bin *l*.17 *35 42 53 85 119 676 *934 1512 = 7*2
BEEST = 2
    Speake olde *Egeon*, if thou bee'st the man   1827
    Oh if thou bee'st the same *Egeon*, speake: 1830
BEFALL = 1
    To day did dine together: so befall my soule,   1685
BEFALNE = 1
    What haue befalne of them and they till now.   126
BEFORE = 7*4
    Before her selfe (almost at fainting vnder   49
    Before the alwaies winde-obeying deepe   66
    Weeping before for what she saw must come,   74
    Gather the sequell by that went before.   98
    Was carried with more speed before the winde,   112
    S.Dro. I durst haue denied that before you were so | chollericke.   460
    Anti. Are you there Wife? you might haue come | before.   710
    *One that before the Iudgme(n)t carries poore soules to hel.   1149
    Luc. Kneele to the Duke before he passe the Abbey.   1598
    I will determine this before I stirre.   1639
    *And now let's go hand in hand, not one before another. | *Exeunt*.   1918
BEG = 1
    Beg thou, or borrow, to make vp the summe,   156
BEGD = 1
    This foole-beg'd patience in thee will be left.   315
BEGGD = 2
    Luc. That loue I begg'd for you, he begg'd of me.   1117
BEGGE = *1
    *and I thinke when he hath lam'd me, I shall begge with   1319
BEGGER = *1
    *I beare it on my shoulders, as a begger woont her brat: 1318

BEGIN = 1
  But like a shrew you first begin to brawle.   1037
BEGINS = 1
  Duke. Why heere begins his Morning storie right: 1832
BEHEADED = 1
  Beheaded publikely for his offence.   1596
BEHINDE = 2*1
  I and breake it in your face, so he break it not behinde.   734
  *came behinde you sir, like an euill angel, and bid you for- | sake your
  libertie.   1203
  Behinde the ditches of the Abbey heere.   1591
BEHOLD = 1*2
  That would behold in me this shamefull sport.   1393
  Gold. See where they come, we wil behold his death   1597
  Abbesse. Most mightie Duke, behold a man much | wrong'd.   1813
BEING *l*.105 167 225 257 *471 516 539 545 636 808 839 *843 *878 1272
  1276 = 13*3
BELEEUE = 2
  Alas poore women, make vs not beleeue   807
  a man denies, you are now bound to beleeue him.   1787
BELGIA = 1
  Anti. Where stood *Belgia*, the *Netherlands*? | *Dro*. Oh sir, I did not
  looke so low. To conclude,   927
BELIKE = 2
  Belike you thought our loue would last too long   1008
  Belike his wife acquainted with his fits,   1273
BELL = 2
  The clocke hath strucken twelue vpon the bell: 210
  Adria. What, the chaine? | *S.Dro*. No, no, the bell, 'tis time that I were
  gone: 1164
BELOUD = 1
  Of credit infinite, highly belou'd,   1469
BEND = 1
  And therefore homeward did they bend their course.   120
BENEFICIALL = 1
  To seeke thy helpe by beneficiall helpe,   154
BENEFIT = 2
  And by the benefit of his wished light   93
  Of whom I hope to make much benefit: 188
BENT = 1
  Met vs againe, and madly bent on vs   1624
BEREFT = 1
  But if thou liue to see like right bereft,   314
BESEECH = 2
  Adr. Did'st speake him faire? | *Luc*. Haue patience I beseech.   1121
  Ran hether to your Grace, whom I beseech | To giue me ample
  satisfaction   1728
BESEEME = 1
  And ill it doth beseeme your holinesse | To separate the husband and
  the wife.   1579
BESHREW = 1
  Beshrew his hand, I scarce could vnderstand it.   325
BESIDE = 1
  Beside the charge, the shame, imprisonment,   1482
BESIDES = 3*4
  Dro. I am an asse, I am a womans man, and besides | my selfe.   868
  Ant. What womans man? and how besides thy | selfe?   869

16

BESIDES *cont.*

Dro. Marrie sir, besides my selfe, I am due to a woman:	872
Besides I haue some businesse in the towne,	1018
Besides this present instance of his rage,	1270
Mar. Besides, I will be sworne these eares of mine,	1736
Besides her vrging of her wracke at sea,	1835

BESPEAKE = *2

S.Dro. Master, if do expect spoon-meate, or bespeake	a long spoone.	*Ant.* Why *Dromio*?	1243
Adr. He did bespeake a Chain for me, but had it not.	1432

BESPOKE = 2

Anti. Made it for me sir, I bespoke it not.	964
Then fairely I bespoke the Officer	1710

BEST = 1*1

I see the Iewell best enamaled	Will loose his beautie: yet the gold bides still	385
Baltz. In debating which was best, wee shall part	with neither.	717

BESTOW = 2

For there's the house: That chaine will I bestow	778
And buy a ropes end, that will I bestow	998

BESTOWD = 1

In what safe place you haue bestow'd my monie;	243

BESTOWES = *1

S.Dro. Because it is a blessing that hee bestowes on	473

BESTRID = 1

When I bestrid thee in the warres, and tooke	1668

BETRAY = 1

Adri. She did betray me to my owne reproofe,	1559

BETTER = 5*1

That vndiuidable Incorporate	Am better then thy deere selfes better part.	517
Better cheere may you haue, but not with better hart.	650
Ant. No: it is thy selfe, mine owne selfes better part:	850
Adr. Ah but I thinke him better then I say:	1131

BETWEENE = 4

But not a thousand markes betweene you both.	249
Betweene you, I shall haue a holy head.	356
by the salt rheume that ranne betweene *France*, and it.	919
Betweene them they will kill the Coniurer.	1650

BETWIXT *see* 'twixt

BEWARE = 1*1

You would keepe from my heeles, and beware of an asse.	637
*the prophesie like the Parrat, beware the ropes end.	1326

BEYOND = 1

Beyond imagination is the wrong	1677

BID = 6*2

We bid be quiet when we heare it crie.	309
Luc. Dromio, goe bid the seruants spred for dinner.	582
But soft, my doore is lockt; goe bid them let vs in.	651
E.Dro. They stand at the doore, Master, bid them	welcome hither.	719
And with you take the Chaine, and bid my wife	1020
*came behinde you sir, like an euill angel, and bid you for-|sake your libertie.	1203
Ant. To what end did I bid thee hie thee home?	1296
And bid the Lady Abbesse come to me:	1638

BIDES = 1
I see the Iewell best enameled | Will loose his beautie: yet the gold
bides still   385
BIGGE = 1
She is too bigge I hope for me to compasse,   1100
BIN *l*.1748 1808 = 2
B!NDE = 5*2
Enter three or foure, and offer to binde him: | *Hee striues.*   1394
Adr. Oh binde him, binde him, let him not come | neere me.   1396
Pinch. Go binde this man, for he is franticke too.   1405
Binde *Dromio* too, and beare them to my house.   1500
Let vs come in, that we may binde him fast,   1507
We came againe to binde them: then they fled   1626
BLACKE = 1
They'll sucke our breath, or pinch vs blacke and blew.   587
BLAME = 2
The one nere got me credit, the other mickle blame: 675
And I too blame haue held him heere too long.   1033
BLAZD = 1
And euer as it blaz'd, they threw on him   1645
BLESSE = *1
Dro. And he will blesse y crosse with other beating: 355
BLESSED = 1
Some blessed power deliuer vs from hence.   1226
BLESSING = *1
S.Dro. Because it is a blessing that hee bestowes on   473
BLEW = 1
They'll sucke our breath, or pinch vs blacke and blew.   587
BLINDNESSE = 1
Muffle your false loue with some shew of blindnesse: 794
BLISSE = 1
Thus haue you heard me seuer'd from my blisse,   121
BLOOD = 2*1
*a rush, a haire, a drop of blood, a pin, a nut, a cherrie-|stone: 1255
Deepe scarres to saue thy life; euen for the blood   1669
And all the Conduits of my blood froze vp: 1794
BLOT = 1
I am possest with an adulterate blot,   535
BLOUD = 1
My bloud is mingled with the crime of lust: 536
BLOUDS = 1
Haue seal'd his rigorous statutes with their blouds,   13
BLOW = 2*1
E.Dro. So come helpe, well strooke, there was blow | for blow.   696
And if the winde blow any way from shore,   938
BLOWES = 4*3
*feele his blowes; and withall so doubtfully, that I could | scarce
vnderstand them.   329
That he did buffet thee, and in his blowes,   552
By the wrongs I suffer, and the blowes I beare,   635
Blowes faire from land: they stay for nought at all,   1080
not feele your blowes.   1307
Anti. Thou art sensible in nothing but blowes, and | so is an Asse.   1308
*for my seruice but blowes. When I am cold, he heates   1313
BLOWS = *2
*I had rather haue it a head, and you vse these blows   431
*If y skin were parchment, & y blows you gaue were ink,   631

18

BLUNT = 1
   Vicious, vngentle, foolish, blunt, vnkinde,   1127
BLUNTS = 1
   Vnkindnesse blunts it more then marble hard.   369
BOATE = 1
   The Sailors sought for safety by our boate,   79
BODIE = 1
   Soule-killing Witches, that deforme the bodie: 266
BODIED = 1
   Ill-fac'd, worse bodied, shapelesse euery where: 1126
BODY = 3*1
   And that this body consecrate to thee,   527
   *Dro. A very reuerent body: I such a one, as a man   881
   Anti. In what part of her body stands *Ireland*?   907
   And therewithall tooke measure of my body.   1192
BOGGES = 1
   *Dro. Marry sir in her buttockes, I found it out by | the bogges.   908
BOIES = *1
   *S.Dro. By my troth your towne is troubled with vn-|ruly boies.   708
BOND = 2
   I will discharge my bond, and thanke you too.   994
   Dro. Master, I am heere entred in bond for you.   1417
BONDMAN = 3
   With him his bondman, all as mad as he,   1613
   And is not that your bondman *Dromio*?   1767
   E.Dro. Within this houre I was his bondman sir, 1768
BONDS = 2
   Till gnawing with my teeth my bonds in sunder, 1726
   Abb. Who euer bound him, I will lose his bonds, 1825
BONES = *1
   *Dro. In veritie you did, my bones beares witnesse, 1364
BOORD = 2
   And let her read it in thy lookes at boord: 804
   At boord he fed not for my vrging it: 1533
BORE = 2
   They fell vpon me, bound me, bore me thence, 1723
   That bore thee at a burthen two faire sonnes?   1829
BORNE = 7
   Nay more, if any borne at *Ephesus* | Be seene at any *Siracusian* Marts
   and Fayres: 20
   Againe, if any *Siracusian* borne | Come to the Bay of *Ephesus*, he dies:
                                  22
   In *Syracusa* was I borne, and wedde   40
   My wife, more carefull for the latter borne,   81
   Which being violently borne vp,   105
   Let him be brought forth, and borne hence for helpe. 1632
   That he is borne about inuisible,   1662
BORROW = 2
   Beg thou, or borrow, to make vp the summe,   156
   Ant. Well, Ile breake in: go borrow me a crow. 741
BOTH = 12*3
   Both by the *Siracusians* and our selues,   18
   Of such a burthen Male, twins both alike: 59
   Fortune had left to both of vs alike,   108
   But not a thousand markes betweene you both.   249
   S.Dro. Nay Master, both in minde, and in my shape. 592
   *E.Dro. O villaine, thou hast stolne both mine office | and my name, 673
   Both winde and tide stayes for this Gentleman, 1032

BOTH *cont.*

Both one and other he denies me now:	1268
Pinch. Mistris, both Man and Master is possest,	1380
Adr. Dissembling Villain, thou speak'st false in both	1388
My Master and his man are both broke loose,	1642
Gold. O periur'd woman! They are both forsworne,	1689
There left me and my man, both bound together,	1725
Fath. I am sure you both of you remember me.	1771
The Duke my husband, and my children both,	1893

BOUGHT = 3*1

I bought, and brought vp to attend my sonnes.	61
*It would make a man mad as a Bucke to be so bought | and sold.	727
I haue conuei'd aboord, and I haue bought	1077
And show'd me Silkes that he had bought for me,	1191

BOUND = 13*2

To him one of the other twins was bound,	84
But hath his bound in earth, in sea, in skie.	291
Nor now I had not, but that I am bound | To *Persia*, and want Gilders for my voyage:	984
For he is bound to Sea, and stayes but for it.	1016
They must be bound and laide in some darke roome.	1382
Dro. Will you be bound for nothing, be mad good | Master, cry the diuell.	1420
Let's call more helpe to haue them bound againe. | *Runne all out.*	1444
Once did I get him bound, and sent him home,	1617
Beaten the Maids a-row, and bound the Doctor,	1643
They fell vpon me, bound me, bore me thence,	1723
There left me and my man, both bound together,	1725
For lately we were bound as you are now.	1773
a man denies, you are now bound to beleeue him.	1787
S.Drom. Oh my olde Master, who hath bound him | heere?	1823
Abb. Who euer bound him, I will lose his bonds,	1825

BOUNDS = 1

Roming cleane through the bounds of *Asia*,	136

BOY = 2

Merch. My yongest boy, and yet my eldest care,	127
Fa. But seuen yeares since, in *Siracusa* boy	1801

BOYES = 1

My wife, not meanely prowd of two such boyes,	62

BRAGS = 1

What simple thiefe brags of his owne attaine?	802

BRAKE = 1

But till this afternoone his passion | Ne're brake into extremity of rage.	1514

BRALLES = 1

Thou sayest his sports were hindred by thy bralles.	1546

BRANCH = 1

It is a branch and parcell of mine oath,	1575

BRANDS = 1

Whose beard they haue sindg'd off with brands of fire,	1644

BRAT = *1

*I beare it on my shoulders, as a begger woont her brat:	1318

BRAWLE = 1

But like a shrew you first begin to brawle.	1037

BRAWLES *see* bralles

BREACH = 1

Your breach of promise to the *Porpentine*,	1035

BREAK = 1*1
*Ant. Go fetch me something, Ile break ope the gate.   729
I and breake it in your face, so he break it not behinde.   734
BREAKE = 8*4
Duk. Nay forward old man, doe not breake off so,   99
Or I shall breake that merrie sconce of yours   244
*Adri. Backe slaue, or I will breake thy pate a-crosse.   354
And breake it with a deepe-diuorcing vow?   533
Adr. I, and let none enter, least I breake your pate.   614
*S.Dro. Breake any breaking here, and Ile breake your | knaues pate.   730
*E.Dro. A man may breake a word with your sir, and | words are but
winde: 732
I and breake it in your face, so he break it not·behinde.   734
Ant. Well, Ile breake in: go borrow me a crow.   741
If by strong hand you offer to breake in   759
An. Feare me not man, I will not breake away,   1281
BREAKES = 1*1
But, too vnruly Deere, he breakes the pale,   376
*any man to answer it that breakes his Band: one that   1214
BREAKING = 1*2
A drop of water in the breaking gulfe,   521
*S.Dro. Breake any breaking here, and Ile breake your | knaues pate.   730
*S.Dro. It seemes thou want'st breaking, out vpon thee | hinde.   735
BREATH = 4*1
They'll sucke our breath, or pinch vs blacke and blew.   587
When the sweet breath of flatterie conquers strife.   814
*to the hot breath of Spaine, who sent whole Ar-|madoes of Carrects to
be ballast at her nose.   925
Ant. Fie, now you run this humor out of breath,   1043
Luc. How hast thou lost thy breath? | S.Dro. By running fast.   1138
BREATHD = 1
I haue not breath'd almost since I did see it.   1654
BRED = 1
Thereof the raging fire of feauer bred,   1544
BREDTH = 1
Anti. Then she beares some bredth?   903
BREST = *1
*my brest had not beene made of faith, and my heart of   934
BRETH = *1
Ant. Where Spaine? | *Dro. Faith I saw it not: but I felt it hot in her
breth.   920
BRIDLE = 1
Luc. Oh, know he is the bridle of your will.   287
BRIDLED = 1
Adr. There's none but asses will be bridled so.   288
BRIEFE = 1
Duk. Well Siracusian; say in briefe the cause   32
BRIER = 1
Vsurping Iuie, Brier, or idle Mosse,   572
BRIGET = 1
E.Dro. Maud, Briget, Marian, Cisley, Gillian, Ginn.   652
BRING = 7*2
And that to morrow you will bring it home.   623
Bring it I pray you to the Porpentine,   777
Buy thou a rope, and bring it home to me.   1002
*Gold. Then you will bring the Chaine to her your | selfe.   1023
And bring thy Master home imediately.   1180

BRING *cont.*

Come Iailor, bring me where the Goldsmith is,	1438
Ad. Then let your seruants bring my husband forth	1562
Promising to bring it to the Porpentine,	1699
And *Dromio* my man did bring them me:	1874

BRINGING = 1

I should haue chid you for not bringing it,	1036

BRINGS = 1 *1

S.Dro. I sir, the Serieant of the Band: he that brings	1213
Heere comes my Man, I thinke he brings the monie.	1289

BROKE = 3

You haue no stomacke, hauing broke your fast:	215
He broke from those that had the guard of him,	1621
My Master and his man are both broke loose,	1642

BROOKE = 1

Mar. My businesse cannot brooke this dalliance,	1045

BROTHER = 9*2

After his brother; and importun'd me	129
Reft of his brother, but retain'd his name,	131
So I, to finde a Mother and a Brother,	203
Luci. Fie brother, how the world is chang'd with you:	547
Then gentle brother get you in againe;	811
I would not spare my brother in this case,	1065
Did call me brother. What I told you then,	1862
Embrace thy brother there, reioyce with him. *Exit*	1905
E.D. Me thinks you are my glasse, & not my brother:	1909
E.Dro. Nay then thus: | We came into the world like brother and brother:	1916

BROTHERS = 1

Exeunt omnes. Manet the two Dromio's and | two Brothers.	1898

BROUGHT = 4*3

I bought, and brought vp to attend my sonnes.	61
S.Dro. Why sir, I brought you word an houre since,	1219
Till I haue brought him to his wits againe,	1565
Let him be brought forth, and borne hence for helpe.	1632
*They brought one *Pinch*, a hungry leane-fac'd Villaine;	1714
E.Ant. Brought to this Town by that most famous | Warriour,	1853
By *Dromio*, but I thinke he brought it not. | *E.Dro.* No, none by me.	1871

BROW = 1

And teare the stain'd skin of my Harlot brow,	531

BRUISD = 1

A wretched soule bruis'd with aduersitie,	308

BUCKE = *1

*It would make a man mad as a Bucke to be so bought | and sold.	727

BUD = 1

And as a bud Ile take thee, and there lie:	836

BUFFE = 1*1

A Wolfe, nay worse, a fellow all in buffe:	1145
*but is in a suite of buffe which rested him, that can I tell,	1155

BUFFET = 1

That he did buffet thee, and in his blowes,	552

BUILDINGS = 2

Peruse the traders, gaze vpon the buildings,	175
Shall loue in buildings grow so ruinate?	790

BURDENED = 1

Her part, poore soule, seeming as burdened	110

BURDNED = 1
But were we burdned with like waight of paine,   310
BURIED = 1
Buried some deere friend, hath not else his eye   1517
BURND = 1
The Pigge quoth I, is burn'd: my gold, quoth he: 343
BURNE = 2*3
Your meat doth burne, quoth I: my gold quoth he: 340
*warrant, her ragges and the Tallow in them, will burne   889
*a *Poland* Winter: If she liues till doomesday, she'l burne | a weeke
longer then the whole World.   890
*effect of fire, and fire will burne: *ergo*, light wenches will | burne, come
not neere her.   1239
BURNES = 1
The Capon burnes, the Pig fals from the spit;   209
BURTHEN = 4
Of such a burthen Male, twins both alike: 59
And this is false you burthen me withall.   1745
That bore thee at a burthen two faire sonnes?   1829
My heauie burthen are deliuered: 1892
BURTHENS = 1
As this is false he burthens me withall.   1686
BUSINESSE = 4
My present businesse cals me from you now.   192
Luc. Because their businesse still lies out adore.   285
Besides I haue some businesse in the towne,   1018
Mar. My businesse cannot brooke this dalliance,   1045
BUT *l*.41 53 56 68 70 97 111 131 140 149 151 161 216 *239 249 288 291
301 *302 310 314 316 331 335 376 377 381 426 *433 435 449 *476 *478
*498 *502 526 543 566 598 624 *629 644 *649 650 651 732 753 773 779
828 841 *878 *883 *887 *893 *899 *917 *918 *920 946 949 953 *965 974
984 1001 1007 1016 1037 1069 1075 1081 1131 *1155 1162 1184 1193
*1200 *1254 *1256 1292 *1308 *1313 1374 1379 1387 1392 *1432 1437
*1456 1465 1484 1514 1525 1530 1545 1547 1556 1569 1688 1732 1733
1769 1781 *1786 1801 1802 1843 1871 1890 = 83*27
BUTTOCKES = *1
Dro. Marry sir in her buttockes, I found it out by | the bogges.   908
BUTTOND = 1
On whose hard heart is button'd vp with steele: 1143
BUY = 7
And not being able to buy out his life,   167
And buy a ropes end, that will I bestow   998
Buy thou a rope, and bring it home to me.   1002
Dro. I buy a thousand pound a yeare, I buy a rope. | *Exit Dromio*   1003
But sirrah, you shall buy this sport as deere,   1069
Some offer me Commodities to buy.   1189
BY = 67*15, 1
But by and by, rude Fishermen of *Corinth*   1843
BYTH = *1
*By'th'way, we met my wife, her sister, and a rabble more | Of vilde
Confederates: Along with them   1712
CAKE = *1
*Your cake here is warme within: you stand here in the | cold.   725
CALD = 1
Euen now a tailor cal'd me in his shop,   1190
CALL = 11*2
S.Dro. Sconce call you it? so you would leaue batte-|ring,   430

CALL *cont*.

Thy selfe I call it, being strange to me:	516
Ant. How can she thus then call vs by our names?	Vnlesse it be by inspiration.	560
Comfort my sister, cheere her, call her wife;	812
Luc. Why call you me loue? Call my sister so.	847
Ant. Call thy selfe sister sweet, for I am thee:	855
She that doth call me husband, euen my soule	948
And euerie one doth call me by my name:	1186
Let's call more helpe to haue them bound againe.	*Runne all out*.	1444
Duke. Why this is straunge: Go call the Abbesse hi-|ther.	1758
S.Ant. And so do I, yet did she call me so:	1860
Did call me brother. What I told you then,	1862

CALLD = 3*1

*this drudge or Diuiner layd claime to mee, call'd mee	929
Enter Adriana, Luciana, Courtizan, and a Schoole-|master, call'd Pinch.	1321
Fath. Is not your name sir call'd *Antipholus*?	1766
That hadst a wife once call'd *Aemilia*,	1828

CALLED = *1

S.Dro. If thy name be called *Luce*, *Luce* thou hast an-|swer'd him well.	690

CALME = 1

The seas waxt calme, and we discouered	94

CALS = 1

My present businesse cals me from you now.	192

CALST = *1

*Dost thou coniure for wenches, that y calst for such store,	656

CALUES-SKIN = *1

*calues-skin, that was kil'd for the Prodigall: hee that	1202

CAME = 13*3

Vnwilling I agreed, alas, too soone wee came aboord.	64
But ere they came, oh let me say no more,	97
And coasting homeward, came to *Ephesus*:	137
S.Dro. Let him walke from whence he came, lest hee	catch cold on's feet.	660
But neither Chaine nor Goldsmith came to me:	1007
If it were chain'd together: and therefore came not.	1009
*came behinde you sir, like an euill angel, and bid you for-|sake your libertie.	1203
By *Dromio* heere, who came in hast for it.	1372
Adri. He came to me, and I deliuer'd it.	1376
Came to my house, and tooke away my Ring,	1434
Ab. And thereof came it, that the man was mad.	1537
We came againe to binde them: then they fled	1626
E.Ant. I neuer came within these Abbey wals,	1742
S.Ant. No sir, not I, I came from *Siracuse*.	1849
E.Ant. I came from *Corinth* my most gracious Lord	*E.Dro*. And I with him.	1851
E.Dro. Nay then thus:	We came into the world like brother and brother:	1916

CAMST = 2

And for what cause thou cam'st to *Ephesus*.	34
Duke. *Antipholus* thou cam'st from *Corinth* first.	1848

CAN *l*.152 307 320 372 *379 560 *688 699 *1155 1486 1655 1805 = 9*3

CANNOT = 9*1

Cannot amount vnto a hundred Markes,	28
Commends me to the thing I cannot get:	198

24

CANNOT *cont.*

Since that my beautie cannot please his eie,	390
Anti. There is something in the winde, that we can-|not get in.	721
Ant. What I should thinke of this, I cannot tell:	973
Mar. My businesse cannot brooke this dalliance,	1045
Adr. I cannot, nor I will not hold me still.	1123
It cannot be that she hath done thee wrong.	1607
All these old witnesses, I cannot erre.	1798
What then became of them, I cannot tell:	1846

CANST *l.534 = 1*

CAPON = 1 *1

The Capon burnes, the Pig fals from the spit;	209
S.Dro. Mome, Malthorse, Capon, Coxcombe, Idi-|ot, Patch,	653

CARBUNCLES = *1

*Rubies, Carbuncles, Saphires, declining their rich As-|pect	924

CARE = 6

And he great care of goods at randone left,	46
Fixing our eyes on whom our care was fixt,	87
Merch. My yongest boy, and yet my eldest care,	127
When I am dull with care and melancholly,	183
It seemes he hath great care to please his wife.	332
Is wandred forth in care to seeke me out	397

CAREFULL = 2

My wife, more carefull for the latter borne,	81
And carefull houres with times deformed hand,	1779

CARES = 1

Knowes not my feeble key of vntun'd cares?	1791

CARKANET = 1

To see the making of her Carkanet,	622

CARRECTS = *1

*to the hot breath of Spaine, who sent whole Ar-|madoes of Carrects to	
be ballast at her nose.	925

CARRIAGE = 1

Teach sinne the carriage of a holy Saint,	800

CARRIED = 2

Was carried towards *Corinth*, as we thought.	90
Was carried with more speed before the winde,	112

CARRIES = *1

*One that before the Iudgme(n)t carries poore soules to hel.	1149

CARUD = 1

Vnlesse I spake, or look'd, or touch'd, or caru'd to thee.	513

CASE = 5 *2

That his attendant, so his case was like,	130
If I last in this seruice, you must case me in leather.	361
I would not spare my brother in this case,	1065
What obseruation mad'st thou in this case?	1108
S.Dro. I doe not know the matter, hee is rested on | the case.	1151
S.Dro. No? why 'tis a plaine case: he that went like	1206
*a Base-Viole in a case of leather; the man sir, that when	1207

CATCH = 1

S.Dro. Let him walke from whence he came, lest hee | catch cold on's	
feet.	660

CATES = *1

*But though my cates be meane, take them in good part,	649

CAUSE = 5

Duk. Well *Siracusian*; say in briefe the cause	32
And for what cause thou cam'st to *Ephesus*.	34

CAUSE *cont.*
    They can be meeke, that haue no other cause: 307
    Plead on your part some cause to you vnknowne;   752
    Gold. Vpon what cause? | *Mar.* To see a reuerent *Siracusian* Merchant,   1592
CENTAUR = 4*2
    Ile to the Centaur to goe seeke this slaue,   270
    Safe at the *Centaur*, and the heedfull slaue   396
    You know no *Centaur*? you receiu'd no gold?   404
    Home to the *Centaur* with the gold you gaue me.   411
    *Ant. Come to the Centaur, fetch our stuffe from | thence: 1451
    *S.Dro. Your goods that lay at host sir in the Centaur.   1902
CENTAURE = 1
    Ant. Goe beare it to the Centaure, where we host,   171
CERTAINE = 3
    E.Mar. I am inuited sir to certaine Marchants,   187
    S.Dro. Certaine ones then. | *An.* Name them.   489
    For certaine Duckets: he with none return'd.   1709
CERTIS = 1
    Dro. Certis she did, the kitchin vestall scorn'd you.   1362
CHACD = 1
    Chac'd vs away: till raising of more aide   1625
CHAIN = *1
    *Adr. He did bespeake a Chain for me, but had it not.   1432
CHAIND = 1
    If it were chain'd together: and therefore came not.   1009
CHAINE = 37*8
    Sister, you know he promis'd me a chaine,   382
    And fetch the chaine, by this I know 'tis made,   776
    For there's the house: That chaine will I bestow   778
    Enter Angelo with the Chaine.   955
    Ang. I know it well sir, loe here's the chaine,   958
    The chaine vnfinish'd made me stay thus long.   960
    And then receiue my money for the chaine.   969
    For feare you ne're see chaine, nor mony more.   971
    That would refuse so faire an offer'd Chaine.   975
    He had of me a Chaine, at fiue a clocke   991
    I promised your presence, and the Chaine,   1006
    But neither Chaine nor Goldsmith came to me: 1007
    **How much your Chaine weighs to the vtmost charect,   1011
    And with you take the Chaine, and bid my wife   1020
    *Gold. Then you will bring the Chaine to her your | selfe.   1023
    *Gold. Well sir, I will? Haue you the Chaine about | you?   1027
    *Gold. Nay come I pray you sir, giue me the Chaine: 1031
    *Gold. You heare how he importunes me, the Chaine.   1039
    Either send the Chaine, or send me by some token.   1042
    Come where's the Chaine, I pray you let me see it.   1044
    Gold. The monie that you owe me for the Chaine.   1049
    Ant. I owe you none, till I receiue the Chaine.   1050
    A chaine, a chaine, doe you not here it ring.   1163
    Adria. What, the chaine? | *S.Dro.* No, no, the bell, 'tis time that I were
    gone: 1164
    Is that the chaine you promis'd me to day.   1230
    Or for my Diamond the Chaine you promis'd,   1252
    **but she more couetous, wold haue a chaine: Ma-|ster   1256
    **be wise, and if you giue it her, the diuell will shake | her Chaine, and
    fright vs with it.   1257
    Cur. I pray you sir my Ring, or else the Chaine,   1259

CHAINE *cont*.

And for the same he promis'd me a Chaine,	1267
Off. Due for a Chaine your husband had of him.	1431
Straight after did I meete him with a Chaine.	1436
But I protest he had the Chaine of me,	1465
Gold. 'Tis so: and that selfe chaine about his necke,	1474
This Chaine, which now you weare so openly.	1481
This Chaine you had of me, can you deny it?	1486
Who parted with me to go fetch a Chaine,	1698
That I this day of him receiu'd the Chaine,	1705
Duke. But had he such a Chaine of thee, or no?	1733
These people saw the Chaine about his necke.	1735
Heard you confesse you had the Chaine of him,	1737
I neuer saw the Chaine, so helpe me heauen:	1744
Goldsmith. That is the Chaine sir, which you had of | mee.	1865
E.Ant. And you sir for this Chaine arrested me.	1868

CHALKLE = *1

Dro. I look'd for the chalkle Cliffes, but I could find	917

CHANCE = 1

What now? How chance thou art return'd so soone.	207

CHANGD = 1 *3

Luci. Fie brother, how the world is chang'd with you:	547
Luc. If thou art chang'd to ought, 'tis to an Asse.	595
*Thou wouldst haue chang'd thy face for a name, or thy | name for an asse.	677
Fa. Oh! griefe hath chang'd me since you saw me last,	1778

CHANGE = 1

Darke working Sorcerers that change the minde:	265

CHARECT = *1

*How much your Chaine weighs to the vtmost charect,	1011

CHARGD = 1

And charg'd him with a thousand markes in gold,	626

CHARGE = 5 *3

So great a charge from thine owne custodie.	226
Where is the gold I gaue in charge to thee?	235
And tell me how thou hast dispos'd thy charge.	238
E.Dro. My charge was but to fetch you fro(m) the Mart	239
Offi. I do, and charge you in the Dukes name to o-|bey me.	1057
Ant. Sathan auoide, I charge thee tempt me not.	1231
Pinch. I charge thee Sathan, hous'd within this man,	1338
Beside the charge, the shame, imprisonment,	1482

CHARGEFULL = 1

The finenesse of the Gold, and chargefull fashion,	1012

CHARGETH = 1

In this the Madman iustly chargeth them.	1690

CHARITABLE = 1

A charitable dutie of my order,	1576

CHAT = 1

Doe vse you for my foole, and chat with you,	422

CHEAP = *1

Bal. I hold your dainties cheap sir, & your welcom deer.	640

CHEATE = 1

I hope you do not meane to cheate me so?	1260

CHEATERS = 1

Disguised Cheaters, prating Mountebankes;	267

CHEEKE = 2

My Mistris made it one vpon my cheeke:	211

CHEEKE *cont.*

From my poore cheeke? then he hath wasted it. 366

CHEER = *1

E.An. Y'are sad signior *Balthazar*, pray God our cheer 638

CHEERE = 3*2

Bal. Small cheere and great welcome, makes a mer-|rie feast. 646
Better cheere may you haue, but not with better hart. 650
Angelo. Heere is neither cheere sir, nor welcome, we | would faine
haue either. 715
Comfort my sister, cheere her, call her wife; 812
E.Ant. There take it, and much thanks for my good | cheere. 1881

CHERRIE = *1

*a rush, a haire, a drop of blood, a pin, a nut, a cherrie-|stone: 1255

CHID = 1

I should haue chid you for not bringing it, 1036

CHILDREN = 3

The children thus dispos'd, my wife and I, 86
These are the parents to these children, 1836
The Duke my husband, and my children both, 1893

CHIN = *1

*no whitenesse in them. But I guesse, it stood in her chin 918

CHOLLERICKE = 1*1

S.Dro. Lest it make you chollericke, and purchase me | another drie
basting. 456
S.Dro. I durst haue denied that before you were so | chollericke. 460

CHOOSE = 1

My Ring away. This course I fittest choose, 1278

CHRISTIAN = 1

Ant. Now as I am a Christian answer me, 242

CHURLE = *1

Bal. Good meat sir is co(m)mon that euery churle affords. 643

CIRCES = 1

I thinke you all haue drunke of *Circes* cup: 1747

CIRCUMSTANCE = 1

With circumstance and oaths, so to denie 1480

CISLEY = 1

E.Dro. Maud, Briget, Marian, Cisley, Gillian, Ginn. 652

CITIE = 3

And wander vp and downe to view the Citie. 194
Mar. How is the man esteem'd heere in the Citie? 1467
Second to none that liues heere in the Citie: 1470

CITIZENS = 1

Doing displeasure to the Citizens, 1614

CITY = 1

Ant. The Duke, and all that know me in the City, 1804

CIZERS = 1

His man with Cizers nickes him like a foole: 1648

CLAIME = 3*3

My sole earths heauen, and my heauens claime. 853
Anti. What claime laies she to thee? 875
Dro. Marry sir, such claime as you would lay to your 876
*a beast she would haue me, but that she being a ve-|rie beastly
creature layes claime to me. 878
*this drudge or Diuiner layd claime to mee, call'd mee 929
Where Dowsabell did claime me for her husband, 1099

CLAIMES = *2

*One that claimes me, one that haunts me, one that will | haue me. 873

CLAIMES *cont.*
  *the Mountaine of mad flesh that claimes mariage of me,   1457
CLAMORS = 1
  The venome clamors of a iealous woman,   1538
CLAPPER = *1
  *A back friend, a shoulder-clapper, one that counterma(n)ds   1146
CLEANE = 1*1
  Roming cleane through the bounds of *Asia*,   136
  *so cleane kept: for why? she sweats a man may goe o-│uer-shooes in
  the grime of it.   894
CLEERE = 1*1
  Luc. Gaze when you should, and that will cleere │ your sight.   844
  Mine eies cleere eie, my deere hearts deerer heart;   851
CLIFFES = *1
  Dro. I look'd for the chalkle Cliffes, but I could find   917
CLOCKE = 4*1
  I craue your pardon, soone at fiue a clocke,   189
  The clocke hath strucken twelue vpon the bell: 210
  Sure *Luciana* it is two a clocke.   277
  He had of me a Chaine, at fiue a clocke   991
  *It was two ere I left him, and now the clocke strikes one.   1166
COASTING = 1
  And coasting homeward, came to *Ephesus*:   137
COCKE = *1
  S.Dro. Flie pride saies the Pea-cocke, Mistris that │ you know. *Exit.*   1262
COILE = *1
  Luce. What a coile is there *Dromio*? who are those │ at the gate?   680
COLD = 2*1
  S.Dro. Let him walke from whence he came, lest hee │ catch cold on's
  feet.   660
  *Your cake here is warme within: you stand here in the │ cold.   725
  *for my seruice but blowes. When I am cold, he heates   1313
COLDE = 2
  She is so hot because the meate is colde: 212
  The meate is colde, because you come not home: 213
COLDLY = 1
  If he were mad, he would not pleade so coldly: 1749
COME = 34*15
  Againe, if any *Siracusian* borne │ Come to the Bay of *Ephesus*, he dies: 22
  Weeping before for what she saw must come,   74
  And stay there *Dromio*, till I come to thee;   172
  The meate is colde, because you come not home: 213
  You come not home, because you haue no stomacke: 214
  I from my Mistris come to you in post: 228
  Ant. Come *Dromio*, come, these iests are out of season,   233
  Ant. Come on sir knaue, haue done your foolishnes,   237
  She that doth fast till you come home to dinner: 254
  They'll goe or come; if so, be patient Sister.   283
  Luc. Till he come home againe, I would forbeare.   305
  When I desir'd him to come home to dinner,   337
  Will you come, quoth I: my gold, quoth he;   341
  Come I will fasten on this sleeue of thine: 567
  Adr. Come, come, no longer will I be a foole,   599
  Come sir to dinner, *Dromio* keepe the gate: 602
  Come sister, *Dromio* play the Porter well.   607
  Luc. Come, come, *Antipholus*, we dine to late.   615
  S.Dro. Nor to day here you must not come againe │ when you may.   667

COME *cont.*

*E.Dro. So come helpe, well strooke, there was blow | for blow.	696
*Anti. Are you there Wife? you might haue come | before.	710
And about euening come your selfe alone,	757
If any Barke put forth, come to the Mart,	940
*Anti. No beare it with you, least I come not time e-|nough.	1025
*Gold. Nay come I pray you sir, giue me the Chaine:	1031
*Gold. Come, come, you know I gaue it you euen now.	1041
Come where's the Chaine, I pray you let me see it.	1044
On Officer to prison, till it come. *Exeunt*	1097
Adr. The houres come backe, that did I neuer here.	1167
Come sister, I am prest downe with conceit:	1181
**effect of fire, and fire will burne: *ergo*, light wenches will | burne, come not neere her.	1239
Ant. Auant thou witch: Come *Dromio* let vs go.	1261
*Ant. Come goe along, my wife is comming yon-|der.	1323
*Adr. Oh binde him, binde him, let him not come | neere me.	1396
Come Iailor, bring me where the Goldsmith is,	1438
Adr. And come with naked swords,	1443
*Ant. Come to the Centaur, fetch our stuffe from | thence:	1451
Let vs come in, that we may binde him fast,	1507
Adr. Come go, I will fall prostrate at his feete,	1583
Haue won his grace to come in person hither,	1585
*Gold. See where they come, we wil behold his death	1597
And bid the Lady Abbesse come to me:	1638
*Duke. Come stand by me, feare nothing: guard with | Halberds.	1659
From whence I thinke you are come by Miracle.	1741
Come go with vs, wee'l looke to that anon,	1904

COMEDIE = 1

The Comedie of Errors.	1921

COMES = 10*4

Here comes the almanacke of my true date:	206
Heere comes your man, now is your husband nie.	317
I sent him from the Mart? see here he comes.	400
How comes it now, my Husband, oh how comes it,	514
*Luce. Faith no, hee comes too late, and so tell your | Master.	683
*Offi. That labour may you saue: See where he comes.	996
That staies but till her Owner comes aboord,	1075
That time comes stealing on by night and day?	1175
**And here she comes in the habit of a light wench, and	1235
**thereof comes, that the wenches say God dam me, That's	1236
Heere comes my Man, I thinke he brings the monie.	1289
And thereof comes it that his head is light.	1541
Comes this way to the melancholly vale;	1589

COMFORT = 2*1

*Mer. Yet this my comfort, when your words are done,	30
Comfort my sister, cheere her, call her wife;	812
Conceit, my comfort and my iniurie. *Exit.*	1182

COMFORTLESSE = 1

Kinsman to grim and comfortlesse dispaire,	1549

COMMAND = 2\|

Therefore most gracious Duke with thy command,	1631
S.Dromio. I Sir am *Dromio*, command him away.	1820

COMMEND = *1

*E.Mar. Sir, I commend you to your owne content. | *Exeunt.*	195

COMMENDS = 2

Ant. He that commends me to mine owne content,	197

CONDUITS = 1
And all the Conduits of my blood froze vp: 1794
CONFEDERATE = 1
And art confederate with a damned packe, 1390
CONFEDERATES = 2
Among my wife, and their confederates, 999
*By'th'way, we met my wife, her sister, and a rabble more | Of vilde
Confederates: Along with them 1712
CONFERENCE = 1
Adr. It was the copie of our Conference. 1531
CONFESSE = 2
But I confesse sir, that we were lock'd out. 1387
Heard you confesse you had the Chaine of him, 1737
CONFIRMES = 1
Adri. His inciuility confirmes no lesse: 1329
CONFISCATE = 2
His goods confiscate to the Dukes dispose, 24
Lest that your goods too soone be confiscate: 164
CONFOUNDS = 1
(Vnseene, inquisitiue) confounds himselfe. 202
CONFUSION = 1
Infect thy sap, and liue on thy confusion. 574
CONIURE = 2*1
*Dost thou coniure for wenches, that y calst for such store, 656
I coniure thee to leaue me, and be gon. 1250
I coniure thee by all the Saints in heauen. 1341
CONIURER = 3
Good Doctor *Pinch*, you are a Coniurer, 1330
Betweene them they will kill the Coniurer. 1650
Forsooth tooke on him as a Coniurer: 1719
CONQUERS = 1
When the sweet breath of flatterie conquers strife. 814
CONSECRATE = 1
And that this body consecrate to thee, 527
CONSENT = 2
Either consent to pay this sum for me, | Or I attach you by this Officer. 1060
Ant. Consent to pay thee that I neuer had: 1062
CONSEQUENCE = 1
The consequence is then, thy iealous fits 1554
CONSIDER = 1
Consider how it stands vpon my credit. 1055
CONSORT = 1
And afterward consort you till bed time: 191
CONSUMING = 1
In sap-consuming Winters drizled snow, 1793
CONTAGION = 1
Being strumpeted by thy contagion: 539
CONTAMINATE = 1
By Ruffian Lust should be contaminate? 528
CONTEMPT = 1
But wrong not that wrong with a more contempt. 566
CONTENT = 1*1
E.Mar. Sir, I commend you to your owne content. | *Exeunt.* 195
Ant. He that commends me to mine owne content, 197
CONTRARIES = 1
Adr. Is't good to sooth him in these contraries? 1366

CONTROUERSIE = 1
  Who but for staying on our Controuersie,   1484
CONTROULES = 1
  Are their males subiects, and at their controules: 293
CONUAY = 1
  Did but conuay vnto our fearefull mindes   70
CONUEID = 1
  I haue conuei'd aboord, and I haue bought   1077
CONUERSE = 1
  Ant. Did you conuerse sir with this gentlewoman: 554
CONUEYD = 1
  Good Master Doctor see him safe conuey'd   1414
COOKE = *1
  *Me thinkes your maw, like mine, should be your cooke, 231
COOLES = *1
  *me with beating: when I am warme, he cooles me with 1314
COPIE = 1
  Adr. It was the copie of our Conference.   1531
CORDS = 1
  But he I thanke him gnaw'd in two my cords,   1769
CORINTH = 5*1
  Was carried towards *Corinth*, as we thought.   90
  Of *Corinth* that, of *Epidarus* this,   96
  By Fishermen of *Corinth*, as we thought.   114
  But by and by, rude Fishermen of *Corinth*   1843
  Duke. Antipholus thou cam'st from *Corinth* first. 1848
  E.Ant. I came from *Corinth* my most gracious Lord | *E.Dro.* And I
  with him.   1851
CORRUPTION = 1
  By falshood and corruption doth it shame: 389
COSENAGE = 1
  They say this towne is full of cosenage: 263
COST = 1
  Anti. Do so, this iest shall cost me some expence. | *Exeunt.* 784
COUERD = 1
  That's couer'd o're with Turkish Tapistrie,   1093
COUETOUS = *1
  *but she more couetous, wold haue a chaine: Ma-|ster 1256
COULD *l.*35 56 103 142 325 *328 *329 399 597 *897 *905 *917 *1458
  1636 1697 = 8*7
COULDST *l.*326 = *1
COUNTER = 1
  A hound that runs Counter, and yet draws drifoot well, 1148
COUNTERFEIT = 1
  To counterfeit thus grosely with your slaue,   563
COUNTERMANDS = *1
  *A back friend, a shoulder-clapper, one that counterma(n)ds 1146
COUNTRIES = 1
  *to hippe: she is sphericall, like a globe: I could find out | Countries in
  her.   905
COUNTRIMEN = 2
  To Merchants our well-dealing Countrimen,   11
  Twixt thy seditious Countrimen and vs,   16
COURSE = 3
  And therefore homeward did they bend their course. 120
  What is the course and drift of your compact?   555
  My Ring away. This course I fittest choose,   1278

COURTEZAN *see also Curtizan* = *1
   *They draw. Enter Adriana, Luciana, Courtezan, & others.   1497
COURTIZAN = 2
   Enter Adriana, Luciana, Courtezan, and a Schoole-|master, call'd Pinch.   1321
   Exeunt. Manet Offic. Adri. Luci. Courtizan   1426
COURTIZANS = 1
   Enter Antipholus Ephes.Dromio from the Courtizans.   995
COXCOMBE = *1
   *S.Dro. Mome, Malthorse, Capon, Coxcombe, Idi-|ot, Patch,   653
CRACKD = 1
   Hast thou so crack'd and splitted my poore tongue   1789
CRANNIES = 1
   But creepe in crannies, when he hides his beames: 426
CRAUE = 1
   I craue your pardon, soone at fiue a clocke,   189
CREATE = 1
   Are you a god? would you create me new?   826
CREATURE = 3*1
   Say he dines forth, and let no creature enter: 606
   Teach me deere creature how to thinke and speake: 820
   *a beast she would haue me, but that she being a ve-|rie beastly
   creature layes claime to me.   878
   Ab. No, not a creature enters in my house.   1561
CREDIT = 4
   The one nere got me credit, the other mickle blame: 675
   (Being compact of credit) that you loue vs,   808
   Consider how it stands vpon my credit.   1055
   Of credit infinite, highly belou'd,   1469
CREDITOR = 1
   Beare me forthwith vnto his Creditor,   1412
CREEKES = 1
   The passages of allies, creekes, and narrow lands: 1147
CREEPE = 1
   But creepe in crannies, when he hides his beames: 426
CRIE = 1*1
   We bid be quiet when we heare it crie.   309
   *Anti. You'll crie for this minion, if I beat the doore | downe.   702
CRIES = 3
   Farre from her nest the Lapwing cries away;   1133
   He cries for you, and vowes if he can take you,   1655
   Cries out, I was possest. Then altogether   1722
CRIME = 1
   My bloud is mingled with the crime of lust: 536
CROOKED = 1
   He is deformed, crooked, old, and sere,   1125
CROSSE = 1*2
   *Adri. Backe slaue, or I will breake thy.pate a-crosse.   354
   *Dro. And he will blesse y crosse with other beating: 355
   S.Dro. Oh for my beads, I crosse me for a sinner.   583
CROW = 2*3
   Ant. Well, Ile breake in: go borrow me a crow.   741
   *E.Dro. A crow without feather, Master meane you so;   742
   *If a crow help vs in sirra, wee'll plucke a crow together.   744
   Ant. Go, get thee gon, fetch me an iron Crow.   745
CROWNE = 1
   Against my Crowne, my oath, my dignity,   146

CRUPPER = 1
  To pay the Sadler for my Mistris crupper: 221
CRY = 2
  Dro. Will you be bound for nothing, be mad good | Master, cry the
  diuell.   1420
  To scorch your face, and to disfigure you: | *Cry within*.   1656
CUCKOLD = 1
  E.Dro. I meane not Cuckold mad, | But sure he is starke mad: 335
CUP = 1
  I thinke you all haue drunke of *Circes* cup: 1747
CUR = 9
CURSE = 1
  My heart praies for him, though my tongue doe curse.   1134
CURT = 1*1
CURTIZAN see also *Cur*., *Curt*. = 1
  Enter a Curtizan.   1227
CURTULL = *1
  *steele, she had transform'd me to a Curtull dog, & made | me turne
  i'th wheele.   935
CUSTODIE = 2
  Iaylor, take him to thy custodie. | *Iaylor*. I will my Lord.   158
  So great a charge from thine owne custodie.   226
CUSTOMERS = *1
  Anti. You Minion you, are these your Customers?   1344
CUT = 1
  And from my false hand cut the wedding ring,   532
CUTS = *1
  S.Dro. Wee'l draw Cuts for the Signior, till then, | dead thou first.   1914
DAIES = 1
  That by this simpathized one daies error   1887
DAILY = 1
  Made daily motions for our home returne: 63
DAINTIES = *1
  Bal. I hold your dainties cheap sir, & your welcom deer.   640
DAINTY = 1
  A table full of welcome, makes scarce one dainty dish.   642
DALLIANCE = 1*1
  Anti. Good Lord, you vse this dalliance to excuse   1034
  Mar. My businesse cannot brooke this dalliance,   1045
DALLY = 1
  Tell me, and dally not, where is the monie?   224
DAM = 1*1
  S.Dro. Nay, she is worse, she is the diuels dam: 1234
  *thereof comes, that the wenches say God dam me, That's   1236
DAME = *1
  Antip. Plead you to me faire dame? I know you not: 542
DAMNED = 1
  And art confederate with a damned packe,   1390
DANGERS = 1
  I see thy age and dangers make thee dote.   1810
DANKISH = 1
  And in a darke and dankish vault at home   1724
DARE = 1
  Mar. I dare and do defie thee for a villaine.   1496
DARKE = 3
  Darke working Sorcerers that change the minde: 265
  They must be bound and laide in some darke roome.   1382

DARKE *cont.*
And in a darke and dankish vault at home   1724
DARKNESSE = 1
And to thy state of darknesse hie thee straight,   1340
DARST = 3
We being strangers here, how dar'st thou trust   225
Arrest me foolish fellow if thou dar'st.   1063
Against thee presently, if thou dar'st stand: 1495
DATE = 1
Here comes the almanacke of my true date: 206
DAY = 26*3
Therefore Marchant, Ile limit thee this day   153
This very day a *Syracusian* Marchant | Is apprehended for a riuall here,   165
Are penitent for your default to day.   217
Luci. Well, I will marry one day but to trie: 316
Husband Ile dine aboue with you to day,   603
Ant. Wherefore? for my dinner: I haue not din'd to | day.   665
S.Dro. Nor to day here you must not come againe | when you may.   667
If thou hadst beene *Dromio* to day in my place,   676
Now in the stirring passage of the day,   760
For locking me out of my doores by day: 1000
That time comes stealing on by night and day?   1175
Hath he not reason to turne backe an houre in a day?   1177
Is that the chaine you promis'd me to day.   1230
Is a mad tale he told to day at dinner,   1271
My wife is in a wayward moode to day,   1284
Reuell and feast it at my house to day,   1346
Ant. Say wherefore didst thou locke me forth to day,   1383
Home to my house, oh most vnhappy day.   1415
Cur. When as your husband all in rage to day   1433
Had hoisted saile, and put to sea to day: 1485
At your important Letters this ill day,   1610
That she this day hath shamelesse throwne on me.   1678
E.Ant. This day (great Duke) she shut the doores | vpon me,   1680
To day did dine together: so befall my soule,   1685
Luc. Nere may I looke on day, nor sleepe on night,   1687
This woman lock'd me out this day from dinner;   1695
That I this day of him receiu'd the Chaine,   1705
Adr. Which of you two did dine with me to day? | *S.Ant.* I, gentle Mistris.   1856
That kitchin'd me for you to day at dinner: 1907
DEAD = 2
And dwell vpon your graue when you are dead;   765
A liuing dead man. This pernicious slaue,   1718
DEADLY = 2
I know it by their pale and deadly lookes,   1381
Poisons more deadly then a mad dogges tooth.   1539
DEAFE = 1
My dull deafe eares a little vse to heare: 1797
DEALER = *1
S.Dro. The plainer dealer, the sooner lost; yet he loo-|seth it in a
kinde of iollitie.   482
DEALERS = *1
Ant. Why thou didst conclude hairy men plain dea-|lers without wit.   480
DEALING = 1
To Merchants our well-dealing Countrimen,   11

DEATH = 5*3
  *And by the doome of death end woes and all.   6
  To *Epidamium*, till my factors death,   45
  A doubtfull warrant of immediate death,   71
  And happy were I in my timelie death,   141
  But though thou art adiudged to the death,   149
  He gaines by death, that hath such meanes to die: 838
  Gold. See where they come, we wil behold his death   1597
  Mar.Fat. Vnlesse the feare of death doth make me | dote, I see my
  sonne *Antipholus* and *Dromio*.   1671
DEBATE = 1
  Ant. I will debate this matter at more leisure   1089
DEBATING = *1
  Baltz. In debating which was best, wee shall part | with neither.   717
DEBT = 4*1
  Thus he vnknowne to me should be in debt: 1160
  Adri. As if time were in debt: how fondly do'st thou | reason?   1170
  If I be in debt and theft, and a Serieant in the way,   1176
  The debt he owes will be requir'd of me.   1410
  And knowing how the debt growes I will pay it.   1413
DEBTED = 1
  Then I stand debted to this Gentleman,   1014
DECAIED = *1
  *he sir, that takes pittie on decaied men, and giues them   1209
DECAYED = 1
  Of my defeatures. My decayed faire,   374
DECEIT = 1
  The foulded meaning of your words deceit: 823
DECEIUE = 2
  As nimble Iuglers that deceiue the eie: 264
  Adr. I see two husbands, or mine eyes deceiue me.   1816
DECIPHERS = 1
  And which the spirit? Who deciphers them?   1819
DECLINE = 1
  Farre more, farre more, to you doe I decline: 831
DECLINING = *1
  *Rubies, Carbuncles, Saphires, declining their rich As-|pect   924
DECREED = 1
  It hath in solemne Synodes beene decreed,   17
DEEDS = 1
  Ill deeds is doubled with an euill word: 806
DEEPE = 3
  Before the alwaies winde-obeying deepe   66
  Deepe scarres to saue thy life; euen for the blood   1669
  For these deepe shames, and great indignities.   1730
DEEPE-DIUORCING = 1
  And breake it with a deepe-diuorcing vow?   533
DEER = *1
  Bal. I hold your dainties cheap sir, & your welcom deer.   640
DEERE = 6
  But, too vnruly Deere, he breakes the pale,   376
  That vndiuidable Incorporate | Am better then thy deere selfes better
  part.   517
  Teach me deere creature how to thinke and speake: 820
  Mine eies cleere eie, my deere hearts deerer heart;   851
  But sirrah, you shall buy this sport as deere,   1069
  Buried some deere friend, hath not else his eye   1517

DEERELY = 1
How deerely would it touch thee to the quicke,   525
DEERER = 1
Mine eies cleere eie, my deere hearts deerer heart;   851
DEFAULT = 1
Are penitent for your default to day.   217
DEFEATURES = 2
Of my defeatures. My decayed faire,   374
Haue written strange defeatures in my face: 1780
DEFIE = 1
Mar. I dare and do defie thee for a villaine.   1496
DEFORME = 1
Soule-killing Witches, that deforme the bodie: 266
DEFORMED = 2
He is deformed, crooked, old, and sere,   1125
And carefull houres with times deformed hand,   1779
DELAY = *1
Delay: Here are the angels that you sent for to deliuer | you.   1222
DELAYES = 1
Forst me to seeke delayes for them and me,   77
DELIGHT = 2
What to delight in, what to sorrow for,   109
Hast thou delight to see a wretched man   1407
DELIUER = 3*1
Didst thou deliuer to me on the Mart.   558
Delay: Here are the angels that you sent for to deliuer | you.   1222
Some blessed power deliuer vs from hence.   1226
And pay the sum that may deliuer me.   1764
DELIUERD = 1
Adri. He came to me, and I deliuer'd it.   1376
DELIUERED = 2
A meane woman was deliuered   58
My heauie burthen are deliuered: 1892
DEMAND = 1
And I will please you what you will demand.   1332
DEMEAND = 1
When he demean'd himselfe, rough, rude, and wildly,   1557
DEMEANE = 1
Else would he neuer so demeane himselfe,   1265
DEMEANOR = 1
And fashion your demeanor to my lookes,   428
DENIDE = 1
Luc. First he deni'de you had in him no right.   1110
DENIE = 7
Ant. Villaine, thou didst denie the golds receit,   412
And that I did denie my wife and house;   627
And why dost thou denie the bagge of gold?   1384
Though most dishonestly he doth denie it.   1466
With circumstance and oaths, so to denie   1480
Ant. Who heard me to denie it or forsweare it?   1489
S.Ant. I thinke it be sir, I denie it not.   1867
DENIED = 2*1
S.Dro. I durst haue denied that before you were so | chollericke.   460
Denied my house for his, me for his wife.   553
And I denied to enter in my house.   1348
DENIES = 3
Both one and other he denies me now: 1268

DENIES *cont.*
    Denies that saying. Sirra, what say you? 1751
    a man denies, you are now bound to beleeue him. 1787
DENY = 3
    This Chaine you had of me, can you deny it? 1486
    Ant. I thinke I had, I neuer did deny it. 1487
    Gold. I thinke I did sir, I deny it not. 1869
DENYING = 1
    Gold. You wrong me more sir in denying it. 1054
DEPART = 5
    Be rul'd by me, depart in patience, 755
    Anti. You haue preuail'd, I will depart in quiet, 768
    Ant. And did not I in rage depart from thence? 1363
    Therefore depart, and leaue him heere with me. 1577
    Ab. Be quiet and depart, thou shalt not haue him. 1581
DEPARTEDST = 1
    Why thou departedst from thy natiue home? 33
DEPTH = 1
    The place of depth, and sorrie execution, 1590
DESERT = 1
    My wife (but I protest without desert) 773
DESIRD = 1
    When I desir'd him to come home to dinner, 337
DESKE = 2*1
    Giue her this key, and tell her in the Deske 1092
    Dro. Here goe: the deske, the purse, sweet now make | haste. 1136
    *will you send him Mistris redemption, the monie in | his deske. 1156
DESPIGHT = 1
    And in despight of mirth meane to be merrie: 769
DESPRATELY = 1
    That desp'rately he hurried through the streete, 1612
DETAINE = 1
    Would that alone, a loue he would detaine, 383
DETERMINE = 1
    I will determine this before I stirre. 1639
DEUILL *see* diuell
DEUISE = 1
    Ant. Vpon my life by some deuise or other, 261
DIALL = 1
    Mar. By this I thinke the Diall points at fiue: 1587
DIAMOND = 2
    Or for my Diamond the Chaine you promis'd, 1252
    Cur. Sir I must haue that Diamond from you. 1880
DID *l.*68 69 70 120 350 407 410 *496 552 554 627 791 *927 1099 1104
    1106 *1111 *1118 1120 1167 1296 1345 1354 1358 *1360 1362 1363
    *1364 1377 1385 *1432 1436 1437 1487 1488 *1490 1510 1525 1536 1559
    1616 1617 1654 1667 1685 1700 1704 1707 1708 1754 1856 1860 1862
    1869 1874 1875 = 48*8
DIDST = 8*4
    Adr. Say, didst thou speake with him? knowst thou | his minde? 322
    That thus so madlie thou did didst answere me? 407
    Ant. Villaine, thou didst denie the golds receit, 412
    Ant. Why thou didst conclude hairy men plain dea-|lers without wit. 480
    Adr. By thee, and this thou didst returne from him. 551
    Didst thou deliuer to me on the Mart. 558
    Thou drunkard thou, what didst thou meane by this? 628
    Adr. Did'st speake him faire? | *Luc.* Haue patience I beseech. 1121

DIDST *cont*.

Ant. Say wherefore didst thou locke me forth to day,   1383
When thou didst make him Master of thy bed,   1635
Duke. A greeuous fault: say woman, didst thou so?   1683
Nor euer didst thou draw thy sword on me: 1743
DIE = 5

Therefore by Law thou art condemn'd to die.   29
And liue: if no, then thou art doom'd to die: 157
Ile weepe (what's left away) and weeping die.   391
He gaines by death, that hath such meanes to die: 838
He shall not die, so much we tender him.   1604
DIES = 2

Againe, if any *Siracusian* borne | Come to the Bay of *Ephesus*, he dies: 22
Dies ere the wearie sunne set in the West: 169
DIET = 1

Diet his sicknesse, for it is my Office,   1568
DIFFERENT = 1

And much different from the man he was: 1513
DIGEST = 1

I doe digest the poison of thy flesh,   538
DIGESTIONS = 1

Vnquiet meales make ill digestions,   1543
DIGNITY = 1

Against my Crowne, my oath, my dignity,   146
DILATE = 1

Doe me the fauour to dilate at full,   125
DIMINISHING = 1

And take vnmingled thence that drop againe | Without addition or diminishing,   522
DIND = 3*3

Ant. Wherefore? for my dinner: I haue not din'd to | day.   665
S.Dromio. To *Adriana*, that is where we din'd,   1098
Adr. O husband, God doth know you din'd at home   1349
Anti. Din'd at home? Thou Villaine, what sayest | thou?   1352
That he din'd not at home, but was lock'd out.   1732
You say he din'd at home, the Goldsmith heere   1750
DINDE = *1

E.Dro. Sir he din'de with her there, at the Porpen-|tine.   1752
DINE = 9

And then goe to my Inne and dine with me?   186
Good Sister let vs dine, and neuer fret;   280
Husband Ile dine aboue with you to day,   603
Luc. Come, come, *Antipholus*, we dine to late.   615
There will we dine: this woman that I meane   772
Dro: Sir sooth to say, you did not dine at home.   1354
To day did dine together: so befall my soule,   1685
Where *Balthasar* and I did dine together.   1700
Adr. Which of you two did dine with me to day? | *S.Ant*. I, gentle Mistris.   1856
DINES = 1

Say he dines forth, and let no creature enter: 606
DINNER = 22*2

Within this houre it will be dinner time,   173
E.Dro. I pray you iest sir as you sit at dinner: 227
Home to your house, the *Phoenix* sir, to dinner;   240
She that doth fast till you come home to dinner: 254
And praies that you will hie you home to dinner.   255

DISHONORED = 1
That hath abused and dishonored me,   1675
DISLOYALTIE = 1
Looke sweet, speake faire, become disloyaltie: 797
DISPAIRE = 1
Kinsman to grim and comfortlesse dispaire,   1549
DISPARAGEMENT = 1
But to our honours great disparagement: 151
DISPATCH = 1
Mar. The houre steales on, I pray you sir dispatch.   1038
DISPENCE = *1
Ad. Vnfeeling fools can with such wrongs dispence: 379
DISPERST = 1
Disperst those vapours that offended vs,   92
DISPLEASD = 1
For which I hope thou feltst I was displeas'd.   414
DISPLEASURE = 2
Do outrage and displeasure to himselfe?   1408
Doing displeasure to the Citizens,   1614
DISPOSD = 2
The children thus dispos'd, my wife and I,   86
And tell me how thou hast dispos'd thy charge.   238
DISPOSE = 1
His goods confiscate to the Dukes dispose,   24
DISSEMBLING = 1 *1
Adr. Dissembling Villain, thou speak'st false in both   1388
Ant. Dissembling harlot, thou art false in all,   1389
DISTAIND = 1
I liue distain'd, thou vndishonoured.   541
DISTEMPERATURES = 1
Of pale distemperatures, and foes to life?   1551
DISTINGUISHD = 1
As could not be distinguish'd but by names.   56
DISTRACT = 1
Ant. The fellow is distract, and so am I,   1224
DISTRACTED = 1
Adr. To fetch my poore distracted husband hence,   1506
DISTRESSED = *1
Adr. Oh that thou wer't not, poore distressed soule.   1343
DISTURBD = 1
To be disturb'd, would mad or man, or beast: 1553
DISTURBED = 1
Neither disturbed with the effect of Wine,   1692
DITCHES = 1
Behinde the ditches of the Abbey heere.   1591
DIUELL = 4 *1
A diuell in an euerlasting garment hath him;   1142
S.Dro. Master, is this Mistris *Sathan?* | *Ant.* It is the diuell. 1232
S.Dro. Marrie he must haue a long spoone that must | eate with the
diuell.   1246
*be wise, and if you giue it her, the diuell will shake | her Chaine, and
fright vs with it.   1257
Dro. Will you be bound for nothing, be mad good | Master, cry the
diuell.   1420
DIUELS = 1 *1
S.Dro. Nay, she is worse, she is the diuels dam: 1234
S.Dro. Some diuels aske but the parings of ones naile,   1254

DIUINE = 2
  Man more diuine, the Master of all these,   294
  Then our earths wonder, more then earth diuine.   819
DIUINER = *1
  *this drudge or Diuiner layd claime to mee, call'd mee   929
DIUORCE = 1
  So that in this vniust diuorce of vs,   107
DIUORCING = 1
  And breake it with a deepe-diuorcing vow?   533
DO *l*.363 420 784 817 897 946 961 988 *1057 1067 1068 *1243 1260 1406
  1408 1427 *1454 1496 1636 1757 1772 *1786 1860 = 19*4
DOCTOR = 3
  Good Doctor *Pinch*, you are a Coniurer,   1330
  Good Master Doctor see him safe conuey'd   1414
  Beaten the Maids a-row, and bound the Doctor,   1643
DOE *l*.99 125 359 370 422 468 519 534 538 *692 793 830 831 840 841 *864
  1134 *1151 1163 *1210 *1422 = 16*5
DOG = *1
  *steele, she had transform'd me to a Curtull dog, & made | me turne
  i'th wheele.   935
DOGGES = 1
  Poisons more deadly then a mad dogges tooth.   1539
DOING = 1
  Doing displeasure to the Citizens,   1614
DONE *l*.*30 101 *237 1483 1607 1701 = 4*2
DOOMD = 1
  And liue: if no, then thou art doom'd to die: 157
DOOME = *1
  *And by the doome of death end woes and all.   6
DOOMESDAY = *1
  *a *Poland* Winter: If she liues till doomesday, she'l burne | a weeke
  longer then the whole World.   890
DOORE *see also* adore = 4*3
  But soft, my doore is lockt; goe bid them let vs in.   651
  E.Drom. Master, knocke the doore hard.   700
  Anti. You'll crie for this minion, if I beat the doore | downe.   702
  Adr. Who is that at the doore y keeps all this noise?   707
  E.Dro. They stand at the doore, Master, bid them | welcome hither.   719
  it from doore to doore.   1320
DOORES = 5*4
  Since mine owne doores refuse to entertaine me,   781
  For locking me out of my doores by day: 1000
  Of his owne doores being shut against his entrance.   1272
  On purpose shut the doores against his way: 1274
  *it when I sit, driuen out of doores with it when I goe   1316
  Whil'st vpon me the guiltie doores were shut,   1347
  Ant. Were not my doores lockt vp, and I shut out?   1355
  Dro. Perdie, your doores were lockt, and you shut | out.   1356
  E.Ant. This day (great Duke) she shut the doores | vpon me,   1680
DORE = 1*4
  Luc. Because their businesse still lies out adore.   285
  *Either get thee from the dore, or sit downe at the hatch: 655
  *When one is one too many, goe get thee from the dore.   657
  E.Ant. Who talks within there? hoa, open the dore.   662
  Adri. Your wife sir knaue? go get you from the dore.   712
DORES = 1
  Why at this time the dores are made against you.   754

DOST *l*.417 435 *656 885 *1170 *1198 1384 *1418 1652 1781 1784 = 7*4
DOTE = 3

Sing Siren for thy selfe, and I will dote: 834
Mar.Fat. Vnlesse the feare of death doth make me | dote, I see my
sonne *Antipholus* and *Dromio*.   1671
I see thy age and dangers make thee dote.   1810
DOTH *l*.160 254 340 380 389 633 948 949 1013 1184 1186 *1349 1466
1547 1579 *1671 = 14*2
DOTING = 1

Anti. Peace doting wizard, peace; I am not mad.   1342
DOUBLE = 1

'Tis double wrong to truant with your bed,   803
DOUBLED = 1

Ill deeds is doubled with an euill word: 806
DOUBT = 3

And doubt not sir, but she will well excuse   753
To your notorious shame, I doubt it not.   1072
Cur. Now out of doubt *Antipholus* is mad,   1264
DOUBTFULL = 1

A doubtfull warrant of immediate death,   71
DOUBTFULLY = *2

Luc. Spake hee so doubtfully, thou couldst not feele | his meaning.   326
*feele his blowes; and withall so doubtfully, that I could | scarce
vnderstand them.   329
DOWNE = 6*1

And wander vp and downe to view the Citie.   194
But here's a villaine that would face me downe   624
*Either get thee from the dore, or sit downe at the hatch: 655
Anti. You'll crie for this minion, if I beat the doore | downe.   702
Pleaseth you walke with me downe to his house,   993
Come sister, I am prest downe with conceit: 1181
There did this periur'd Goldsmith sweare me downe,   1704
DOWSABELL = 1

Where Dowsabell did claime me for her husband,   1099
DRAW = 4*2

And draw within the compasse of suspect   748
Good sir draw neere to me, Ile speake to him: 1476
They draw. Enter Adriana, Luciana, Courtezan, & others.   1497
Mar. I am sorry now that I did draw on him.   1510
Nor euer didst thou draw thy sword on me: 1743
S.Dro. Wee'l draw Cuts for the Signior, till then, | lead thou first.   1914
DRAWNE = 2

Enter Antipholus Siracusia with his Rapier drawne, | *and Dromio Sirac.* 1440
Each one with irefull passion, with drawne swords   1623
DRAWS = 1

A hound that runs Counter, and yet draws drifoot well,   1148
DREAME = 3

What, was I married to her in my dreame?   577
Fa. If I dreame not, thou art *Aemilia*,   1838
If this be not a dreame I see and heare.   1864
DREW = 3

Drew me from kinde embracements of my spouse;   47
Namely, some loue that drew him oft from home.   1523
And thereupon I drew my sword on you: 1739
DRIE = 2

Ant. Well sir, then 'twill be drie.   453

DROMIO *cont.*

By *Dromio* heere, who came in hast for it.	1372
Enter Antipholus Siracusia with his Rapier drawne, | and Dromio Sirac.	1440
Enter Antipholus and Dromio againe.	1473
Binde *Dromio* too, and beare them to my house.	1500
Enter Antipholus, and E.Dromio of Ephesus.	1665
*Mar.Fat. Vnlesse the feare of death doth make me | dote, I see my	
sonne *Antipholus* and *Dromio.*	1671
And is not that your bondman *Dromio*?	1767
Now am I *Dromio*, and his man, vnbound.	1770
Ant. Neither. | *Fat. Dromio*, nor thou?	1782
Enter the Abbesse with Antipholus Siracusa, | and Dromio Sir.	1811
S.Dromio. I Sir am *Dromio*, command him away.	1820
E.Dro. I Sir am *Dromio*, pray let me stay.	1821
And the twin *Dromio*, all were taken vp;	1842
By force tooke *Dromio*, and my sonne from them,	1844
By *Dromio*, but I thinke he brought it not. | *E.Dro.* No, none by me.	1871
And *Dromio* my man did bring them me:	1874
*E.An. Dromio, what stuffe of mine hast thou imbarkt	1901
*S.Ant. He speakes to me, I am your master *Dromio.*	1903

DROMIOS = 2

And these two *Dromio's*, one in semblance:	1834
Exeunt omnes. Manet the two Dromio's and | two Brothers.	1898

DROP = 4*2

I to the world am like a drop of water,	199
That in the Ocean seekes another drop,	200
**trying: the other, that at dinner they should not drop in | his porrage.	492
A drop of water in the breaking gulfe,	521
And take vnmingled thence that drop againe | Without addition or	
diminishing,	522
**a rush, a haire, a drop of blood, a pin, a nut, a cherrie-|stone:	1255

DROSSE = 1

If ought possesse thee from me, it is drosse,	571

DROWNE = 1

To drowne me in thy sister floud of teares:	833

DROWNED = 1

Let Loue, being light, be drowned if she sinke.	839

DRUDGE = *1

**this drudge or Diuiner layd claime to mee, call'd mee	929

DRUGGES = 1

With wholsome sirrups, drugges, and holy prayers	1573

DRUNKARD = 1

Thou drunkard thou, what didst thou meane by this?	628

DRUNKE = 1

I thinke you all haue drunke of *Circes* cup:	1747

DRUNKEN = 1

Ant. Thou drunken slaue, I sent thee for a rope,	1085

DUCKETS = 8*2

Which doth amount to three odde Duckets more	1013
There is a purse of Duckets, let her send it:	1094
A Ring he hath of mine worth fortie Duckets,	1266
For fortie Duckets is too much to loose.	1279
Ant. Fiue hundred Duckets villaine for a rope?	1294
*Ant. Wentst not thou to her for a purse of Duckets.	1375
Off. Two hundred Duckets. | *Adr.* Say, how growes it due.	1429
For certaine Duckets: he with none return'd.	1709
S.Ant. This purse of Duckets I receiu'd from you,	1873

DUCKETS *cont.*
E.Ant. These Duckets pawne I for my father heere.   1878
DUE = 3*2
*no wife, no mistresse: so that my arrant due vnto my   348
Dro. Marrie sir, besides my selfe, I am due to a woman: 872
Mar. You know since Pentecost the sum is due,   982
Off. Two hundred Duckets. | *Adr.* Say, how growes it due.   1429
Off. Due for a Chaine your husband had of him.   1431
DUK = 2
DUKE see also *Duk.* = 16*5, 8*8
*Enter the Duke of Ephesus, with the Merchant of Siracusa, | Iaylor, and
other attendants.*   2
Sprung from the rancorous outrage of your Duke,   10
Luc. Complaine vnto the Duke of this indignity.   1582
Anon I'me sure the Duke himselfe in person   1588
Luc. Kneele to the Duke before he passe the Abbey.   1598
Enter the Duke of Ephesus, and the Merchant of Siracuse   1599
Adr. Iustice most sacred Duke against the Abbesse.   1605
Therefore most gracious Duke with thy command,   1631
E.Ant. Iustice most gracious Duke, oh grant me iu-|(stice,   1666
E.Ant. This day (great Duke) she shut the doores | vpon me,   1680
Fa. Most mighty Duke, vouchsafe me speak a word: 1762
Ant. The Duke, and all that know me in the City,   1804
Abbesse. Most mightie Duke, behold a man much | wrong'd.   1813
Duke *Menaphon* your most renowned Vnckle.   1855
Abb. Renowned Duke, vouchsafe to take the paines   1883
The Duke my husband, and my children both,   1893
DUKES = 1*1
His goods confiscate to the Dukes dispose,   24
Offi. I do, and charge you in the Dukes name to o-|bey me.   1057
DULL = 4
When I am dull with care and melancholly,   183
Are my discourses dull? Barren my wit,   367
Sweet recreation barr'd, what doth ensue | But moodie and dull
melancholly,   1547
My dull deafe eares a little vse to heare: 1797
DURANCE = *1
*suites of durance: he that sets vp his rest to doe more ex-|ploits 1210
DURING = 1
During which time, he ne're saw *Siracusa*:   1809
DURST = *1
S.Dro. I durst haue denied that before you were so | chollericke. 460
DUTIE = 1
A charitable dutie of my order,   1576
DWELL = 1
And dwell vpon your graue when you are dead;   765
E *l.*1665 = 1
EACH = 2
Each one with irefull passion, with drawne swords   1623
I see we still did meete each others man,   1875
EAN = 1*2
EANT = 6*9
EANTI = 1*1
EARE = 3
E.Dro. I, I, he told his minde vpon mine eare,   324
That neuer words were musicke to thine eare,   509
Ant. There is my hand, and let it feele your eare.   1337

EARES = 6*3

E.Dro. Nay, hee's at too hands with mee, and that my | two eares can witnesse. 320
What error driues our eies and eares amisse? 579
Ile stop mine eares against the Mermaids song. 954
And teach your eares to list me with more heede: 1090
I tell you 'twill sound harshly in her eares. 1287
*my long eares. I haue serued him from the houre of my 1311
Mar. These eares of mine thou knowst did hear thee: 1490
Mar. Besides, I will be sworne these eares of mine, 1736
My dull deafe eares a little vse to heare: 1797

EARNEST = 1*1

S.Dr. Hold sir, for Gods sake, now your iest is earnest, 419
That he did plead in earnest, yea or no: 1106

EARTH = 4

At length the sonne gazing vpon the earth, 91
But hath his bound in earth, in sea, in skie. 291
Ant. Am I in earth, in heauen, or in hell? 608
Then our earths wonder, more then earth diuine. 819

EARTHIE = 1

Lay open to my earthie grosse conceit: 821

EARTHS = 2

Then our earths wonder, more then earth diuine. 819
My sole earths heauen, and my heauens claime. 853

EASIE = 1

For know my loue: as easie maist thou fall 520

EAT = 1

S.Dro. If it be sir, I pray you eat none of it. | *Ant*. Your reason? 454

EATE = 1

S.Dro. Marrie he must haue a long spoone that must | eate with the diuell. 1246

ED = *1

EDR = *1

EDRO = 18*25

EDROM = 1

EDROMIO = *1

EFFECT = 1*1

*effect of fire, and fire will burne: *ergo*, light wenches will | burne, come not neere her. 1239
Neither disturbed with the effect of Wine, 1692

EGEAN = 1

Merch. Hopelesse and helpelesse doth *Egean* wend, 160

EGEON = 4

Duke. Haplesse *Egeon* whom the fates haue markt 143
S.Ant. *Egeon* art thou not? or else his ghost. 1822
Speake olde *Egeon*, if thou bee'st the man 1827
Oh if thou bee'st the same *Egeon*, speake: 1830

EIE = 6

As nimble Iuglers that deceiue the eie: 264
Since that my beautie cannot please his eie, 390
To put the finger in the eie and weepe; 600
Luc. It is a fault that springeth from your eie. 842
Mine eies cleere eie, my deere hearts deerer heart; 851
Might'st thou perceiue austeerely in his eie, 1105

EIES = 4

What error driues our eies and eares amisse? 579
Mine eies cleere eie, my deere hearts deerer heart; 851

EIES *cont.*

And yet would herein others eies were worse:	1132
Who giue their eies the liberty of gazing.	1520

EIGHTEENE = 1

At eighteene yeeres became inquisitiue	128

EITHER *see also* eyther = 4*1

E.An. Oh signior *Balthazar*, either at flesh or fish,	641
*Either get thee from the dore, or sit downe at the hatch:	655
Angelo. Heere is neither cheere sir, nor welcome, we | would faine haue either.	715
Either send the Chaine, or send me by some token.	1042
Either consent to pay this sum for me, | Or I attach you by this Officer.	1060

ELDER = 1

S.Dro. Not I sir, you are my elder. | *E.Dro.* That's a question, how shall we trie it.	1912

ELDEST = 1

Merch. My yongest boy, and yet my eldest care,	127

ELL = *1

*an Ell and three quarters, will not measure her from hip | to hip.	901

ELME = 1

Thou art an Elme my husband, I a Vine:	568

ELSE = 8*2

Or else, what lets it but he would be here?	381
*to, or else I shall seek my wit in my shoulders, but I pray | sir, why am I beaten?	433
'Tis so, I am an Asse, else it could neuer be,	597
S.Anti. Sweete Mistris, what your name is else I | know not;	815
Luc. All this my sister is, or else should be.	854
Or else you may returne without your money.	1030
Cur. I pray you sir my Ring, or else the Chaine,	1259
Else would he neuer so demeane himselfe,	1265
Buried some deere friend, hath not else his eye	1517
S.Ant. *Egeon* art thou not? or else his ghost.	1822

ELSE-WHERE = 2

Ile knocke else-where, to see if they'll disdaine me.	782
Or if you like else-where doe it by stealth,	793

EMAR = 1*1

EMBARKD *see* imbarkt

EMBELLISHED = 1

Ant. Where *America*, the *Indies*? | *Dro.* Oh sir, vpon her nose, all ore embellished with	922

EMBRACD *see* imbrac'd

EMBRACE = 1

Embrace thy brother there, reioyce with him. *Exit*	1905

EMBRACEMENTS = 1

Drew me from kinde embracements of my spouse;	47

EMILIA see Aemilia

ENAMALED = 1

I see the Iewell best enamaled | Will loose his beautie: yet the gold bides still	385

ENCHANTING *see* inchanting

ENCOUNTRED = 1

We were encountred by a mighty rocke,	104

END = 12*5

*And by the doome of death end woes and all.	6
My woes end likewise with the euening Sonne.	31
Yet that the world may witnesse that my end	37

END *cont.*

ENTER *cont.*
    Enter Antipholus Ephes. with a Iailor.   1280
    Enter Dromio Eph. with a ropes end.   1288
    Enter Adriana, Luciana, Courtizan, and a Schoole-|master, call'd Pinch.   1321
    And I denied to enter in my house.   1348
    Enter three or foure, and offer to binde him: | Hee striues.   1394
    Enter Antipholus Siracusia with his Rapier drawne, | and Dromio Sirac.   1440
    Enter the Merchant and the Goldsmith.   1463
    Enter Antipholus and Dromio againe.   1473
    *They draw. Enter Adriana, Luciana, Courtezan, & others.   1497
    Enter Ladie Abbesse.   1504
    Good people enter, and lay hold on him.   1560
    Enter the Duke of Ephesus, and the Merchant of Siracuse   1599
    Enter a Messenger.   1640
    Enter Antipholus, and E.Dromio of Ephesus.   1665
    Duke. Saw'st thou him enter at the Abbey heere?   1756
    Enter the Abbesse with Antipholus Siracusa, | and Dromio Sir.   1811
ENTERS = 1
    Ab. No, not a creature enters in my house.   1561
ENTERTAINE = 2
    Ile entertaine the free'd fallacie.   581
    Since mine owne doores refuse to entertaine me,   781
ENTRANCE = 1
    Of his owne doores being shut against his entrance.   1272
ENTRED = 1
    Dro. Master, I am heere entred in bond for you.   1417
EP = 1
    Exeunt Dromio Ep.   260
EPH = 2
    Enter Dromio Eph.   318
    Enter Dromio Eph. with a ropes end.   1288
EPHANT = *1
EPHES = 2
    Enter Antipholus Ephes.Dromio from the Courtizans.   995
    Enter Antipholus Ephes. with a Iailor.   1280
EPHESUS see also *E.An., E.D., E.Dr., E.Dro., E.Drom., E.Dromio.,*
    E.Mar., Eph.Ant., Ephes., Ephes.Dromio. = 11*2
    *Enter the Duke of Ephesus, with the Merchant of Siracusa, | Iaylor, and
    other attendants.   2
    Nay more, if any borne at *Ephesus* | Be seene at any *Siracusian* Marts
    and Fayres: 20
    Againe, if any *Siracusian* borne | Come to the Bay of *Ephesus*, he dies: 22
    And for what cause thou cam'st to *Ephesus*.   34
    And coasting homeward, came to *Ephesus*:   137
    Try all the friends thou hast in *Ephesus*,   155
    Enter Dromio of Ephesus.   205
    In *Ephesus* I am but two houres old,   543
    *Enter Antipholus of Ephesus, his man Dromio, Angelo the | Goldsmith,
    and Balthaser the Merchant.   617
    Gold. Sir, sir, I shall haue Law in *Ephesus*,   1071
    That I should be attach'd in *Ephesus*,   1286
    Enter the Duke of Ephesus, and the Merchant of Siracuse   1599
    Enter Antipholus, and E.Dromio of Ephesus.   1665
EPIDAMIUM = 7
    To *Epidamium*, till my factors death,   45
    A league from *Epidamium* had we saild   65
    Mer. Therefore giue out you are of *Epidamium*,   163

EPIDAMIUM *cont.*
  Dro. Master, there's a Barke of *Epidamium,*   1074
  What ship of *Epidamium* staies for me.   1083
  Abb. By men of *Epidamium,* he, and I,   1841
  And me they left with those of *Epidamium.*   1845
EPIDARUS = 1
  Of *Corinth* that, of *Epidarus* this,   96
ERE = 6*1
  But ere they came, oh let me say no more,   97
  For ere the ships could meet by twice fiue leagues,   103
  Dies ere the wearie sunne set in the West: 169
  Luc. Ere I learne loue, Ile practise to obey.   303
  *It was two ere I left him, and now the clocke strikes one.   1166
  Ile giue thee ere I leaue thee so much money | To warrant thee as I am
    rested for.   1282
  Adr. I will discharge thee ere I go from thee,   1411
ERGO = *1
  *effect of fire, and fire will burne: *ergo,* light wenches will | burne, come
    not neere her.   1239
EROTES = 1
  Enter Antipholis Erotes, a Marchant, and Dromio.   162
ERRAND *see* arrant
ERRE = 1
  All these old witnesses, I cannot erre.   1798
ERROR = 2
  What error driues our eies and eares amisse?   579
  That by this simpathized one daies error.   1887
ERRORS = 3
  Smothred in errors, feeble, shallow, weake,   822
  And thereupon these errors are arose.   1877
  The Comedie of Errors.   1921
ERROTIS *see also* E.Ant., E.Anti. = 1
  Enter Antipholis Errotis.   394
ESCAPE = 1
  Anon I wot not, by what strong escape   1620
ESTABLISH = 1
  Establish him in his true sence againe,   1331
ESTEEMD = 1
  Mar. How is the man esteem'd heere in the Citie?   1467
ESTIMATION = 1
  Against your yet vngalled estimation,   763
ESTRANGED = 1
  That thou art then estranged from thy selfe?   515
EUEN = 9*3
  E.Ant. Euen now, euen here, not halfe an howre since.   409
  Ant. Villaine thou liest, for euen her verie words,   557
  Euen in the spring of Loue, thy Loue-springs rot?   789
  She that doth call me husband, euen my soule   948
  Gold. Euen iust the sum that I do owe to you,   988
  Gold. Come, come, you know I gaue it you euen now.   1041
  Euen now a tailor cal'd me in his shop,   1190
  Euen now we hous'd him in the Abbey heere.   1663
  Euen for the seruice that long since I did thee,   1667
  Deepe scarres to saue thy life; euen for the blood   1669
  Euen in the strength and height of iniurie: 1676
EUENING = 2
  My woes end likewise with the euening Sonne.   31

EUENING *cont.*
   And about euening come your selfe alone,   757
EUER = 4*1
   S.Dro. Was there euer anie man thus beaten out of   442
   For euer hows'd, where it gets possession.   767
   And euer as it blaz'd, they threw on him   1645
   Nor euer didst thou draw thy sword on me: 1743
   Abb. Who euer bound him, I will lose his bonds,   1825
EUERIE = 2
   If euerie one knowes vs, and we know none,   942
   And euerie one doth call me by my name: 1186
EUERIEONE *see* euerie
EUERLASTING = 1
   A diuell in an euerlasting garment hath him;   1142
EUERY = 2*2
   S.Dro. I sir, and wherefore; for they say, euery why | hath a wherefore.   438
   Who euery word by all my wit being scan'd,   545
   Bal. Good meat sir is co(m)mon that euery churle affords.   643
   Ill-fac'd, worse bodied, shapelesse euery where: 1126
EUILL = 2*1
   Ill deeds is doubled with an euill word: 806
   No euill lost is wail'd, when it is gone.   1130
   *came behinde you sir, like an euill angel, and bid you for-|sake your
   libertie.   1203
EXCEEDING = 1
   Those, for their parents were exceeding poore,   60
EXCELLENT = 1
   I know a wench of excellent discourse,   770
EXCEPT = 1
   Adr. To none of these, except it be the last,   1522
EXCLUDES = 1
   Excludes all pitty from our threatning lookes: 14
EXCREMENT = 1
   it is) so plentifull an excrement?   472
EXCUSE = 1*2
   E.Anti. Good signior *Angelo* you must excuse vs all,   619
   And doubt not sir, but she will well excuse   753
   Anti. Good Lord, you vse this dalliance to excuse   1034
EXECUTION = 1
   The place of depth, and sorrie execution,   1590
EXEMPT = 1
   Be it my wrong, you are from me exempt,   565
EXEUNT = 11
   But to procrastinate his liuelesse end. *Exeunt.*   161
   E.Mar. Sir, I commend you to your owne content. | *Exeunt.* 195
   Exeunt Dromio Ep.   260
   Anti. Do so, this iest shall cost me some expence. | *Exeunt.* 784
   On Officer to prison, till it come. *Exeunt*   1097
   Exeunt. Manet Offic. Adri. Luci. Courtizan   1426
   Off. Away, they'l kill vs. | *Exeunt omnes, as fast as may be, frighted.* 1446
   Therefore away, to get our stuffe aboord. *Exeunt*   1461
   This is some Priorie, in, or we are spoyl'd. | *Exeunt to the Priorie.* 1502
   Exeunt omnes. Manet the two Dromio's and | *two Brothers.* 1898
   *And now let's go hand in hand, not one before another. | *Exeunt.* 1918
EXIT = 14
   And goe indeede, hauing so good a meane. | *Exit Dromio.* 180
   I greatly feare my monie is not safe. *Exit.*   271

FACE *cont.*
  But here's a villaine that would face me downe 624
  *Thou wouldst haue chang'd thy face for a name, or thy | name for an 677
  asse.
  I and breake it in your face, so he break it not behinde. 734
  Dro. Swart like my shoo, but her face nothing like 893
  Oh, his hearts Meteors tilting in his face. 1109
  Did this Companion with the saffron face 1345
  To scorch your face, and to disfigure you: | *Cry within.* 1656
  And with no-face (as 'twere) out-facing me, 1721
  Haue written strange defeatures in my face: 1780
  Though now this grained face of mine be hid 1792
FACING = 1
  And with no-face (as 'twere) out-facing me, 1721
FACTORS = 1
  To *Epidamium*, till my factors death, 45
FADING = 1
  My wasting lampes some fading glimmer left; 1796
FAINE = 1
  Angelo. Heere is neither cheere sir, nor welcome, we | would faine 715
  haue either.
FAINTING = 1
  Before her selfe (almost at fainting vnder 49
FAIRE = 11*3
  Of my defeatures. My decayed faire, 374
  So he would keepe faire quarter with his bed: 384
  Keepe then faire league and truce with thy true bed, 540
  Antip. Plead you to me faire dame? I know you not: 542
  Looke sweet, speake faire, become disloyaltie: 797
  Beare a faire presence, though your heart be tainted, 799
  Ant. For gazing on your beames faire sun being by. 843
  Doth for a wife abhorre. But her faire sister 949
  That would refuse so faire an offer'd Chaine. 975
  Blowes faire from land: they stay for nought at all, 1080
  Adr. Did'st speake him faire? | *Luc.* Haue patience I beseech. 1121
  *vs no harme: you saw they speake vs faire, giue vs gold: 1455
  That bore thee at a burthen two faire sonnes? 1829
  And this faire Gentlewoman her sister heere 1861
FAIRELY = 1
  Then fairely I bespoke the Officer 1710
FAIRIE = 2
  This is the Fairie land, oh spight of spights, 584
  A Feind, a Fairie, pittilesse and ruffe: 1144
FAITH = *4
  Luce. Faith no, hee comes too late, and so tell your | Master. 683
  Ant. Where *Spaine*? | *Dro.* Faith I saw it not: but I felt it hot in her 920
  breth.
  *my brest had not beene made of faith, and my heart of 934
  Dro. Faith stay heere this night, they will surely do 1454
FALL = 3
  Marchant. | Proceed *Solinus* to procure my fall, 4
  For know my loue: as easie maist thou fall 520
  Adr. Come go, I will fall prostrate at his feete, 1583
FALLACIE = 1
  Ile entertaine the free'd fallacie. 581
FALLING = 1
  Who falling there to finde his fellow forth, 201

FALS = 1

The Capon burnes, the Pig fals from the spit;   209
FALSE = 9*1

And from my false hand cut the wedding ring,   532
For if we two be one, and thou play false,   537
Muffle your false loue with some shew of blindnesse: 794
Be secret false: what need she be acquainted?   801
*Adr. Dissembling Villain, thou speak'st false in both   1388
Ant. Dissembling harlot, thou art false in all,   1389
But with these nailes, Ile plucke out these false eyes,   1392
And that is false thou dost report to vs.   1652
As this is false he burthens me withall.   1686
And this is false you burthen me withall.   1745
FALSHOOD = 1

By falshood and corruption doth it shame: 389
FALSING = 1

An. Nay, not sure in a thing falsing.   488
FAME = 1

Shame hath a bastard fame, well managed,   805
FAMILIARLIE = 1

Antiph. Because that I familiarlie sometimes   421
FAMOUS = *1

*E.Ant. Brought to this Town by that most famous | Warriour,   1853
FAR = *1

*Gold. My Lord, in truth, thus far I witnes with him: 1731
FARE = 1

Ang. You are a merry man sir, fare you well. Exit.   972
FAREWELL = 1

Ant. Farewell till then: I will goe loose my selfe,   193
FARING = 1

Such as sea-faring men prouide for stormes: 83
FARRE = 4

Two shippes from farre, making amaine to vs: 95
Farre more, farre more, to you doe I decline: 831
Farre from her nest the Lapwing cries away;   1133
FARTHEST = 1

Fiue Sommers haue I spent in farthest Greece,   135
FASHION = 3

That mourn'd for fashion, ignorant what to feare,   76
And fashion your demeanor to my lookes,   428
The finenesse of the Gold, and chargefull fashion,   1012
FAST = 7

You haue no stomacke, hauing broke your fast: 215
But we that know what 'tis to fast and pray,   216
She that doth fast till you come home to dinner: 254
*Ant. Why how now Dromio, where run'st thou so | fast?   862
Luc. How hast thou lost thy breath? | S.Dro. By running fast.   1138
Off. Away, they'l kill vs. | Exeunt omnes, as fast as may be, frighted.   1446
Let vs come in, that we may binde him fast,   1507
FASTEN = 1

Come I will fasten on this sleeue of thine: 567
FASTNED = 2

Had fastned him vnto a small spare Mast,   82
Fastned our selues at eyther end the mast,   88
FAT = 1, 3

*but leane lucke in the match, and yet is she a wondrous | fat marriage.   883
Anti. How dost thou meane a fat marriage?   885

FAT *cont.*
  S.Dro. There is a fat friend at your masters house,   1906
FATALL = 1
  That floated with thee on the fatall rafte.   1840
FATES = 1
  Duke. Haplesse *Egeon* whom the fates haue markt   143
FATH = 3
FATHER see also *Fa., Fat., Fath., Mar.Fat.* = *1, 3*1
  *S.Dro. Marry sir, by a rule as plaine as the plaine bald | pate of Father
  time himselfe.   463
  Ant. I neuer saw my Father in my life.   1800
  *E.Ant. These Duckets pawne I for my father heere.   1878
  Duke. It shall not neede, thy father hath his life.   1879
FAULT = 5
  For she will scoure your fault vpon my pate: 230
  That's not my fault, hee's master of my state.   371
  Luc. It is a fault that springeth from your eie.   842
  Anti. That's a fault that water will mend.   896
  Duke. A greeuous fault: say woman, didst thou so?   1683
FAUOUR = 2
  Doe me the fauour to dilate at full,   125
  Yet will I fauour thee in what I can;   152
FAYRES = 1
  Nay more, if any borne at *Ephesus* | Be seene at any *Siracusian* Marts
  and Fayres: 20
FEARE = 5*2
  That mourn'd for fashion, ignorant what to feare,   76
  I greatly feare my monie is not safe. *Exit.*   271
  For feare you ne're see chaine, nor mony more.   971
  *S.Dro. Oh yes, if any houre meete a Serieant, a turnes | backe for verie
  feare.   1168
  An. Feare me not man, I will not breake away,   1281
  *Duke. Come stand by me, feare nothing: guard with | Halberds.   1659
  *Mar.Fat. Vnlesse the feare of death doth make me | dote, I see my
  sonne *Antipholus* and *Dromio.*   1671
FEAREFULL = 1
  Did but conuay vnto our fearefull mindes   70
FEAST = 3*1
  *Bal. Small cheere and great welcome, makes a mer-|rie feast.   646
  Reuell and feast it at my house to day,   1346
  Go to a Gossips feast, and go with mee,   1895
  Duke. With all my heart, Ile Gossip at this feast.   1897
FEASTED = 1
  While she with Harlots feasted in my house.   1682
FEATHER = *1
  *E.Dro. A crow without feather, Master meane you so;   742
FEATHERS = *1
  *S.Dro. I, when fowles haue no feathers, and fish haue | no fin.   739
FEAUER = 2
  Thereof the raging fire of feauer bred,   1544
  And what's a Feauer, but a fit of madnesse?   1545
FED = 1
  At boord he fed not for my vrging it: 1533
FEE = 1
  Gold. Heere is thy fee, arrest him Officer.   1064
FEEBLE = 2
  Smothred in errors, feeble, shallow, weake,   822

FEEBLE *cont*.
Knowes not my feeble key of vntun'd cares?	1791

FEEDES = 1
And feedes from home; poore I am but his stale.	377

FEELE = 2*3
Luc. Spake hee so doubtfully, thou couldst not feele | his meaning.	326
*feele his blowes; and withall so doubtfully, that I could | scarce vnderstand them.	329
not feele your blowes.	1307
Pinch. Giue me your hand, and let mee feele your | pulse.	1335
Ant. There is my hand, and let it feele your eare.	1337

FEELING = 1
And gazing in mine eyes, feeling my pulse,	1720

FEET = 1
S.Dro. Let him walke from whence he came, lest hee | catch cold on's feet.	660

FEETE = 1
Adr. Come go, I will fall prostrate at his feete,	1583

FEIND = 1
A Feind, a Fairie, pittilesse and ruffe:	1144

FELL = 1
They fell vpon me, bound me, bore me thence,	1723

FELLOW = 5
Who falling there to finde his fellow forth,	201
Arrest me foolish fellow if thou dar'st.	1063
A Wolfe, nay worse, a fellow all in buffe:	1145
Ant. The fellow is distract, and so am I,	1224
Pinch. It is no shame, the fellow finds his vaine,	1367

FELT = 1*1
Ant. Where *Spaine*? | *Dro*. Faith I saw it not: but I felt it hot in her breth.	920
That since haue felt the vigor of his rage.	1365

FELTST = 1
For which I hope thou feltst I was displeas'd.	414

FEMALES = 1
Are masters to their females, and their Lords:	298

FETCH = 8*6
E.Dro. My charge was but to fetch you fro(m) the Mart	239
Adri. Go back againe, thou slaue, & fetch him home.	351
Adri. Hence prating pesant, fetch thy Master home.	357
Ant. Go fetch me something, Ile break ope the gate.	729
Ant. Go, get thee gon, fetch me an iron Crow.	745
And fetch the chaine, by this I know 'tis made,	776
Ile fetch my sister to get her good will. *Exit*.	860
Ant. Why giue it to my wife, and fetch your mony.	1040
Adr. Go fetch it Sister: this I wonder at. | *Exit Luciana*.	1158
Ant. Come to the Centaur, fetch our stuffe from | thence:	1451
Adr. To fetch my poore distracted husband hence,	1506
And will not suffer vs to fetch him out,	1629
Who parted with me to go fetch a Chaine,	1698
S.Dro. Mast.(er) shall I fetch your stuffe from shipbord?	1900

FETHER = *1
*For a fish without a finne, ther's a fowle without a fether,	743

FIE = 4*1
Luci. Fie how impatience lowreth in your face.	362
Luci. Selfe-harming Iealousie; fie beat it hence.	378
Luci. Fie brother, how the world is chang'd with you:	547

FIE *cont.*
   Ant. Fie, now you run this humor out of breath,   1043
   Fie on thee wretch, 'tis pitty that thou liu'st   1491
FIELD = 1
   To make it wander in an vnknowne field?   825
FIEND *see also* feind = *2
   Ant. Auoid then fiend, what tel'st thou me of sup-|(ping?   1248
   Pinch. More company, the fiend is strong within him   1398
FIERY = 1
   Luc. Alas how fiery, and how sharpe he lookes.   1333
FIN = 1
   S.Dro. I, when fowles haue no feathers, and fish haue | no fin.   739
FIND = *2
   *to hippe: she is sphericall, like a globe: I could find out | Countries in
   her.   905
   Dro. I look'd for the chalkle Cliffes, but I could find   917
FINDE = 4*1
   Hopelesse to finde, yet loth to leaue vnsought   138
   Who falling there to finde his fellow forth,   201
   So I, to finde a Mother and a Brother,   203
   *I could finde in my heart to stay heere still, and turne | Witch.   1458
   Duke. Discouer how, and thou shalt finde me iust.   1679
FINDS = 1
   Pinch. It is no shame, the fellow finds his vaine,   1367
FINE = 1*1
   Ant. May he not doe it by fine and recouerie?   468
   S.Dro. Yes, to pay a fine for a perewig, and recouer | the lost haire of
   another man.   469
FINEM = *1
   E.Dro. Mistris *respice finem*, respect your end, or ra-|ther   1325
FINENESSE = 1
   The finenesse of the Gold, and chargefull fashion,   1012
FINGER = 3
   To put the finger in the eie and weepe;   600
   The Ring I saw vpon his finger now,   1435
   Cur. He did, and from my finger snacht that Ring.   1754
FINIS *l.*1920 = 1
FINNE = *1
   *For a fish without a finne, ther's a fowle without a fether,   743
FIRE = 2*2
   *effect of fire, and fire will burne: *ergo*, light wenches will | burne, come
   not neere her.   1239
   Thereof the raging fire of feauer bred,   1544
   Whose beard they haue sindg'd off with brands of fire,   1644
FIRST = 7*1
   I could not speake with *Dromio*, since at first   399
   Ant. Why first for flowting me, and then wherefore,   440
   But like a shrew you first begin to brawle.   1037
   Luc. First he deni'de you had in him no right.   1110
   First, he did praise my beautie, then my speech.   1120
   After you first forswore it on the Mart,   1738
   Duke. *Antipholus* thou cam'st from *Corinth* first.   1848
   S.Dro. Wee'l draw Cuts for the Signior, till then, | lead thou first.   1914
FISH = 2*2
   Of more preheminence then fish and fowles,   297
   E.An. Oh signior *Balthazar*, either at flesh or fish,   641
   S.Dro. I, when fowles haue no feathers, and fish haue | no fin.   739

FISH *cont*.

*For a fish without a finne, ther's a fowle without a fether,   743
FISHERMEN = 2

By Fishermen of *Corinth*, as we thought.   114
But by and by, rude Fishermen of *Corinth*   1843
FISHERS = 1

And would haue reft the Fishers of their prey,   118
FISHES = 1

The beasts, the fishes, and the winged fowles   292
FIT = 2

And what's a Feauer, but a fit of madnesse?   1545
A most outragious fit of madnesse tooke him: 1611
FITS = 2

Belike his wife acquainted with his fits,   1273
The consequence is then, thy iealous fits   1554
FITTEST = 1

My Ring away. This course I fittest choose,   1278
FIUE = 7

For ere the ships could meet by twice fiue leagues,   103
Fiue Sommers haue I spent in farthest *Greece*,   135
I craue your pardon, soone at fiue a clocke,   189
He had of me a Chaine, at fiue a clocke   991
Ant. Fiue hundred Duckets villaine for a rope?   1294
E.Dro. Ile serue you sir fiue hundred at the rate.   1295
Mar. By this I thinke the Diall points at fiue: 1587
FIXING = 1

Fixing our eyes on whom our care was fixt,   87
FIXT = 1

Fixing our eyes on whom our care was fixt,   87
FLATTERIE = 1

When the sweet breath of flatterie conquers strife.   814
FLED = 2

We came againe to binde them: then they fled   1626
And then you fled into this Abbey heere,   1740
FLESH = 2*1

I doe digest the poison of thy flesh,   538
E.An. Oh signior *Balthazar*, either at flesh or fish,   641
*the Mountaine of mad flesh that claimes mariage of me,   1457
FLIE = 2*1

So flie I from her that would be my wife. *Exit*   945
S.Dro. Flie pride saies the Pea-cocke, Mistris that | you know. *Exit*.   1262
Harke, harke, I heare him Mistris: flie, be gone.   1658
FLOATED = 1

That floated with thee on the fatall rafte.   1840
FLOATING = 1

And floating straight, obedient to the streame,   89
FLOOD = *1

Dro. No sir, 'tis in graine, *Noahs* flood could not | do it.   897
FLOUD = 1

To drowne me in thy sister floud of teares: 833
FLOUT = 1

Ant. What wilt thou flout me thus vnto my face   256
FLOWT = 1

Ant. Yea, dost thou ieere & flowt me in the teeth?   417
FLOWTING = *1

Ant. Why first for flowting me, and then wherefore,   440

FOES = 1
Of pale distemperatures, and foes to life?   1551
FOLLOWERS = 1
therefore to the worlds end, will haue bald followers.   501
FOLLOWING = 1
Had made prouision for her following me,   51
FOND = 1
Luci. How manie fond fooles serue mad Ielousie? | *Exit.*   392
FONDLY = *1
Adri. As if time were in debt: how fondly do'st thou | reason?   1170
FOOD = 1
In food, in sport, and life-preseruing rest   1552
FOODE = 1
My foode, my fortune, and my sweet hopes aime;   852
FOOLE = 3*1
Doe vse you for my foole, and chat with you,   422
Adr. Come, come, no longer will I be a foole,   599
His man with Cizers nickes him like a foole: 1648
Adr. Peace foole, thy Master and his man are here,   1651
FOOLERIE = 1
Ant. Well sir, there rest in your foolerie: 1217
FOOLES = 1
Luci. How manie fond fooles serue mad Ielousie? | *Exit.*   392
FOOLE-BEGD = 1
This foole-beg'd patience in thee will be left.   315
FOOLISH = 3
When the sunne shines, let foolish gnats make sport,   425
Arrest me foolish fellow if thou dar'st.   1063
Vicious, vngentle, foolish, blunt, vnkinde,   1127
FOOLISHNES = *1
Ant. Come on sir knaue, haue done your foolishnes,   237
FOOLS = *1
Ad. Vnfeeling fools can with such wrongs dispence: 379
FOOT = *1
Dro. No longer from head to foot, then from hippe   904
FOOT-BALL = 1
That like a foot-ball you doe spurne me thus: 359
FOR *l.*15 34 41 51 60 63 69 74 76 77 78 79 81 83 100 103 109 124 148 165
177 217 221 230 241 *258 338 350 353 364 414 *419 422 *432 *438 *440
441 445 446 449 458 *466 *469 484 494 520 537 549 553 557 573 *575
582 583 596 605 *644 *656 *665 *671 677 696 699 *702 *743 766 767
778 779 791 *792 834 *843 855 *894 *917 944 949 *962 964 969 971 978
984 992 1000 1016 1032 1036 1049 1060 1080 1081 1083 1085 1087 1088
1099 1100 1102 1115 1117 1134 1168 1188 1191 *1196 *1202 *1221
*1222 1252 1267 1279 1282 1290 1293 1294 *1301 *1313 1372 *1375
1379 1405 1417 *1420 1431 *1432 1442 *1456 1460 1484 1496 1498
*1501 1508 1524 1532 1533 1563 1568 1571 1596 1603 1618 1632 1655
1667 1669 1670 1697 1706 1709 1730 1773 1868 1876 *1878 *1881 1907
*1914 = 133*36
FORBEARE = 1
Luc. Till he come home againe, I would forbeare.   305
FORBID = 1
Being forbid? There take you that sir knaue.   257
FORCE = 1
By force tooke *Dromio,* and my sonne from them,   1844

FORGOT = 1
Iulia. And may it be that you haue quite forgot | A husbands office?
shall *Antipholus*   787
FORHEAD = *1
*Dro. In her forhead, arm'd and reuerted, making | warre against her
heire.   914
FORMALL = 1
To make of him a formall man againe: 1574
FORME = 1
Ant. Thou hast thine owne forme. | *S.Dro*. No, I am an Ape.   593
FORSAKE = *1
*came behinde you sir, like an euill angel, and bid you for-|sake your
libertie.   1203
FORSOOTH = 1
Forsooth tooke on him as a Coniurer: 1719
FORST = 1
Forst me to seeke delayes for them and me,   77
FORSWEARE = 1
Ant. Who heard me to denie it or forsweare it?   1489
FORSWORE = 3
Which he forswore most monstrously to haue.   1475
Mar. Yes that you did sir, and forswore it too.   1488
After you first forswore it on the Mart,   1738
FORSWORNE = *2
*Adr. And true he swore, though yet forsworne hee | were.   1113
*Gold. O periur'd woman! They are both forsworne,   1689
FORTH = 7*4
Who falling there to finde his fellow forth,   201
Is wandred forth in care to seeke me out   397
Say he dines forth, and let no creature enter: 606
If any Barke put forth, come to the Mart,   940
*Is there any ships puts forth to night? may we be gone?   1218
*that the Barke *Expedition* put forth to night, and then   1220
*Ant. Say wherefore didst thou locke me forth to day,   1383
Adr. I did not gentle husband locke thee forth.   1385
*Ad. Then let your seruants bring my husband forth   1562
Nor send him forth, that we may beare him hence.   1630
Let him be brought forth, and borne hence for helpe.   1632
FORTHWITH = 1
Beare me forthwith vnto his Creditor,   1412
FORTIE = 2
A Ring he hath of mine worth fortie Duckets,   1266
For fortie Duckets is too much to loose.   1279
FORTUNE = 3
Fortune had left to both of vs alike,   108
My foode, my fortune, and my sweet hopes aime;   852
I, to this fortune that you see mee in.   1847
FORTUNES = 1
And heare at large discoursed all our fortunes,   1885
FORTUNE-TELLER = 1
A thred-bare Iugler, and a Fortune-teller,   1716
FORWARD = 1
Duk. Nay forward old man, doe not breake off so,   99
FOULDED = 1
The foulded meaning of your words deceit: 823
FOULE = 1
That may with foule intrusion enter in,   764

FOUND = 2*2
    What ruines are in me that can be found,   372
    *Dro. Marry sir in her buttockes, I found it out by | the bogges.   908
    *Dro. I found it by the barrennesse, hard in the palme | of the hand.   911
    I see sir you haue found the Gold-smith now: 1229
FOURE = 1
    Enter three or foure, and offer to binde him: | *Hee striues.*   1394
FOWLE = *1
    *For a fish without a finne, ther's a fowle without a fether,   743
FOWLES = 2*1
    The beasts, the fishes, and the winged fowles   292
    Of more preheminence then fish and fowles,   297
    *S.Dro. I, when fowles haue no feathers, and fish haue | no fin.   739
FRANCE = 2
    Ant. Where *France*?   913
    by the salt rheume that ranne betweene *France*, and it.   919
FRANTICKE = 1
    Pinch. Go binde this man, for he is franticke too.   1405
FRAUGHTAGE = 1
    And then sir she beares away. Our fraughtage sir,   1076
FREE = 1
    Free from these slanders, and this open shame.   1351
FREED = 1
    Ile entertaine the free'd fallacie.   581
FREEDOME = 1
    I gain'd my freedome; and immediately   1727
FREELY = 1
    Duke. Speake freely *Siracusian* what thou wilt.   1765
FRENSIE = 1
    And yeelding to him, humors well his frensie.   1368
FRET = 1
    Good Sister let vs dine, and neuer fret;   280
FRIEND = 6*1
    *A back friend, a shoulder-clapper, one that counterma(n)ds   1146
    As if I were their well acquainted friend,   1185
    You haue done wrong to this my honest friend,   1483
    Buried some deere friend, hath not else his eye   1517
    If any friend will pay the summe for him,   1603
    Haply I see a friend will saue my life,   1763
    S.Dro. There is a fat friend at your masters house,   1906
FRIENDS = 1
    Try all the friends thou hast in *Ephesus*,   155
FRIGHT = 1
    *be wise, and if you giue it her, the diuell will shake | her Chaine, and
    fright vs with it.   1257
FRIGHTED = 1
    Off. Away, they'l kill vs. | *Exeunt omnes, as fast as may be, frighted.*   1446
FROM *l.*10 14 33 47 48 65 95 121 192 209 226 228 *239 279 366 377 400
    515 519 524 532 *551 565 571 637 *655 *657 *660 *669 *712 842 *888
    *901 *904 *933 938 944 945 995 1073 1080 1133 1226 *1311 *1317 1320
    1351 1363 1411 *1449 *1451 1513 1523 1555 1564 1586 1621 1695 1741
    1754 1844 1848 1849 *1851 1873 1880 *1900 = 50*18
FROWNE = 1
    Adri. I, I, *Antipholus*, looke strange and frowne,   505
FROZE = 1
    And all the Conduits of my blood froze vp: 1794

FULFILL = 1
  For seruants must their Masters mindes fulfill. *Exit*   1102
FULL = 4
  Doe me the fauour to dilate at full,   125
  They say this towne is full of cosenage: 263
  A table full of welcome, makes scarce one dainty dish.   642
  And we shall make full satisfaction.   1889
FURIE = 1
  That heere and there his furie had committed,   1619
FURNISHD = 1
  Anti. I am not furnish'd with the present monie: 1017
GAIND = 1
  I gain'd my freedome; and immediately   1727
GAINE = 1
  And gaine a husband by his libertie: 1826
GAINES = 1
  He gaines by death, that hath such meanes to die: 838
GARMENT = 1
  A diuell in an euerlasting garment hath him;   1142
GARMENTS = *1
  *E.Dro. You would say so Master, if your garments | were thin.   723
GATE = 4*1
  Come sir to dinner, *Dromio* keepe the gate: 602
  S.Dro. Master, shall I be Porter at the gate?   613
  *Luce. What a coile is there *Dromio*? who are those | at the gate?   680
  *Ant. Go fetch me something, Ile break ope the gate.   729
  Go some of you, knocke at the Abbey gate,   1637
GATES = 1
  And heere the Abbesse shuts the gates on vs,   1628
GATHER = 3
  Gather the sequell by that went before.   98
  The reason that I gather he is mad,   1269
  All gather to see them.   1815
GAUE = 10*4
  Gaue any Tragicke Instance of our harme: 67
  Gaue healthfull welcome to their ship-wrackt guests,   117
  Where haue you left the mony that I gaue you.   219
  Where is the gold I gaue in charge to thee?   235
  E.Dro. To me sir? why you gaue no gold to me?   236
  Where is the thousand markes I gaue thee villaine?   342
  Ant. The gold I gaue to *Dromio* is laid vp   395
  Home to the *Centaur* with the gold you gaue me.   411
  *S.Dro. Marry sir, for this something that you gaue me | for nothing.   446
  **If y skin were parchment, & y blows you gaue were ink,   631
  *Gold. Come, come, you know I gaue it you euen now.   1041
  Gold. You know I gaue it you halfe an houre since.   1051
  *Ant. You gaue me none, you wrong mee much to | say so.   1052
  E.Dro. Why sir, I gaue the Monie for the Rope.   1293
GAUST = 1
  She whom thou gau'st to me to be my wife;   1674
GAY = 1
  Doe their gay vestments his affections baite?   370
GAZE = 1*1
  Peruse the traders, gaze vpon the buildings,   175
  *Luc. Gaze when you should, and that will cleere | your sight.   844
GAZING = 3*1
  At length the sonne gazing vpon the earth,   91

GAZING *cont.*

*Ant. For gazing on your beames faire sun being by.	843
Who giue their eies the liberty of gazing.	1520
And gazing in mine eyes, feeling my pulse,	1720

GENIUS = 1

Duke. One of these men is *genius* to the other:	1817

GENTLE = 6*1

Prettie and wittie; wilde, and yet too gentle;	771
Then gentle brother get you in againe;	811
Possest with such a gentle soueraigne grace,	950
Adr. I did not gentle husband locke thee forth.	1385
Dro. And gentle Mr I receiu'd no gold:	1386
*me thinkes they are such a gentle Nation, that but for	1456
Adr. Which of you two did dine with me to day? | *S.Ant.* I, gentle	
Mistris.	1856

GENTLEMAN = 3

Then I stand debted to this Gentleman,	1014
Both winde and tide stayes for this Gentleman,	1032
And in his companie that Gentleman.	1703

GENTLEMEN = *1

*gentlemen are tired giues them a sob, and rests them:	1208

GENTLEWOMAN = 2

Ant. Did you conuerse sir with this gentlewoman:	554
And this faire Gentlewoman her sister heere	1861

GET = 10*5

For with long trauaile I am stiffe and wearie. | Get thee away.	177
Commends me to the thing I cannot get:	198
*long, I must get a sconce for my head, and Insconce it	432
*Either get thee from the dore, or sit downe at the hatch:	655
*When one is one too many, goe get thee from the dore.	657
Adri. Your wife sir knaue? go get you from the dore.	712
Anti. There is something in the winde, that we can-|not get in.	721
Ant. Go, get thee gon, fetch me an iron Crow.	745
To her will we to dinner, get you home	775
Then gentle brother get you in againe;	811
Ile fetch my sister to get her good will. *Exit.*	860
But soft I see the Goldsmith; get thee gone,	1001
Therefore away, to get our stuffe aboord. *Exeunt*	1461
Some get within him, take his sword away:	1499
Once did I get him bound, and sent him home,	1617

GETS = 1

For euer hows'd, where it gets possession.	767

GHOST = 1

S.Ant. Egeon art thou not? or else his ghost.	1822

GIFTS = 1

When in the streets he meetes such Golden gifts:	977

GILDERS = 2

Who wanting gilders to redeeme their liues,	12
Nor now I had not, but that I am bound | To *Persia*, and want Gilders	
for my voyage:	984

GILLIAN = 1

E.Dro. Maud, Briget, Marian, Cisley, Gillian, Ginn.	652

GINN = 1

E.Dro. Maud, Briget, Marian, Cisley, Gillian, Ginn.	652

GIUE = 10*7

Mer. Therefore giue out you are of *Epidamium*,	163
Vpon what bargaine do you giue it me?	420

GIUE *cont.*

. *Ant.* Ile make you amends next, to giue you nothing | 448
. Thou hast no husband yet, nor I no wife: | Giue me thy hand. | 857
Gold. Nay come I pray you sir, giue me the Chaine: | 1031
Ant. Why giue it to my wife, and fetch your mony. | 1040
Ant. I do obey thee, till I giue thee baile. | 1068
Giue her this key, and tell her in the Deske | 1092
Some other giue me thankes for kindnesses; | 1188
*thinkes a man alwaies going to bed, and saies, God giue | you good rest. | 1215
Cur. Giue me the ring of mine you had at dinner, | 1251
*be wise, and if you giue it her, the diuell will shake | her Chaine, and fright vs with it. | 1257
Ile giue thee ere I leaue thee so much money | To warrant thee as I am rested for. | 1282
Pinch. Giue me your hand, and let mee feele your | pulse. | 1335
*vs no harme: you saw they speake vs faire, giue vs gold: | 1455
Who giue their eies the liberty of gazing. | 1520
Ran hether to your Grace, whom I beseech | To giue me ample satisfaction | 1728

GIUEN = 1
*beasts, and what he hath scanted them in haire, hee hath | giuen them in wit. | 474

GIUES = 1*2
Ile vtter what my sorrow giues me leaue. | 39
*gentlemen are tired giues them a sob, and rests them: | 1208
*he sir, that takes pittie on decaied men, and giues them | 1209

GLAD = 1
S.Dro. I am glad to see you in this merrie vaine, | 415

GLADLY = 1
Which though my selfe would gladly haue imbrac'd, | 72

GLANCED = 1
In company I often glanced it: | 1535

GLASSE = *1
E.D. Me thinks you are my glasse, & not my brother: | 1909

GLIMMER = 1
My wasting lampes some fading glimmer left; | 1796

GLOBE = *1
*to hippe: she is sphericall, like a globe: I could find out | Countries in her. | 905

GLORIOUS = 1
And in that glorious supposition thinke, | 837

GNATS = 1
When the sunne shines, let foolish gnats make sport, | 425

GNAWD = 1
But he I thanke him gnaw'd in two my cords, | 1769

GNAWING = 1
Till gnawing with my teeth my bonds in sunder, | 1726

GO = 20*9
Adri. Go back againe, thou slaue, & fetch him home. | 351
And in this mist at all aduentures go. | 612
Adri. Your wife sir knaue? go get you from the dore. | 712
Ant. Go fetch me something, Ile break ope the gate. | 729
Ant. Well, Ile breake in: go borrow me a crow. | 741
Ant. Go, get thee gon, fetch me an iron Crow. | 745
Anti. Go hie thee presently, post to the rode, | 937
Go home with it, and please your Wife withall, | 967

GO *cont*.

*Ant. While I go to the Goldsmiths house, go thou	997
Adr. Go fetch it Sister: this I wonder at. | *Exit Luciana*.	1158
*Adr. Go *Dromio*, there's the monie, beare it straight,	1179
Ant. Auant thou witch: Come *Dromio* let vs go.	1261
*Offi. Masters let him go: he is my prisoner, and you | shall not haue	
him.	1403
Pinch. Go binde this man, for he is franticke too.	1405
Offi. He is my prisoner, if I let him go,	1409
Adr. I will discharge thee ere I go from thee,	1411
Adr. Go beare him hence, sister go you with me:	1424
Adr. Come go, I will fall prostrate at his feete,	1583
Go some of you, knocke at the Abbey gate,	1637
Who parted with me to go fetch a Chaine,	1698
To go in person with me to my house.	1711
*Duke. Why this is straunge: Go call the Abbesse hi- |ther.	1758
To go with vs into the Abbey heere,	1884
Go to a Gossips feast, and go with mee,	1895
Come go with vs, wee'l looke to that anon,	1904
**And now let's go hand in hand, not one before another. | *Exeunt*.	1918

GOBLINS = 1

We talke with Goblins, Owles and Sprights;	585

GOD = 5*7

*E.Dro. What meane you sir, for God sake hold your | (hands:	258
*E.An. Y'are sàd signior *Balthazar*, pray God our cheer	638
Are you a god? would you create me new?	826
*thinkes a man alwaies going to bed, and saies, God giue | you good	
rest.	1215
*thereof comes, that the wenches say God dam me, That's	1236
*as much to say, God make me a light wench: It is writ-|ten,	1237
*Adr. O husband, God doth know you din'd at home	1349
Dro. God and the Rope-maker beare me witnesse,	1378
*Luc. God helpe poore soules, how idlely doe they | talke.	1422
Luc. God for thy mercy, they are loose againe.	1442
Adr. Hold, hurt him not for God sake, he is mad,	1498
Which God he knowes, I saw not. For the which,	1706

GODS = 2*2

Merch. Oh had the gods done so, I had not now	101
For Gods sake send some other messenger.	353
*S.Dr. Hold sir, for Gods sake, now your iest is earnest,	419
*S.Dro. Runne master run, for Gods sake take a house,	1501

GOE = 12*5

Ant. Goe beare it to the Centaure, where we host,	171
And goe indeede, hauing so good a meane. | *Exit Dromio*.	180
And then goe to my Inne and dine with me?	186
Ant. Farewell till then: I will goe loose my selfe,	193
Ile to the Centaur to goe seeke this slaue,	270
They'll goe or come; if so, be patient Sister.	283
Dro. Goe backe againe, and be new beaten home?	352
Luc. *Dromio*, goe bid the seruants spred for dinner.	582
But soft, my doore is lockt; goe bid them let vs in.	651
*When one is one too many, goe get thee from the dore.	657
*E.Dro. If you went in paine Master, this knaue wold | goe sore.	713
*so cleane kept: for why? she sweats a man may goe o-|uer-shooes in	
the grime of it.	894
*Dro. Here goe: the deske, the purse, sweet now make | haste.	1136
Will you goe with me, wee'll mend our dinner here?	1242

GOE *cont*.
*it when I sit, driuen out of doores with it when I goe	1316
Ant. Come goe along, my wife is comming yon-|der.	1323
Haue suffer'd wrong. Goe, keepe vs companie,	1888

GOES = *1
*that *Adam* that keepes the prison; hee that goes in the	1201

GOING = *1
*thinkes a man alwaies going to bed, and saies, God giue | you good rest.	1215

GOLD = 14*9, 16*3
Where is the gold I gaue in charge to thee?	235
E.Dro. To me sir? why you gaue no gold to me?	236
He ask'd me for a hundred markes in gold:	338
'Tis dinner time, quoth I: my gold, quoth he:	339
Your meat doth burne, quoth I: my gold quoth he:	340
Will you come, quoth I: my gold, quoth he;	341
The Pigge quoth I, is burn'd: my gold, quoth he:	343
I see the Iewell best enamaled | Will loose his beautie: yet the gold bides still	385
Where gold and no man that hath a name,	388
Ant. The gold I gaue to *Dromio* is laid vp	395
You know no *Centaur*? you receiu'd no gold?	404
Home to the *Centaur* with the gold you gaue me.	411
And charg'd him with a thousand markes in gold,	626
The finenesse of the Gold, and chargefull fashion,	1012
S.Dro. Master, here's the gold you sent me for: what	1196
Ant. What gold is this? What *Adam* do'st thou | meane?	1198
And why dost thou denie the bagge of gold?	1384
Dro. And gentle Mr I receiu'd no gold:	1386
*vs no harme: you saw they speake vs faire, giue vs gold:	1455

GOLDEN = 2
Spread ore the siluer waues thy golden haires;	835
When in the streets he meetes such Golden gifts:	977

GOLDS = 1
Ant. Villaine, thou didst denie the golds receit,	412

GOLDSMITH see also Gold. = *1, 10*1
Enter Antipholus of Ephesus, his man Dromio, Angelo the | Goldsmith, and Balthaser the Merchant.	617
Enter a Merchant, Goldsmith, and an Officer.	981
But soft I see the Goldsmith; get thee gone,	1001
But neither Chaine nor Goldsmith came to me:	1007
Ant. Thou hast subborn'd the Goldsmith to arrest | mee.	1369
Off. One *Angelo* a Goldsmith, do you know him?	1427
Come Iailor, bring me where the Goldsmith is,	1438
Enter the Merchant and the Goldsmith.	1463
That Goldsmith there, were he not pack'd with her,	1696
There did this periur'd Goldsmith sweare me downe,	1704
You say he din'd at home, the Goldsmith heere	1750

GOLDSMITHS = *1
Ant. While I go to the Goldsmiths house, go thou	997

GOLD-SMITH = 1
I see sir you haue found the Gold-smith now:	1229

GON = 2
Ant. Go, get thee gon, fetch me an iron Crow.	745
I coniure thee to leaue me, and be gon.	1250

GONE = 10*1
If it proue so, I will be gone the sooner:	269

GONE *cont*.

And from the Mart he's somewhere gone to dinner:	279
'Tis time I thinke to trudge, packe, and be gone.	943
But soft I see the Goldsmith; get thee gone,	1001
And that shall baile me: hie thee slaue, be gone,	1096
No euill lost is wail'd, when it is gone.	1130
Adria. What, the chaine? | *S.Dro.* No, no, the bell, 'tis time that I were gone:	1164
*Is there any ships puts forth to night? may we be gone?	1218
And Ile be gone sir, and not trouble you.	1253
Harke, harke, I heare him Mistris: flie, be gone.	1658
Thirtie three yeares haue I but gone in trauaile	1890

GOOD = 17*12

And goe indeede, hauing so good a meane. | *Exit Dromio.*	180
Good Sister let vs dine, and neuer fret;	280
Ant. In good time sir: what's that? | *S.Dro.* Basting.	451
Ant. Well sir, learne to iest in good time, there's a | time for all things.	458
E.Anti. Good signior *Angelo* you must excuse vs all,	619
*May answer my good will, and your good welcom here.	639
Bal. Good meat sir is co(m)mon that euery churle affords.	643
*But though my cates be meane, take them in good part,	649
Vpon mine hostesse there, good sir make haste:	780
Ant. As good to winke sweet loue, as looke on night.	846
Ile fetch my sister to get her good will. *Exit.*	860
Good Signior take the stranger to my house,	1019
Anti. Good Lord, you vse this dalliance to excuse	1034
Good sir say, whe'r you'l answer me, or no:	1046
*thinkes a man alwaies going to bed, and saies, God giue | you good rest.	1215
Ant. And to that end sir, I will welcome you. | *Offi.* Good sir be patient.	1299
Offi. Good now hold thy tongue.	1303
Good Doctor *Pinch*, you are a Coniurer,	1330
Adr. Is't good to sooth him in these contraries?	1366
Dro. Monie by me? Heart and good will you might,	1373
Good Master Doctor see him safe conuey'd	1414
Dro. Will you be bound for nothing, be mad good | Master, cry the diuell.	1420
Good sir draw neere to me, Ile speake to him:	1476
Good people enter, and lay hold on him.	1560
To do him all the grace and good I could.	1636
Adr. No my good Lord. My selfe, he, and my sister,	1684
I hope I shall haue leisure to make good,	1863
E.Ant. There take it, and much thanks for my good | cheere.	1881

GOODLY = 1

A ioyfull mother of two goodly sonnes:	54

GOODS = 3*1

His goods confiscate to the Dukes dispose,	24
And he great care of goods at randone left,	46
Lest that your goods too soone be confiscate:	164
S.Dro. Your goods that lay at host sir in the Centaur.	1902

GOSSIP = 1

Duke. With all my heart, Ile Gossip at this feast.	1897

GOSSIPPING = 1

Will you walke in to see their gossipping?	1911

GOSSIPS = 1

Go to a Gossips feast, and go with mee,	1895

GOT = 2

The one nere got me credit, the other mickle blame: 675
haue you got the picture of old *Adam* new apparel'd? 1197

GRACE = 6*2

Adri. His company must do his minions grace, 363
*Lesse in your knowledge, and your grace you show not, 818
Possest with such a gentle soueraigne grace, 950
Haue won his grace to come in person hither, 1585
Adr. May it please your Grace, *Antipholus* my husba(n)d, 1608
To do him all the grace and good I could. 1636
Ran hether to your Grace, whom I beseech | To giue me ample
satisfaction 1728
Curt. As sure (my Liege) as I do see your Grace. 1757

GRACIOUS = 1*2

Therefore most gracious Duke with thy command, 1631
E.Ant. Iustice most gracious Duke, oh grant me iu- |(stice, 1666
E.Ant. I came from *Corinth* my most gracious Lord | *E.Dro.* And I
with him. 1851

GRAINE = *1

Dro. No sir, 'tis in graine, *Noahs* flood could not | do it. 897

GRAINED = 1

Though now this grained face of mine be hid 1792

GRANT = 2*1

For what obscured light the heauens did grant, 69
E.Ant. Iustice most gracious Duke, oh grant me iu- |(stice, 1666
That then I lost for thee, now grant me iustice. 1670

GRASSE = 1

S.Dro. 'Tis true she rides me, and I long for grasse. 596

GRAUE = 1

And dwell vpon your graue when you are dead; 765

GRAUITIE = 1

Adri. How ill agrees it with your grauitie, 562

GREASE = *1

Dro. Marry sir, she's the Kitchin wench, & al grease, 886

GREAT = 6*3

And he great care of goods at randone left, 46
But to our honours great disparagement: 151
So great a charge from thine owne custodie. 226
It seemes he hath great care to please his wife. 332
Bal. Small cheere and great welcome, makes a mer- |rie feast. 646
*the Mole in my necke, the great Wart on my left arme, 932
Great pailes of puddled myre to quench the haire; 1646
E.Ant. This day (great Duke) she shut the doores | vpon me, 1680
For these deepe shames, and great indignities. 1730

GREATLY = 1

I greatly feare my monie is not safe. *Exit.* 271

GREECE = 1

Fiue Sommers haue I spent in farthest *Greece*, 135

GREEFE = 1

After so long greefe such Natiuitie. 1896

GREEUE = 1

So thou that hast no vnkinde mate to greeue thee, 312

GREEUOUS = 1

Duke. A greeuous fault: say woman, didst thou so? 1683

GRIEFE = *1

Fa. Oh! griefe hath chang'd me since you saw me last, 1778

GRIEFES = 1
    Then I to speake my griefes vnspeakeable: 36
GRIM = 1
    Kinsman to grim and comfortlesse dispaire,   1549
GRIME = *1
    *so cleane kept: for why? she sweats a man may goe o-|uer-shooes in
    the grime of it.   894
GROSELY = 1
    To counterfeit thus grosely with your slaue,   563
GROSSE = 1
    Lay open to my earthie grosse conceit: 821
GROUND = 1
    By him not ruin'd? Then is he the ground   373
GROW = 1
    Shall loue in buildings grow so ruinate?   790
GROWES = 3
    *S.Dro. There's no time for a man to recouer his haire | that growes
    bald by nature.   466
    And knowing how the debt growes I will pay it.   1413
    Off. Two hundred Duckets. | *Adr.* Say, how growes it due.   1429
GROWING = 1
    Is growing to me by *Antipholus*,   989
GUARD = 1*1
    He broke from those that had the guard of him,   1621
    Duke. Come stand by me, feare nothing: guard with | Halberds.   1659
GUESSE = *1
    *no whitenesse in them. But I guesse, it stood in her chin   918
GUEST = *1
    Anti. I, to a niggardly Host, and more sparing guest: 648
GUESTS = 1
    Gaue healthfull welcome to their ship-wrackt guests,   117
GUILTIE = 1
    Whil'st vpon me the guiltie doores were shut,   1347
GUILTY = 1
    But least my selfe be guilty to selfe wrong,   953
GULFE = 1
    A drop of water in the breaking gulfe,   521
HABIT = *1
    *And here she comes in the habit of a light wench, and   1235
HAD *l*.42 51 53 65 82 85 101 108 115 119 170 220 222 *431 *931 *934
    *935 984 991 1062 1110 1191 1251 1350 1431 *1432 1465 1485 1486
    1487 1609 1619 1621 1733 1734 1737 1755 *1865 = 33*6
HADST *l*.246 676 1828 = 3
HAIRE = 3*6
    *S.Dro. There's no time for a man to recouer his haire | that growes
    bald by nature.   466
    *S.Dro. Yes, to pay a fine for a perewig, and recouer | the lost haire of
    another man.   469
    *Ant. Why, is Time such a niggard of haire, being (as   471
    *beasts, and what he hath scanted them in haire, hee hath | giuen them
    in wit.   474
    *Ant. Why, but theres manie a man hath more haire | then wit.   476
    *S.Dro. Not a man of those but he hath the wit to lose | his haire.   478
    *S.Dro. Marry and did sir: namely, in no time to re-|couer haire lost
    by Nature.   496
    *a rush, a haire, a drop of blood, a pin, a nut, a cherrie-|stone: 1255
    Great pailes of puddled myre to quench the haire;   1646

HAIRES = 1
Spread ore the siluer waues thy golden haires;   835
HAIRY = *1
*Ant. Why thou didst conclude hairy men plain dea-|lers without wit.   480
HALBERDS = 1
*Duke. Come stand by me, feare nothing: guard with | Halberds.   1659
HALFE = 1*1
*E.Ant. Euen now, euen here, not halfe an howre since.   409
Gold. You know I gaue it you halfe an houre since.   1051
HAND = 9*4
Adr. Say, is your tardie master now at hand?   319
Beshrew his hand, I scarce could vnderstand it.   325
That neuer touch well welcome to thy hand,   511
And from my false hand cut the wedding ring,   532
*That you beat me at the Mart I haue your hand to show;   630
If by strong hand you offer to breake in   759
Thou hast no husband yet, nor I no wife: | Giue me thy hand.   857
*Dro. I found it by the barrennesse, hard in the palme | of the hand.   911
*Pinch. Giue me your hand, and let mee feele your | pulse.   1335
Ant. There is my hand, and let it feele your eare.   1337
And carefull houres with times deformed hand,   1779
*And now let's go hand in hand, not one before another. | Exeunt.   1918
HANDS = 2*3
*E.Dro. What meane you sir, for God sake hold your | (hands: 258
*E.Dro. Nay, hee's at too hands with mee, and that my | two eares can
witnesse.   320
*E.Dro. Nay, rather perswade him to hold his hands.   1304
*Natiuitie to this instant, and haue nothing at his hands   1312
And it shall priuiledge him from your hands,   1564
HAND-WRITING = *1
*Your owne hand-writing would tell you what I thinke.   632
HANG = 1
My mistresse, sir, quoth I: hang vp thy Mistresse: 344
HAP = 2
And by me; had not our hap beene bad: 42
And knowing whom it was their hap to saue,   116
HAPLESSE = 1
Duke. Haplesse Egeon whom the fates haue markt   143
HAPLY = 2
Ab. Haply in priuate. | Adr. And in assemblies too.   1528
Haply I see a friend will saue my life,   1763
HAPPY = 2
Vnto a woman, happy but for me,   41
And happy were I in my timelie death,   141
HARBENGER = 1
Apparell vice like vertues harbenger: 798
HARBOUR = 1
I will not harbour in this Towne to night.   939
HARBOURS = 1
Or that, or any place that harbours men: 139
HARD = 3*1
Vnkindnesse blunts it more then marble hard.   369
E.Drom. Master, knocke the doore hard.   700
*Dro. I found it by the barrennesse, hard in the palme | of the hand.   911
On whose hard heart is button'd vp with steele: 1143
HARKE = 2
Harke, harke, I heare him Mistris: flie, be gone.   1658

HARLOT = 2
  And teare the stain'd skin of my Harlot brow,   531
  Ant. Dissembling harlot, thou art false in all,   1389
HARLOTS = 1
  While she with Harlots feasted in my house.   1682
HARME = 1*1
  Gaue any Tragicke Instance of our harme: 67
  *vs no harme: you saw they speake vs faire, giue vs gold: 1455
HARMING = 1
  Luci. Selfe-harming Iealousie; fie beat it hence.   378
HARSHLY = 1
  I tell you 'twill sound harshly in her eares.   1287
HART = 1
  Better cheere may you haue, but not with better hart.   650
HAST *l.*155 238 *252 312 593 *673 *690 857 1138 *1369 1407 1789
  *1901 = 8*5, 1
  By *Dromio* heere, who came in hast for it.   1372
HASTE *see also* hast = 3
  That in such haste I sent to seeke his Master?   276
  Vpon mine hostesse there, good sir make haste: 780
  Dro. Here goe: the deske, the purse, sweet now make | haste.   1136
HATCH = *1
  *Either get thee from the dore, or sit downe at the hatch: 655
HATH *l.*17 210 278 291 332 365 366 388 438 *474 *476 *478 506 774 805
  838 952 1142 1177 1266 *1319 1511 1512 *1516 1517 1555 1607 1675
  1678 *1778 1795 *1823 1879 = 26*8
HAUE *l.*13 *35 72 118 121 126 135 143 214 215 219 *237 243 247 307 356
  405 *431 450 *460 *494 501 *630 650 *665 *677 *685 *688 694 *710 715
  *739 746 768 787 809 873 *877 *878 *882 959 *962 965 983 1018 *1027
  1029 1033 1036 1071 1077 1121 1124 1174 1197 1229 *1246 *1256 1290
  *1311 *1312 1365 1403 1444 1464 1475 1483 1524 1565 1569 1570 1572
  1581 1585 1644 1654 1747 1748 1780 1808 1863 1880 1888 1890 = 66*22
HAUING = 2
  And goe indeede, hauing so good a meane. | *Exit Dromio.*   180
  You haue no stomacke, hauing broke your fast: 215
HAUNTS = *1
  *One that claimes me, one that haunts me, one that will | haue me.   873
HAZARDED = 1
  I hazarded the losse of whom I lou'd.   134
HE *see also* a = 107*33
HEAD = 3*3
  Betweene you, I shall haue a holy head.   356
  *I had rather haue it a head, and you vse these blows   431
  *long, I must get a sconce for my head, and Insconce it   432
  Dro. No longer from head to foot, then from hippe   904
  And thereof comes it that his head is light.   1541
  bare head, with the Headsman, & other | *Officers.*   1600
HEADIE-RASH = 1
  Nor headie-rash prouoak'd with raging ire,   1693
HEADSMAN = 1
  bare head, with the Headsman, & other | *Officers.*   1600
HEADSTRONG = 1
  Luc. Why, headstrong liberty is lasht with woe: 289
HEALTHFULL = 1
  Gaue healthfull welcome to their ship-wrackt guests,   117
HEAR = *1
  Mar. These eares of mine thou knowst did hear thee: 1490

HEARD = 4

Thus haue you heard me seuer'd from my blisse,	121
Nay, he's a theefe too: haue you not heard men say,	1174
Ant. Who heard me to denie it or forsweare it?	1489
Heard you confesse you had the Chaine of him,	1737

HEARE *see also* here = 9*2

We bid be quiet when we heare it crie.	309
Ant. Let's heare it.	465
Shouldst thou but heare I were licencious?	526
Or sleepe I now, and thinke I heare all this?	578
Anti. Doe you heare you minion, you'll let vs in I | hope?	692
Gold. You heare how he importunes me, the Chaine.	1039
Offic. I do arrest you sir, you heare the suite.	1067
Harke, harke, I heare him Mistris: flie, be gone.	1658
My dull deafe eares a little vse to heare:	1797
If this be not a dreame I see and heare.	1864
And heare at large discoursed all our fortunes,	1885

HEART *see also* hart = 6*3

Beare a faire presence, though your heart be tainted,	799
Mine eies cleere eie, my deere hearts deerer heart;	851
*my brest had not beene made of faith, and my heart of	934
My tongue, though not my heart, shall haue his will.	1124
My heart praies for him, though my tongue doe curse.	1134
On whose hard heart is button'd vp with steele:	1143
Dro. Monie by me? Heart and good will you might,	1373
*I could finde in my heart to stay heere still, and turne | Witch.	1458
Duke. With all my heart, Ile Gossip at this feast.	1897

HEARTS = 2

Mine eies cleere eie, my deere hearts deerer heart;	851
Oh, his hearts Meteors tilting in his face.	1109

HEATES = *1

*for my seruice but blowes. When I am cold, he heates	1313

HEAUEN = 4

Ant. Am I in earth, in heauen, or in hell?	608
My sole earths heauen, and my heauens claime.	853
I coniure thee by all the Saints in heauen.	1341
I neuer saw the Chaine, so helpe me heauen:	1744

HEAUENS = 3

For what obscured light the heauens did grant,	69
There's nothing situate vnder heauens eye,	290
My sole earths heauen, and my heauens claime.	853

HEAUIE = 2

Adr. This weeke he hath beene heauie, sower sad,	1512
My heauie burthen are deliuered:	1892

HEAUIER = *1

Mer. A heauier taske could not haue beene impos'd,	35

HEE *l.*326 *328 *473 *474 *660 *683 *1113 *1151 *1201 *1202
1394 = 1*10

HEEDE = 1

And teach your eares to list me with more heede:	1090

HEEDFULL = 2

Whil'st I had beene like heedfull of the other.	85
Safe at the *Centaur*, and the heedfull slaue	396

HEELES = 3

Nay, and you will not sir, Ile take my heeles.	259
You would keepe from my heeles, and beware of an asse.	637
And at her heeles a huge infectious troope	1550

HEERE = 28*5

But heere must end the story of my life,	140
Heere comes your man, now is your husband nie.	317
*Angelo. Heere is neither cheere sir, nor welcome, we | would faine	
haue either.	715
Anti. There's none but Witches do inhabite heere,	946
I see a man heere needs not liue by shifts,	976
And I too blame haue held him heere too long.	1033
Gold. Heere is thy fee, arrest him Officer.	1064
Luc. Then swore he that he was a stranger heere.	1112
Heere comes my Man, I thinke he brings the monie.	1289
By Dromio heere, who came in hast for it.	1372
Dro. Master, I am heere entred in bond for you.	1417
*Dro. Faith stay heere this night, they will surely do	1454
*I could finde in my heart to stay heere still, and turne | Witch.	1458
Mar. How is the man esteem'd heere in the Citie?	1467
Second to none that liues heere in the Citie:	1470
Therefore depart, and leaue him heere with me.	1577
*Adr. I will not hence, and leaue my husband heere:	1578
Behinde the ditches of the Abbey heere.	1591
That heere and there his furie had committed,	1619
And heere the Abbesse shuts the gates on vs,	1628
Euen now we hous'd him in the Abbey heere,	1663
Gold. He had my Lord, and when he ran in heere,	1734
And then you fled into this Abbey heere,	1740
If heere you hous'd him, heere he would haue bin.	1748
You say he din'd at home, the Goldsmith heere	1750
Duke. Saw'st thou him enter at the Abbey heere?	1756
In seuen short yeares, that heere my onely sonne	1790
*S.Drom. Oh my olde Master, who hath bound him | heere?	1823
Duke. Why heere begins his Morning storie right:	1832
And this faire Gentlewoman her sister heere	1861
*E.Ant. These Duckets pawne I for my father heere.	1878
To go with vs into the Abbey heere,	1884

HEEREIN = 1

Heerein you warre against your reputation,	747

HEEREOF = 1

I long to know the truth heereof at large.	1439

HEES = 1*1

*E.Dro. Nay, hee's at too hands with mee, and that my | two eares can	
witnesse.	320
That's not my fault, hee's master of my state.	371

HEIGHT = 1

Euen in the strength and height of iniurie:	1676

HEIRE = 1

*Dro. In her forhead, arm'd and reuerted, making | warre against her	
heire.	914

HEL = *1

*One that before the Iudgme(n)t carries poore soules to hel.	1149

HELD = 2

And I too blame haue held him heere too long.	1033
Ab. How long hath this possession held the man.	1511

HELL = 2

Ant. Am I in earth, in heauen, or in hell?	608
S.Dro. No, he's in Tartar limbo, worse then hell:	1141

HELP = *1

*If a crow help vs in sirra, wee'll plucke a crow together.	744

HELPE = 6*2
To seeke thy helpe by beneficiall helpe,	154
*E.Dro. So come helpe, well strooke, there was blow | for blow.	696
*Luc. God helpe poore soules, how idlely doe they | talke.	1422
Let's call more helpe to haue them bound againe. | *Runne all out.*	1444
Let him be brought forth, and borne hence for helpe.	1632
And sure (vnlesse you send some present helpe)	1649
I neuer saw the Chaine, so helpe me heauen:	1744

HELPEFULL = 1
Our helpefull ship was splitted in the midst;	106

HELPELESSE = 2
Merch. Hopelesse and helpelesse doth *Egean* wend,	160
With vrging helpelesse patience would releeue me;	313

HENCE = 11*1
Adri. Hence prating pesant, fetch thy Master home.	357
You spurne me hence, and he will spurne me hither,	360
Luci. Selfe-harming Iealousie; fie beat it hence.	378
S.Dro. I did not see you since you sent me hence	410
Ang. Ile meet you at that place some houre hence.	783
And therefore 'tis hie time that I were hence:	947
Some blessed power deliuer vs from hence.	1226
Adr. Go beare him hence, sister go you with me:	1424
Adr. To fetch my poore distracted husband hence,	1506
Adr. I will not hence, and leaue my husband heere:	1578
Nor send him forth, that we may beare him hence.	1630
Let him be brought forth, and borne hence for helpe.	1632

HER *l.*43 49 51 110 241 273 556 557 559 *575 577 598 622 751 775 791
*792 804 812 830 860 *887 *888 *889 *893 899 *901 905 907 *908 914
*918 *920 922 *925 *930 *933 945 949 *1023 1075 1079 1092 1094 1095
1099 1133 1239 1257 1287 *1318 1358 1359 *1360 *1375 1377 1550 1696
*1712 *1752 1755 1835 1861 = 47*25

HERE = 10*10
This very day a *Syracusian* Marchant | Is apprehended for a riuall here,	165
Here comes the almanacke of my true date:	206
We being strangers here, how dar'st thou trust	225
Or else, what lets it but he would be here?	381
I sent him from the Mart? see here he comes.	400
E.Ant. Euen now, euen here, not halfe an howre since.	409
*May answer my good will, and your good welcom here.	639
S.Dro. Nor to day here you must not come againe | when you may.	667
*Your cake here is warme within: you stand here in the | cold.	725
S.Dro. Breake any breaking here, and Ile breake your | knaues pate.	730
Dro. Here goe: the deske, the purse, sweet now make | haste.	1136
A chaine, a chaine, doe you not here it ring.	1163
Adr. The houres come backe, that did I neuer here.	1167
And lapland Sorcerers inhabite here.	1194
Delay: Here are the angels that you sent for to deliuer | you.	1222
And here we wander in illusions:	1225
*And here she comes in the habit of a light wench, and	1235
Will you goe with me, wee'll mend our dinner here?	1242
Adr. Peace foole, thy Master and his man are here,	1651

HEREIN = 1
And yet would herein others eies were worse:	1132

HERES = 4*2
But here's a villaine that would face me downe	624
*E.Dro. Here's too much out vpon thee, I pray thee let | me in.	737
Ang. I know it well sir, loe here's the chaine,	958

76

HERES *cont.*
   Gold. Sauing your merrie humor: here's the note 1010
   **S.Dro.* Master, here's the gold you sent me for: what 1196
   E.Dro. Here's that I warrant you will pay them all. 1291
HERSELFE *see* selfe
HES = 5
   And from the Mart he's somewhere gone to dinner: 279
   S.Dro. No, he's in Tartar limbo, worse then hell: 1141
   **S.Dro.* Time is a verie bankerout, and owes more then | he's worth to
   season. 1172
   Nay, he's a theefe too: haue you not heard men say, 1174
   And now he's there, past thought of humane reason. 1664
HETHER = 1
   Ran hether to your Grace, whom I beseech | To giue me ample
   satisfaction 1728
HID = 1
   Though now this grained face of mine be hid 1792
HIDES = 1
   But creepe in crannies, when he hides his beames: 426
HIE = 8
   And praies that you will hie you home to dinner. 255
   Anti. Go hie thee presently, post to the rode, 937
   And therefore 'tis hie time that I were hence: 947
   To *Adriana* Villaine hie thee straight: 1091
   And that shall baile me: hie thee slaue, be gone, 1096
   My way is now to hie home to his house, 1275
   Ant. To what end did I bid thee hie thee home? 1296
   And to thy state of darknesse hie thee straight, 1340
HIER = 1
   S.Dro. A ship you sent me too, to hier waftage. 1084
HIGH *see* hie
HIGHEST = 1
   Thy substance, valued at the highest rate, 27
HIGHLY = 1
   Of credit infinite, highly belou'd, 1469
HIGHNESSE = 1
   But she tels to your Highnesse simple truth. 1688
HIM *l.*26 82 84 132 158 278 286 *322 337 *349 *351 373 400 *551 564 625
   626 *660 *690 701 1015 1033 1047 1056 1064 1110 1121 1131 1134 1142
   *1155 *1156 *1166 *1304 *1311 1331 1366 1368 1394 *1396 *1398 1403
   1409 1414 1424 1427 1431 1436 1476 1498 1499 1507 1508 1510 1523
   1524 1536 1556 1560 1564 1565 1570 1571 1574 1577 1581 1603 1604
   1611 1613 1617 1621 1629 1630 1632 1635 1636 1645 1647 1648 1658
   1663 1702 1705 1719 *1731 1737 1748 1756 1769 1787 1820 *1823 1825
   1851 1876 1905 = 86*18
HIMSELFE = 7*1
   (Vnseene, inquisitiue) confounds himselfe. 202
   **S.Dro.* Marry sir, by a rule as plaine as the plaine bald | pate of Father
   time himselfe. 463
   **S.Dro.* Thus I mend it: Time himselfe is bald, and 500
   Else would he neuer so demeane himselfe, 1265
   Do outrage and displeasure to himselfe? 1408
   When he demean'd himselfe, rough, rude, and wildly, 1557
   Anon I'me sure the Duke himselfe in person 1588
   And with his mad attendant and himselfe, 1622
HINDE = 1
   **S.Dro.* It seemes thou want'st breaking, out vpon thee | hinde. 735

HINDRED = 3*1
    *were you hindred by the Serieant to tarry for the *Hoy*   1221
    Gold. I am sorry Sir that I haue hindred you,   1464
    It seemes his sleepes were hindred by thy railing,   1540
    Thou sayest his sports were hindred by thy bralles.   1546
HIP = 1*1
    *an Ell and three quarters, will not measure her from hip | to hip.   901
HIPPE = *2
    Dro. No longer from head to foot, then from hippe   904
    *to hippe: she is sphericall, like a globe: I could find out | Countries in
    her.   905
HIRE *see* hier
HIS *see also* on's *l.*13 24 93 129 130 131 161 167 184 201 276 281 291 322
    324 325 326 *329 332 363 370 375 377 380 384 385 390 426 *466 478
    492 552 553 *617 802 993 1105 1109 1124 1156 1190 *1210 1211 *1214
    1270 1272 1273 1274 1275 1276 *1304 *1312 1329 1331 1334 1365 1367
    1368 1412 1435 1440 1471 *1474 1499 1508 1509 1514 1517 1518 1540
    1541 1542 1546 1565 1567 1568 1583 1585 1596 *1597 1613 1616 1619
    1622 1642 1648 *1651 1703 1735 1768 1770 1822 1825 1826 1832
    1879 = 93*10
HIT = 1
    Nor by what wonder you do hit of mine: 817
HITHER *see also* hether = 4*1
    You spurne me hence, and he will spurne me hither,   360
    E.Dro. They stand at the doore, Master, bid them | welcome hither.   719
    Ab. Be quiet people, wherefore throng you hither?   1505
    Haue won his grace to come in person hither,   1585
    Duke. Why this is straunge: Go call the Abbesse hi-|ther.   1758
HOA = *1
    E.Ant. Who talks within there? hoa, open the dore.   662
HOISTED = 1
    Had hoisted saile, and put to sea to day: 1485
HOLD = 5*5
    E.Dro. What meane you sir, for God sake hold your | (hands: 258
    *Thinkst y I iest? hold, take thou that, & that. *Beats Dro.*   418
    S.Dr. Hold sir, for Gods sake, now your iest is earnest,   419
    Bal. I hold your dainties cheap sir, & your welcom deer.   640
    Luc. Oh soft sir, hold you still: 859
    Adr. I cannot, nor I will not hold me still.   1123
    Offi. Good now hold thy tongue.   1303
    E.Dro. Nay, rather perswade him to hold his hands.   1304
    Adr. Hold, hurt him not for God sake, he is mad,   1498
    Good people enter, and lay hold on him.   1560
HOLIE = 1
    To yeeld possession to my holie praiers,   1339
HOLINESSE = 1
    And ill it doth beseeme your holinesse | To separate the husband and
    the wife.   1579
HOLLOW = 1
    A needy-hollow-ey'd-sharpe-looking-wretch;   1717
HOLPE = *1
    Eph.Ant. A man is well holpe vp that trusts to you,   1005
HOLY = 4
    Betweene you, I shall haue a holy head.   356
    Teach sinne the carriage of a holy Saint,   800
    'Tis holy sport to be a little vaine,   813
    With wholsome sirrups, drugges, and holy prayers   1573

HOMAGE = 2
| I know his eye doth homage other-where, | 380 |
| Nor to her bed no homage doe I owe: | 830 |

HOME = 35*6
Why thou departedst from thy natiue home?	33
Made daily motions for our home returne:	63
The meate is colde, because you come not home:	213
You come not home, because you haue no stomacke:	214
And strike you home without a messenger.	232
Home to your house, the *Phoenix* sir, to dinner;	240
She that doth fast till you come home to dinner:	254
And praies that you will hie you home to dinner.	255
Luc. Till he come home againe, I would forbeare.	305
Adri. But say, I prethee, is he comming home?	331
When I desir'd him to come home to dinner,	337
*tongue, I thanke him, I bare home vpon my shoulders:	349
Adri. Go back againe, thou slaue, & fetch him home.	351
Dro. Goe backe againe, and be new beaten home?	352
Adri. Hence prating pesant, fetch thy Master home.	357
Whil'st I at home starue for a merrie looke:	364
And feedes from home; poore I am but his stale.	377
Your Mistresse sent to haue me home to dinner?	405
Home to the *Centaur* with the gold you gaue me.	411
She sent for you by *Dromio* home to dinner.	549
And that to morrow you will bring it home.	623
To her will we to dinner, get you home	775
Go home with it, and please your Wife withall,	967
Buy thou a rope, and bring it home to me.	1002
And bring thy Master home imediately.	1180
My way is now to hie home to his house,	1275
Ant. To what end did I bid thee hie thee home?	1296
*from home, welcom'd home with it when I returne, nay	1317
Adr. O husband, God doth know you din'd at home	1349
Anti. Din'd at home? Thou Villaine, what sayest | thou?	1352
Dro. Sir sooth to say, you did not dine at home.	1354
Home to my house, oh most vnhappy day.	1415
And beare him home for his recouerie.	1508
Namely, some loue that drew him oft from home.	1523
And therefore let me haue him home with me.	1570
Once did I get him bound, and sent him home,	1617
I did obey, and sent my Pesant home	1708
And in a darke and dankish vault at home	1724
That he din'd not at home, but was lock'd out.	1732
You say he din'd at home, the Goldsmith heere	1750

HOMELIE = 1
| Hath homelie age th'alluring beauty tooke | 365 |

HOMEWARD = 2
| And therefore homeward did they bend their course. | 120 |
| And coasting homeward, came to *Ephesus*: | 137 |

HONEST = 2*1
Luc. With words, that in an honest suit might moue.	1119
You haue done wrong to this my honest friend,	1483
To walke where any honest men resort.	1492

HONESTIE = 1
| Ile proue mine honor, and mine honestie | 1494 |

HONOR = 2
| Th'vnuiolated honor of your wife. | 749 |

HONOR *cont.*
Ile proue mine honor, and mine honestie 1494
HONOURS = 1
But to our honours great disparagement: 151
HOPE = 8
But longer did we not retaine much hope; 68
Of whom I hope to make much benefit: 188
For which I hope thou feltst I was displeas'd. 414
Anti. Doe you heare you minion, you'll let vs in I | hope? 692
Ant. And if I haue not sir, I hope you haue: 1029
She is too bigge I hope for me to compasse, 1100
I hope you do not meane to cheate me so? 1260
I hope I shall haue leisure to make good, 1863
HOPELESSE = 2
Hopelesse to finde, yet loth to leaue vnsought 138
Merch. Hopelesse and helpelesse doth *Egean* wend, 160
HOPES = 1
My foode, my fortune, and my sweet hopes aime; 852
HORNE = 1 *1
E.Dro. Why Mistresse, sure my Master is horne mad. 333
Adri. Horne mad, thou villaine? 334
HORSE = *1
*horse, and she would haue me as a beast, not that I bee-|ing 877
HOST = 1 *2
Ant. Goe beare it to the Centaure, where we host, 171
Anti. I, to a niggardly Host, and more sparing guest: 648
S.Dro. Your goods that lay at host sir in the Centaur. 1902
HOSTESSE = 1
Vpon mine hostesse there, good sir make haste: 780
HOSTS = 1
By computation and mine hosts report. 398
HOT = 1 *2
She is so hot because the meate is colde: 212
Ant. Where *Spaine*? | *Dro.* Faith I saw it not: but I felt it hot in her breth. 920
*to the hot breath of Spaine, who sent whole Ar-|madoes of Carrects to be ballast at her nose. 925
HOUND = 1
A hound that runs Counter, and yet draws drifoot well, 1148
HOURE = 8 *3
Within this houre it will be dinner time, 173
Reserue them till a merrier houre then this: 234
Ang. Ile meet you at that place some houre hence. 783
Mar. The houre steales on, I pray you sir dispatch. 1038
Gold. You know I gaue it you halfe an houre since. 1051
S.Dro. Oh yes, if any houre meete a Serieant, a turnes | backe for verie feare. 1168
Hath he not reason to turne backe an houre in a day? 1177
S.Dro. Why sir, I brought you word an houre since, 1219
*my long eares. I haue serued him from the houre of my 1311
E.Dro. Within this houre I was his bondman sir, 1768
Of you my sonnes, and till this present houre 1891
HOURES = 3
In *Ephesus* I am but two houres old, 543
Adr. The houres come backe, that did I neuer here. 1167
And carefull houres with times deformed hand, 1779

HOUSD = 2*1
Pinch. I charge thee Sathan, hous'd within this man,	1338
Euen now we hous'd him in the Abbey heere.	1663
If heere you hous'd him, heere he would haue bin.	1748

HOUSE = 18*3
Home to your house, the *Phoenix* sir, to dinner;	240
E.Dr. Quoth my Master, I know quoth he, no house,	347
My house was at the *Phoenix*? Wast thou mad,	406
Denied my house for his, me for his wife.	553
And that I did denie my wife and house;	627
For there's the house: That chaine will I bestow	778
Pleaseth you walke with me downe to his house,	993
Ant. While I go to the Goldsmiths house, go thou	997
Good Signior take the stranger to my house,	1019
My way is now to hie home to his house,	1275
He rush'd into my house, and tooke perforce	1277
Reuell and feast it at my house to day,	1346
And I denied to enter in my house.	1348
Home to my house, oh most vnhappy day.	1415
Came to my house, and tooke away my Ring,	1434
Binde *Dromio* too, and beare them to my house.	1500
S.Dro. Runne master run, for Gods sake take a house,	1501
Ab. No, not a creature enters in my house.	1561
While she with Harlots feasted in my house,	1682
To go in person with me to my house.	1711
S.Dro. There is a fat friend at your masters house,	1906

HOUSES = 1
| By rushing in their houses: bearing thence | 1615 |

HOW = 27*10
What now? How chance thou art return'd so soone.	207
We being strangers here, how dar'st thou trust	225
And tell me how thou hast dispos'd thy charge.	238
Adr. How if your husband start some other where?	304
Luci. Fie how impatience lowreth in your face.	362
Luci. How manie fond fooles serue mad Ielousie?	*Exit*.	392
How now sir, is your merrie humor alter'd?	402
How comes it now, my Husband, oh how comes it,	514
How deerely would it touch thee to the quicke,	525
Luci. Fie brother, how the world is chang'd with you:	547
Ant. How can she thus then call vs by our names?	Vnlesse it be by inspiration.	560
Adri. How ill agrees it with your grauitie,	562
Teach me deere creature how to thinke and speake:	820
Ant. Not mad, but mated, how I doe not know.	841
Ant. Why how now *Dromio*, where run'st thou so	fast?	862
Ant. What womans man? and how besides thy	selfe?	869
Anti. How dost thou meane a fat marriage?	885
*How much your Chaine weighs to the vtmost charect,	1011
Gold. You heare how he importunes me, the Chaine.	1039
Consider how it stands vpon my credit.	1055
An. How now? a Madman? Why thou peeuish sheep	1082
Luc. How hast thou lost thy breath?	*S.Dro*. By running fast.	1138
Adri. As if time were in debt: how fondly do'st thou	reason?	1170
How now sir? Haue you that I sent you for?	1290
Curt. How say you now? Is not your husband mad?	1328
Luc. Alas how fiery, and how sharpe he lookes.	1333
Cur. Marke, how he trembles in his extasie.	1334

HOW *cont.*

Luc. Aye me poore man, how pale and wan he looks.	1399
And knowing how the debt growes I will pay it.	1413
Luc. God helpe poore soules, how idlely doe they | talke.	1422
Off. Two hundred Duckets. | *Adr*. Say, how growes it due.	1429
Mar. How is the man esteem'd heere in the Citie?	1467
Ab. How long hath this possession held the man.	1511
Duke. Discouer how, and thou shalt finde me iust.	1679
S.Dro. Not I sir, you are my elder. | *E.Dro*. That's a question, how shall we trie it.	1912

HOWRE = 1*1

That very howre, and in the selfe-same Inne,	57
E.Ant. Euen now, euen here, not halfe an howre since.	409

HOWRES = 2

And make a Common of my serious howres,	424
My wife is shrewish when I keepe not howres;	620

HOWSD = 1

For euer hows'd, where it gets possession.	767

HOWSE = 1

Anti. What art thou that keep'st mee out from the | howse I owe?	669

HOY = *1

*were you hindred by the Serieant to tarry for the *Hoy*	1221

HUGE = 1

And at her heeles a huge infectious troope	1550

HUMANE = 1

And now he's there, past thought of humane reason.	1664

HUMOR = 4

Ant. I am not in a sportiue humor now:	223
How now sir, is your merrie humor alter'd?	402
Gold. Sauing your merrie humor: here's the note	1010
Ant. Fie, now you run this humor out of breath,	1043

HUMORS = 1

And yeelding to him, humors well his frensie.	1368

HUMOUR = 1

Lightens my humour with his merry iests:	184

HUNDRED = 5

Cannot amount vnto a hundred Markes,	28
He ask'd me for a hundred markes in gold:	338
Ant. Fiue hundred Duckets villaine for a rope?	1294
E.Dro. Ile serue you sir fiue hundred at the rate.	1295
Off. Two hundred Duckets. | *Adr*. Say, how growes it due.	1429

HUNGRY = *1

*They brought one *Pinch*, a hungry leane-fac'd Villaine;	1714

HURLE = 1

And hurle the name of husband in my face,	530

HURRIED = 1

That desp'rately he hurried through the streete,	1612

HURT = 1

Adr. Hold, hurt him not for God sake, he is mad,	1498

HUSBAND = 22*6

Adr. Neither my husband nor the slaue return'd,	275
Adr. How if your husband start some other where?	304
Heere comes your man, now is your husband nie.	317
How comes it now, my Husband, oh how comes it,	514
And hurle the name of husband in my face,	530
Thou art an Elme my husband, I a Vine:	568
Husband Ile dine aboue with you to day,	603

HUSBAND *cont.*

Thou hast no husband yet, nor I no wife: | Giue me thy hand.	857
She that doth call me husband, euen my soule	948
Where Dowsabell did claime me for her husband,	1099
Curt. How say you now? Is not your husband mad?	1328
Adr. O husband, God doth know you din'd at home	1349
Adr. I did not gentle husband locke thee forth.	1385
Off. Due for a Chaine your husband had of him.	1431
Cur. When as your husband all in rage to day	1433
Adr. To fetch my poore distracted husband hence,	1506
Hath scar'd thy husband from the vse of wits.	1555
Ad. Then let your seruants bring my husband forth	1562
Adr. I will attend my husband, be his nurse,	1567
Adr. I will not hence, and leaue my husband heere:	1578
And ill it doth beseeme your holinesse | To separate the husband and the wife.	1579
And take perforce my husband from the Abbesse.	1586
Adr. May it please your Grace, *Antipholus* my husba(n)d,	1608
Duke. Long since thy husband seru'd me in my wars	1633
Adr. Ay me, it is my husband: witnesse you,	1661
And gaine a husband by his libertie:	1826
Adr. And are not you my husband? | *E.Ant.* No, I say nay to that.	1858
The Duke my husband, and my children both,	1893

HUSBANDS = 2

Iulia. And may it be that you haue quite forgot | A husbands office? shall *Antipholus*	787
Adr. I see two husbands, or mine eyes deceiue me.	1816

I = 371 *94, 9*6

E.Dro. I, I, he told his minde vpon mine eare,	324
S.Dro. I sir, and wherefore; for they say, euery why | hath a wherefore.	438
Adri. I, I, *Antipholus*, looke strange and frowne,	505
Adr. I, and let none enter, least I breake your pate.	614
Anti. I, to a niggardly Host, and more sparing guest:	648
I and breake it in your face, so he breake it not behinde.	734
S.Dro. I, when fowles haue no feathers, and fish haue | no fin.	739
Dro. A very reuerent body: I such a one, as a man	881
Ang. Mr *Antipholus.* | *Anti.* I that's my name.	956
S.Dro. I sir, the Serieant of the Band: he that brings	1213
Adr. Why so I did. | *Ab.* I but not rough enough.	1525
Ab. I, but not enough.	1530
E.Dromio. I sir, but I am sure I do not, and whatso- |euer	1786

IAILOR = 2 *1

Enter Antipholus Ephes. with a Iailor.	1280
Ant. What will you murther me, thou Iailor thou?	1400
Come Iailor, bring me where the Goldsmith is,	1438

IARRES = 1

For since the mortall and intestine iarres	15

IAYLOR = 1, 2

Enter the Duke of Ephesus, with the Merchant of Siracusa, | Iaylor, and other attendants.	2
Iaylor, take him to thy custodie. | *Iaylor.* I will my Lord.	158

IDIOT = *1

S.Dro. Mome, Malthorse, Capon, Coxcombe, Idi- |ot, Patch,	653

IDLE = 2

Vsurping Iuie, Brier, or idle Mosse,	572
And shriue you of a thousand idle prankes:	604

IDLELY = *1
  Luc. God helpe poore soules, how idlely doe they | talke.   1422
IEALOUS = 3
  Luc. Who would be iealous then of such a one?   1129
  The venome clamors of a iealous woman,   1538
  The consequence is then, thy iealous fits   1554
IEALOUSIE = 1
  Luci. Selfe-harming Iealousie; fie beat it hence.   378
IEERE = 1
  Ant. Yea, dost thou ieere & flowt me in the teeth?   417
IELOUSIE = 1
  Luci. How manie fond fooles serue mad Ielousie? | *Exit*.   392
IEST = 6*3
  E.Dro. I pray you iest sir as you sit at dinner: 227
  As you loue stroakes, so iest with me againe: 403
  What meanes this iest, I pray you Master tell me?   416
  *Thinkst y I iest? hold, take thou that, & that. *Beats Dro*.   418
  S.Dr. Hold sir, for Gods sake, now your iest is earnest,   419
  Your sawcinesse will iest vpon my loue,   423
  If you will iest with me, know my aspect,   427
  Ant. Well sir, learne to iest in good time, there's a | time for all things.   458
  Anti. Do so, this iest shall cost me some expence. | *Exeunt*.   784
IESTS = 1*1
  Lightens my humour with his merry iests: 184
  Ant. Come *Dromio*, come, these iests are out of season,   233
IEWELL = 1
  I see the Iewell best enamaled | Will loose his beautie: yet the gold
  bides still   385
IEWELS = 1
  Rings, Iewels, any thing his rage did like.   1616
IF *l*.20 22 157 229 250 269 283 304 314 361 368 427 454 537 571 586 595
  605 *631 676 *690 *702 *713 *723 *744 759 782 791 793 828 839 *890
  *933 938 940 942 979 1009 1029 1047 1063 1066 *1168 *1170 1176 1185
  *1243 *1257 1409 1495 1603 1655 1748 1749 1827 1830 1838 1839
  1864 = 47*12
IGNORANT = 1
  That mourn'd for fashion, ignorant what to feare,   76
ILE *l*.39 153 174 190 259 270 303 391 *448 581 603 611 *663 *729 *730
  741 782 783 827 836 860 954 968 978 987 1047 1253 1282 1295 1392
  1476 1494 1897 = 29*4
ILL = 5
  Adri. How ill agrees it with your grauitie,   562
  Ill deeds is doubled with an euill word: 806
  Vnquiet meales make ill digestions,   1543
  And ill it doth beseeme your holinesse | To separate the husband and
  the wife.   1579
  At your important Letters this ill day,   1610
ILLUSIONS = 1
  And here we wander in illusions: 1225
ILL-FACD = 1
  Ill-fac'd, worse bodied, shapelesse euery where: 1126
IMAGINARIE = 1
  Sure these are but imaginarie wiles,   1193
IMAGINATION = 1
  Beyond imagination is the wrong   1677
IMBARKT = *1
  E.An. *Dromio*, what stuffe of mine hast thou imbarkt   1901

IMBRACD = 1
Which though my selfe would gladly haue imbrac'd,   72
IME = 1
Anon I'me sure the Duke himselfe in person   1588
IMEDIATELY = 1
And bring thy Master home imediately.   1180
IMMEDIATE = 1
A doubtfull warrant of immediate death,   71
IMMEDIATELY = 1
I gain'd my freedome; and immediately   1727
IMPATIENCE = 1
Luci. Fie how impatience lowreth in your face.   362
IMPEACH = 2
Ant. Thou art a Villaine to impeach me thus,   1493
Duke. Why what an intricate impeach is this?   1746
IMPORTANT = 1
At your important Letters this ill day,   1610
IMPORTUND = 2
After his brother; and importun'd me   129
And since I haue not much importun'd you,   983
IMPORTUNES = *1
Gold. You heare how he importunes me, the Chaine.   1039
IMPOSD = *1
Mer. A heauier taske could not haue beene impos'd,   35
IMPRISONMENT = 1
Beside the charge, the shame, imprisonment,   1482
IN *see also* i'th = 176*46
INCESSANT = 1
Yet the incessant weepings of my wife,   73
INCHANTING = 1
Of such inchanting presence and discourse,   951
INCIUILITY = 1
Adri. His inciuility confirmes no lesse: 1329
INCORPORATE = 1
That vndiuidable Incorporate | Am better then thy deere selfes better
part.   517
INCREAST = 1
With her I liu'd in ioy, our wealth increast   43
INDEEDE = 2*1
And goe indeede, hauing so good a meane. | *Exit Dromio*.   180
If I returne I shall be post indeede.   229
E.Dro. I am an Asse indeede, you may prooue it by   1310
INDIES = 1
Ant. Where *America*, the *Indies*? | *Dro*. Oh sir, vpon her nose, all ore
embellished with   ·   922
INDIGNITIES = 1
For these deepe shames, and great indignities.   1730
INDIGNITY = 1
Luc. Complaine vnto the Duke of this indignity.   1582
INDUED = 1
Indued with intellectuall sence and soules,   296
INFECT = 1
Infect thy sap, and liue on thy confusion.   574
INFECTIOUS = 1
And at her heeles a huge infectious troope   1550
INFINITE = 1
Of credit infinite, highly belou'd,   1469

INFRINGE = 1
I am not partiall to infringe our Lawes;   8
INGAGD = 1
And I to thee ingag'd a Princes word,   1634
INHABITE = 2
Anti. There's none but Witches do inhabite heere,   946
And lapland Sorcerers inhabite here.   1194
INIURIE = 2
Conceit, my comfort and my iniurie. *Exit.*   1182
Euen in the strength and height of iniurie: 1676
INK = *1
*If y skin were parchment, & y blows you gaue were ink,   631
INNE = 3
That very howre, and in the selfe-same Inne,   57
And then returne and sleepe within mine Inne,   176
And then goe to my Inne and dine with me?   186
INQUISITIUE = 2
At eighteene yeeres became inquisitiue   128
(Vnseene, inquisitiue) confounds himselfe.   202
INSCONCE = *1
*long, I must get a sconce for my head, and Insconce it   432
INSPIRATION = 1
Ant. How can she thus then call vs by our names? | Vnlesse it be by
inspiration.   560
INSTANCE = 2
Gaue any Tragicke Instance of our harme: 67
Besides this present instance of his rage,   1270
INSTANT = 1*1
And in the instant that I met with you,   990
*Natiuitie to this instant, and haue nothing at his hands   1312
INSUE = 1
If we obay them not, this will insue: 586
INTELLECTUALL = 1
Indued with intellectuall sence and soules,   296
INTESTINE = 1
For since the mortall and intestine iarres   15
INTO *l.*1277 1514 1594 1627 1740 1884 1916 = 7
INTRICATE = 1
Duke. Why what an intricate impeach is this?   1746
INTRUSION = 2
Who all for want of pruning, with intrusion,   573
That may with foule intrusion enter in,   764
INUISIBLE = 1
That he is borne about inuisible,   1662
INUITE = 1
Some tender monie to me, some inuite me;   1187
INUITED = 2
E.Mar. I am inuited sir to certaine Marchants,   187
Luc. Perhaps some Merchant hath inuited him,   278
IOLLITIE = *1
S.Dro. The plainer dealer, the sooner lost; yet he loo-|seth it in a
kinde of iollitie.   482
IOY = 1
With her I liu'd in ioy, our wealth increast   43
IOYFULL = 1
A ioyfull mother of two goodly sonnes: 54

IRE = 1
    Nor headie-rash prouoak'd with raging ire,   1693
IREFULL = 1
    Each one with irefull passion, with drawne swords   1623
IRELAND = 1
    Anti. In what part of her body stands *Ireland*?   907
IRON = 1
    Ant. Go, get thee gon, fetch me an iron Crow.   745
IS *see also* hee's, he's, here's, that's, there's, ther's, 'tis, what's,
    where's = 102*40
IST = 1
    Adr. Is't good to sooth him in these contraries?   1366
IT *see also* is't, 't = 124*34
ITH = 1
    *steele, she had transform'd me to a Curtull dog, & made | me turne
    i'th wheele.   935
IUDGMENT = *1
    *One that before the Iudgme(n)t carries poore soules to hel.   1149
IUGLER = 1
    A thred-bare Iugler, and a Fortune-teller,   1716
IUGLERS = 1
    As nimble Iuglers that deceiue the eie: 264
IUIE = 1
    Vsurping Iuie, Brier, or idle Mosse,   572
IULIA = 1
IULIANA = 1
    Enter Iuliana, with Antipholus of Siracusia.   786
IUST = 2
    Gold. Euen iust the sum that I do owe to you,   988
    Duke. Discouer how, and thou shalt finde me iust.   1679
IUSTICE = 1*4
    Adr. Iustice most sacred Duke against the Abbesse.   1605
    E.Ant. Iustice most gracious Duke, oh grant me iu-|(stice,   1666
    That then I lost for thee, now grant me iustice.   1670
    E.Ant. Iustice (sweet Prince) against y Woman there: 1673
IUSTLY = 1
    In this the Madman iustly chargeth them.   1690
KALENDERS = 1
    And you the Kalenders of their Natiuity,   1894
KEEPE = 8
    There is your monie that I had to keepe.   170
    Adri. This seruitude makes you to keepe vnwed.   300
    So he would keepe faire quarter with his bed: 384
    Keepe then faire league and truce with thy true bed,   540
    Come sir to dinner, *Dromio* keepe the gate: 602
    My wife is shrewish when I keepe not howres;   620
    You would keepe from my heeles, and beware of an asse.   637
    Haue suffer'd wrong. Goe, keepe vs companie,   1888
KEEPES = *1
    *that *Adam* that keepes the prison; hee that goes in the   1201
KEEPS = *1
    Adr. Who is that at the doore y keeps all this noise?   707
KEEPST = *1
    Anti. What art thou that keep'st mee out from the | howse I owe? 669
KEPT = 1*2
    The Sadler had it Sir, I kept it not.   222

KEPT *cont.*

*so cleane kept: for why? she sweats a man may goe o-|uer-shooes in
the grime of it. 894
S.Dro. Not that *Adam* that kept the Paradise: but 1200
KEY = 2
Giue her this key, and tell her in the Deske 1092
Knowes not my feeble key of vntun'd cares? 1791
KICKE = 1
I should kicke being kickt, and being at that passe, 636
KICKT = 1
I should kicke being kickt, and being at that passe, 636
KILD = *1
*calues-skin, that was kil'd for the Prodigall: hee that 1202
KILL = 2
Off. Away, they'l kill vs. | *Exeunt omnes, as fast as may be, frighted.* 1446
Betweene them they will kill the Coniurer. 1650
KILLING = 1
Soule-killing Witches, that deforme the bodie: 266
KINDE = 1*1
Drew me from kinde embracements of my spouse; 47
S.Dro. The plainer dealer, the sooner lost; yet he loo-|seth it in a
kinde of iollitie. 482
KINDNESSE = *1
*Then for her wealths-sake vse her with more kindnesse: 792
KINDNESSES = 1
Some other giue me thankes for kindnesses; 1188
KINSMAN = 1
Kinsman to grim and comfortlesse dispaire, 1549
KITCHEN = *1
Anti. Did not her Kitchen maide raile, taunt, and | scorne me? 1360
KITCHIN = 1*1
Dro. Marry sir, she's the Kitchin wench, & al grease, 886
Dro. Certis she did, the kitchin vestall scorn'd you. 1362
KITCHIND = 1
That kitchin'd me for you to day at dinner: 1907
KNAUE = 1*3
Ant. Come on sir knaue, haue done your foolishnes, 237
Being forbid? There take you that sir knaue. 257
Adri. Your wife sir knaue? go get you from the dore. 712
E.Dro. If you went in paine Master, this knaue wold | goe sore. 713
KNAUES = 1
S.Dro. Breake any breaking here, and Ile breake your | knaues pate. 730
KNEELE = *1
Luc. Kneele to the Duke before he passe the Abbey. 1598
KNEW = 1*1
An. I knew 'twould be a bald conclusion: but soft, | who wafts vs
yonder. 502
Gold. I knew he was not in his perfect wits. 1509
KNOCKE = 4
E.Drom. Master, knocke the doore hard. 700
Luce. Let him knocke till it ake. 701
Ile knocke else-where, to see if they'll disdaine me. 782
Go some of you, knocke at the Abbey gate, 1637
KNOW = 29*13
But we that know what 'tis to fast and pray, 216
Luc. Oh, know he is the bridle of your will. 287
I know not thy mistresse, out on thy mistresse. | *Luci.* Quoth who? 345

KNOW *cont.*

E.Dr. Quoth my Master, I know quoth he, no house,	347
I know his eye doth homage other-where,	380
Sister, you know he promis'd me a chaine,	382
You know no *Centaur*? you receiu'd no gold?	404
If you will iest with me, know my aspect,	427
Ant. Dost thou not know? | *S.Dro.* Nothing sir, but that I am beaten.	435
For know my loue: as easie maist thou fall	520
I know thou canst, and therefore see thou doe it.	534
Antip. Plead you to me faire dame? I know you not:	542
Vntill I know this sure vncertaintie,	580
But I should know her as well as she knowes me.	598
E.Dro. Say what you wil sir, but I know what I know,	629
To know the reason of this strange restraint:	758
I know a wench of excellent discourse,	770
And fetch the chaine, by this I know 'tis made,	776
S.Anti. Sweete Mistris, what your name is else I | know not;	815
But if that I am I, then well I know, | Your weeping sister is no wife of mine,	828
Ant. Not mad, but mated, how I doe not know.	841
S.Dro. Doe you know me sir? Am I *Dromio*? Am I | your man? Am I my selfe?	864
*and I know not what vse to put her too, but to make a	887
If euerie one knowes vs, and we know none,	942
Ang. I know it well sir, loe here's the chaine,	958
Mar. You know since Pentecost the sum is due,	982
Gold. Come, come, you know I gaue it you euen now.	1041
Gold. You know I gaue it you halfe an houre since.	1051
S.Dro. I doe not know the matter, hee is rested on | the case.	1151
S.Dro. I know not at whose suite he is arested well;	1154
S.Dro. Flie pride saies the Pea-cocke, Mistris that | you know. *Exit.*	1262
Adr. O husband, God doth know you din'd at home	1349
I know it by their pale and deadly lookes,	1381
Off. One *Angelo* a Goldsmith, do you know him?	1427
Adr. I know the man: what is the summe he owes?	1428
I long to know the truth heereof at large.	1439
Father. Why looke you strange on me? you know | me well.	1775
But tell me yet, dost thou not know my voice?	1781
Fath. Not know my voice, oh times extremity	1788
Ant. The Duke, and all that know me in the City,	1804
Duke. Stay, stand apart, I know not which is which.	1850

KNOWES = 4

But I should know her as well as she knowes me.	598
If euerie one knowes vs, and we know none,	942
Which God he knowes, I saw not. For the which,	1706
Knowes not my feeble key of vntun'd cares?	1791

KNOWING = 2

And knowing whom it was their hap to saue,	116
And knowing how the debt growes I will pay it.	1413

KNOWLEDGE = *1

*Lesse in your knowledge, and your grace you show not,	818

KNOWNE = 1

Knowne vnto these, and to my selfe disguisde:	610

KNOWST = 1*2

Adr. Say, didst thou speake with him? knowst thou | his minde?	322
Mar. These eares of mine thou knowst did hear thee:	1490
Thou know'st we parted, but perhaps my sonne,	1802

LABOUR = 2*1
    Against my soules pure truth, why labour you,   824
    *Offi. That labour may you saue: See where he comes.   996
    Or loose my labour in assaying it.   1566
LABOURED = 1
    Whom whil'st I laboured of a loue to see,   133
LADIE = 1
    Enter Ladie Abbesse.   1504
LADY = 2
    Duke. She is a vertuous and a reuerend Lady,   1606
    And bid the Lady Abbesse come to me: 1638
LAID = 1
    Ant. The gold I gaue to *Dromio* is laid vp   395
LAIDE = 1
    They must be bound and laide in some darke roome.   1382
LAIES = 1
    Anti. What claime laies she to thee?   875
LAMD = *1
    *and I thinke when he hath lam'd me, I shall begge with 1319
LAMPE = *1
    *Lampe of her, and run from her by her owne light. I 888
LAMPES = 1
    My wasting lampes some fading glimmer left;   1796
LAND = 2
    This is the Fairie land, oh spight of spights,   584
    Blowes faire from land: they stay for nought at all, 1080
LANDS = 1
    The passages of allies, creekes, and narrow lands: 1147
LAPLAND = 1
    And lapland Sorcerers inhabite here.   1194
LAPWING = 1
    Farre from her nest the Lapwing cries away;   1133
LARGE = 2
    I long to know the truth heereof at large.   1439
    And heare at large discoursed all our fortunes,   1885
LASHT = 1
    Luc. Why, headstrong liberty is lasht with woe: 289
LAST = 4*1
    E.Dro. Oh sixe pence that I had a wensday last,   220
    If I last in this seruice, you must case me in leather. 361
    Belike you thought our loue would last too long   1008
    Adr. To none of these, except it be the last,   1522
    Fa. Oh! griefe hath chang'd me since you saw me last, 1778
LATE = 2*2
    The enmity and discord which of late   9
    E.Dro. Return'd so soone, rather approacht too late: 208
    Luc. Come, come, *Antipholus*, we dine to late.   615
    Luce. Faith no, hee comes too late, and so tell your | Master. 683
LATELY = 1
    For lately we were bound as you are now.   1773
LATTER = 1
    My wife, more carefull for the latter borne,   81
LAUGH = *1
    E.Dro. O Lord I must laugh, haue at you with a Pro-|uerbe, 685
LAUGHES = 1
    Whil'st man and Master laughes my woes to scorne: 601

LAW = 2
    Therefore by Law thou art condemn'd to die.   29
    Gold. Sir, sir, I shall haue Law in *Ephesus,*   1071
LAWES = 3
    I am not partiall to infringe our Lawes;   8
    Now trust me, were it not against our Lawes,   145
    Against the Lawes and Statutes of this Towne,   1595
LAY = 2*2
    Lay open to my earthie grosse conceit: 821
    Dro. Marry sir, such claime as you would lay to your   876
    Good people enter, and lay hold on him.   1560
    S.Dro. Your goods that lay at host sir in the Centaur.   1902
LAYD = *1
    *this drudge or Diuiner layd claime to mee, call'd mee   929
LAYES = *1
    *a beast she would haue me, but that she being a ve- | rie beastly
    creature layes claime to me.   878
LEAD = 2
    Thee will I loue, and with thee lead my life;   856
    S.Dro. Wee'l draw Cuts for the Signior, till then, | lead thou first.   1914
LEAGUE = 2
    A league from *Epidamium* had we saild   65
    Keepe then faire league and truce with thy true bed,   540
LEAGUES = 1
    For ere the ships could meet by twice fiue leagues,   103
LEANE = *1
    *but leane lucke in the match, and yet is she a wondrous | fat marriage.   883
LEANE-FACD = *1
    *They brought one *Pinch,* a hungry leane-fac'd Villaine;   1714
LEARNE = 1*1
    Luc. Ere I learne loue, Ile practise to obey.   303
    Ant. Well sir, learne to iest in good time, there's a | time for all things.   458
LEAST = 2*1
    Adr. I, and let none enter, least I breake your pate.   614
    But least my selfe be guilty to selfe wrong,   953
    Anti. No beare it with you, least I come not time e- | nough.   1025
LEATHER = 1*1
    If I last in this seruice, you must case me in leather.   361
    *a Base-Viole in a case of leather; the man sir, that when   1207
LEAUE = 6*2
    Ile vtter what my sorrow giues me leaue.   39
    Hopelesse to finde, yet loth to leaue vnsought   138
    S.Dro. Sconce call you it? so you would leaue batte- | ring,   430
    If not, Ile leaue him to the Officer.   1047
    I coniure thee to leaue me, and be gon.   1250
    Ile giue thee ere I leaue thee so much money | To warrant thee as I am
    rested for.   1282
    Therefore depart, and leaue him heere with me.   1577
    Adr. I will not hence, and leaue my husband heere: 1578
LEFT = 9*2
    And he great care of goods at randone left,   46
    And left the ship then sinking ripe to vs.   80
    Fortune had left to both of vs alike,   108
    Where haue you left the mony that I gaue you.   219
    This foole-beg'd patience in thee will be left.   315
    Ile weepe (what's left away) and weeping die.   391
    *the Mole in my necke, the great Wart on my left arme,   932

LEFT *cont.*
*It was two ere I left him, and now the clocke strikes one.	1166
There left me and my man, both bound together,	1725
My wasting lampes some fading glimmer left;	1796
And me they left with those of *Epidamium.*	1845

LEISURE = 2
Ant. I will debate this matter at more leisure	1089
I hope I shall haue leisure to make good,	1863

LENGTH = 2
At length the sonne gazing vpon the earth,	91
At length another ship had seiz'd on vs,	115

LESSE = 1*1
*Lesse in your knowledge, and your grace you show not,	818
Adri. His inciuility confirmes no lesse:	1329

LESSER = 2
With lesser waight, but not with lesser woe,	111

LEST *see also* least = 1*2
Lest that your goods too soone be confiscate:	164
S.Dro. Lest it make you chollericke, and purchase me | another drie basting.	456
S.Dro. Let him walke from whence he came, lest hee | catch cold on's feet.	660

LET = 26*7
But ere they came, oh let me say no more,	97
Good Sister let vs dine, and neuer fret;	280
Then let your will attend on their accords.	299
When the sunne shines, let foolish gnats make sport,	425
Say he dines forth, and let no creature enter:	606
Adr. I, and let none enter, least I breake your pate.	614
But soft, my doore is lockt; goe bid them let vs in.	651
S.Dro. Let him walke from whence he came, lest hee | catch cold on's feet.	660
E.Dro. Let my Master in *Luce.*	682
Anti. Doe you heare you minion, you'll let vs in I | hope?	692
Anti. Thou baggage let me in.	698
Luce. Let him knocke till it ake.	701
E.Dro. Here's too much out vpon thee, I pray thee let | me in.	737
Balth. Haue patience sir, oh let it not be so,	746
And let vs to the Tyger all to dinner,	756
Let not my sister read it in your eye:	795
And let her read it in thy lookes at boord:	804
Let Loue, being light, be drowned if she sinke.	839
Come where's the Chaine, I pray you let me see it.	1044
There is a purse of Duckets, let her send it:	1094
Ant. Auant thou witch: Come *Dromio* let vs go.	1261
Pinch. Giue me your hand, and let mee feele your | pulse.	1335
Ant. There is my hand, and let it feele your eare.	1337
Adr. Oh binde him, binde him, let him not come | neere me.	1396
Offi. Masters let him go: he is my prisoner, and you | shall not haue him.	1403
Offi. He is my prisoner, if I let him go,	1409
Let vs come in, that we may binde him fast,	1507
Adr. As roughly as my modestie would let me.	1527
Ad. Then let your seruants bring my husband forth	1562
And therefore let me haue him home with me.	1570
Ab. Be patient, for I will not let him stirre,	1571
Let him be brought forth, and borne hence for helpe.	1632

LET *cont.*
    E.Dro. I Sir am *Dromio*, pray let me stay.   1821
LETS = 3*1
    Or else, what lets it but he would be here?   381
    Ant. Let's heare it.   465
    Let's call more helpe to haue them bound againe. | *Runne all out.*   1444
    *And now let's go hand in hand, not one before another. | *Exeunt.*   1918
LETTERS = 1
    At your important Letters this ill day,   1610
LEUIED = 1
    Vnlesse a thousand markes be leuied   25
LIBERTIE = 2*2
    A man is Master of his libertie: 281
    Adr. Why should their libertie then ours be more?   284
    *came behinde you sir, like an euill angel, and bid you for-|sake your
    libertie.   1203
    And gaine a husband by his libertie: 1826
LIBERTIES = 1
    And manie such like liberties of sinne: 268
LIBERTY = 2
    Luc. Why, headstrong liberty is lasht with woe: 289
    Who giue their eies the liberty of gazing.   1520
LICENCIOUS = 1
    Shouldst thou but heare I were licencious?   526
LIE = 1
    And as a bud Ile take thee, and there lie: 836
LIEGE = 3
    E.Ant. My Liege, I am aduised what I say,   1691
    E.Anti. Tis true (my Liege) this Ring I had of her.   1755
    Curt. As sure (my Liege) as I do see your Grace.   1757
LIES = 1
    Luc. Because their businesse still lies out adore.   285
LIEST = 1
    Ant. Villaine thou liest, for euen her verie words,   557
LIFE = 16
    That by misfortunes was my life prolong'd,   122
    But heere must end the story of my life,   140
    And not being able to buy out his life,   167
    Ant. Vpon my life by some deuise or other,   261
    S.Dro. I neuer spake with her in all my life.   559
    Thee will I loue, and with thee lead my life;   856
    Dro. As from a Beare a man would run for life,   944
    Of pale distemperatures, and foes to life?   1551
    Mess. Mistris, vpon my life I tel you true,   1653
    Deepe scarres to saue thy life; euen for the blood   1669
    Haply I see a friend will saue my life,   1763
    E.Ant. I neuer saw you in my life till now.   1777
    Yet hath my night of life some memorie: 1795
    Ant. I neuer saw my Father in my life.   1800
    I ne're saw *Siracusa* in my life.   1806
    Duke. It shall not neede, thy father hath his life.   1879
LIFE-PRESERUING = 1
    In food, in sport, and life-preseruing rest   1552
LIGHT = 4*6
    For what obscured light the heauens did grant,   69
    And by the benefit of his wished light   93
    Let Loue, being light, be drowned if she sinke.   839

LIGHT *cont.*

*Lampe of her, and run from her by her owne light. I	888
*And here she comes in the habit of a light wench, and	1235
*as much to say, God make me a light wench: It is writ-|ten,	1237
*they appeare to men like angels of light, light is an	1238
*effect of fire, and fire will burne: *ergo*, light wenches will | burne, come not neere her.	1239
And thereof comes it that his head is light.	1541

LIGHTENS = 1

Lightens my humour with his merry iests:	184

LIGHTLY = 1

And will not lightly trust the Messenger,	1285

LIKE = 15*8

And, which was strange, the one so like the other,	55
Whil'st I had beene like heedfull of the other.	85
That his attendant, so his case was like,	130
I to the world am like a drop of water,	199
*Me thinkes your maw, like mine, should be your cooke,	231
And manie such like liberties of sinne:	268
But were we burdned with like waight of paine,	310
But if thou liue to see like right bereft,	314
That like a foot-ball you doe spurne me thus:	359
Or if you like else-where doe it by stealth,	793
Apparell vice like vertues harbenger:	798
Dro. Swart like my shoo, but her face nothing like	893
*to hippe: she is sphericall, like a globe: I could find out | Countries in her.	905
But like a shrew you first begin to brawle.	1037
*came behinde you sir, like an euill angel, and bid you for-|sake your libertie.	1203
S.Dro. No? why 'tis a plaine case: he that went like	1206
*they appeare to men like angels of light, light is an	1238
*the prophesie like the Parrat, beware the ropes end.	1326
Rings, Iewels, any thing his rage did like.	1616
His man with Cizers nickes him like a foole:	1648
These two *Antipholus*, these two so like,	1833
E.Dro. Nay then thus: | We came into the world like brother and brother:	1916

LIKEWISE = 1

My woes end likewise with the euening Sonne.	31

LIMBO = 1

S.Dro. No, he's in Tartar limbo, worse then hell:	1141

LIMIT = 1

Therefore Marchant, Ile limit thee this day	153

LINGERD = 1

Say that I lingerd with you at your shop	621

LIST = 1

And teach your eares to list me with more heede:	1090

LITTLE = 2

'Tis holy sport to be a little vaine,	813
My dull deafe eares a little vse to heare:	1797

LIUD = 1

With her I liu'd in ioy, our wealth increast	43

LIUE = 6

Could all my trauells warrant me they liue.	142
And liue: if no, then thou art doom'd to die:	157
But if thou liue to see like right bereft,	314

LIUE *cont.*

I liue distain'd, thou vndishonoured.	541
Infect thy sap, and liue on thy confusion.	574
I see a man heere needs not liue by shifts,	976

LIUELESSE = 1

But to procrastinate his liuelesse end. *Exeunt.*	161

LIUES = 3*1

Who wanting gilders to redeeme their liues,	12
For slander liues vpon succession:	766
*a *Poland* Winter: If she liues till doomesday, she'l burne ∣ a weeke	
longer then the whole World.	890
Second to none that liues heere in the Citie:	1470

LIUING = 1

A liuing dead man. This pernicious slaue,	1718

LIUST = 1

Fie on thee wretch, 'tis pitty that thou liu'st	1491

LOATHSOME = 1

To make a loathsome abiect scorne of me:	1391

LOCKD = 3

But I confesse sir, that we were lock'd out.	1387
This woman lock'd me out this day from dinner;	1695
That he din'd not at home, but was lock'd out.	1732

LOCKE = 1*1

Ant. Say wherefore didst thou locke me forth to day,	1383
Adr. I did not gentle husband locke thee forth.	1385

LOCKING = 1

For locking me out of my doores by day:	1000

LOCKT = 1*2

But soft, my doore is lockt; goe bid them let vs in.	651
Ant. Were not my doores lockt vp, and I shut out?	1355
Dro. Perdie, your doores were lockt, and you shut ∣ out.	1356

LOE = 1

Ang. I know it well sir, loe here's the chaine,	958

LONG = 13*4

There had she not beene long, but she became	53
For with long trauaile I am stiffe and wearie. ∣ Get thee away.	177
*long, I must get a sconce for my head, and Insconce it	432
S.Dro. 'Tis true she rides me, and I long for grasse.	596
Once this your long experience of your wisedome,	750
The chaine vnfinish'd made me stay thus long.	960
Belike you thought our loue would last too long	1008
And I too blame haue held him heere too long.	1033
S.Dro. Master, if do expect spoon-meate, or bespeake ∣ a long	
spoone. ∣ *Ant.* Why *Dromio*?	1243
S.Dro. Marrie he must haue a long spoone that must ∣ eate with the	
diuell.	1246
*my long eares. I haue serued him from the houre of my	1311
I long to know the truth heereof at large.	1439
I long that we were safe and sound aboord.	1453
Ab. How long hath this possession held the man.	1511
Duke. Long since thy husband seru'd me in my wars	1633
Euen for the seruice that long since I did thee,	1667
After so long greefe such Natiuitie.	1896

LONGER = 3*1

But longer did we not retaine much hope;	68
Adr. Come, come, no longer will I be a foole,	599

LONGER *cont.*

*a *Poland* Winter: If she liues till doomesday, she'l burne | a weeke longer then the whole World.	890
*Dro. No longer from head to foot, then from hippe	904

LOOKD = 2*1

Vnlesse I spake, or look'd, or touch'd, or caru'd to thee.	513
*Dro. I look'd for the chalkle Cliffes, but I could find	917
Look'd he or red or pale, or sad or merrily?	1107

LOOKE = 7*3

Adr. Looke when I serue him so, he takes it thus.	286
Whil'st I at home starue for a merrie looke:	364
A sunnie looke of his, would soone repaire.	375
Adri. I, I, *Antipholus*, looke strange and frowne,	505
Looke sweet, speake faire, become disloyaltie:	797
*Ant. As good to winke sweet loue, as looke on night.	846
Anti. Where stood *Belgia*, the *Netherlands*? | *Dro. Oh sir, I did not looke so low. To conclude,	927
Luc. Nere may I looke on day, nor sleepe on night,	1687
*Father. Why looke you strange on me? you know | me well.	1775
Come go with vs, wee'l looke to that anon,	1904

LOOKES = 5

Excludes all pitty from our threatning lookes:	14
And fashion your demeanor to my lookes,	428
And let her read it in thy lookes at boord:	804
Luc. Alas how fiery, and how sharpe he lookes.	1333
I know it by their pale and deadly lookes,	1381

LOOKING = 1

A needy-hollow-ey'd-sharpe-looking-wretch;	1717

LOOKS = *1

*Luc. Aye me poore man, how pale and wan he looks.	1399

LOOSE *see also* lose = 7

Ant. Farewell till then: I will goe loose my selfe,	193
In quest of them (vnhappie a) loose my selfe.	204
I see the Iewell best enamaled | Will loose his beautie: yet the gold bides still	385
For fortie Duckets is too much to loose.	1279
Luc. God for thy mercy, they are loose againe.	1442
Or loose my labour in assaying it.	1566
My Master and his man are both broke loose,	1642

LOOSETH = *1

*S.Dro. The plainer dealer, the sooner lost; yet he loo-|seth it in a kinde of iollitie.	482

LORD = 4*5

Iaylor, take him to thy custodie. | *Iaylor.* I will my Lord.	158
Lord of the wide world, and wilde watry seas,	295
*E.Dro. O Lord I must laugh, haue at you with a Pro-|uerbe,	685
*Anti. Good Lord, you vse this dalliance to excuse	1034
Who I made Lord of me, and all I had,	1609
*Adr. No my good Lord. My selfe, he, and my sister,	1684
*Gold. My Lord, in truth, thus far I witnes with him:	1731
Gold. He had my Lord, and when he ran in heere,	1734
*E.Ant. I came from *Corinth* my most gracious Lord | *E.Dro.* And I with him.	1851

LORDS = 1

Are masters to their females, and their Lords:	298

LOSE *see also* loose = 1*1

*S.Dro. Not a man of those but he hath the wit to lose | his haire.	478

LOSE *cont.*
    Abb. Who euer bound him, I will lose his bonds,   1825
LOSSE = 1
    I hazarded the losse of whom I lou'd.   134
LOST = 4*3
    *S.Dro. Yes, to pay a fine for a perewig, and recouer | the lost haire of
    another man.   469
    *S.Dro. The plainer dealer, the sooner lost; yet he loo-|seth it in a
    kinde of iollitie.   482
    *S.Dro. Marry and did sir: namely, in no time to re-|couer haire lost
    by Nature.   496
    No euill lost is wail'd, when it is gone.   1130
    Luc. How hast thou lost thy breath? | *S.Dro.* By running fast.   1138
    *Ab. Hath he not lost much wealth by wrack of sea,   1516
    That then I lost for thee, now grant me iustice.   1670
LOTH = 1
    Hopelesse to finde, yet loth to leaue vnsought   138
LOUD = 1
    I hazarded the losse of whom I lou'd.   134
LOUE = 17*2
    Whom whil'st I laboured of a loue to see,   133
    Luc. Ere I learne loue, Ile practise to obey.   303
    Would that alone, a loue he would detaine,   383
    As you loue stroakes, so iest with me againe: 403
    Your sawcinesse will iest vpon my loue,   423
    For know my loue: as easie maist thou fall   520
    Euen in the spring of Loue, thy Loue-springs rot?   789
    Shall loue in buildings grow so ruinate?   790
    Muffle your false loue with some shew of blindnesse: 794
    (Being compact of credit) that you loue vs,   808
    Let Loue, being light, be drowned if she sinke.   839
    *Ant. As good to winke sweet loue, as looke on night.   846
    Luc. Why call you me loue? Call my sister so.   847
    Thee will I loue, and with thee lead my life;   856
    Belike you thought our loue would last too long   1008
    Luc. That loue I begg'd for you, he begg'd of me.   1117
    *Adr. With what perswasion did he tempt thy loue?   1118
    Stray'd his affection in vnlawfull loue,   1518
    Namely, some loue that drew him oft from home.   1523
LOUE-SPRINGS = 1
    Euen in the spring of Loue, thy Loue-springs rot?   789
LOW = *1
    Anti. Where stood *Belgia*, the *Netherlands*? | **Dro.* Oh sir, I did not
    looke so low. To conclude,   927
LOWRETH = 1
    Luci. Fie how impatience lowreth in your face.   362
LUC = 27*7
LUCE = 3*4, 2*2
    Enter Luce.   679
    E.Dro. Let my Master in *Luce.*   682
    *S.Dro. If thy name be called *Luce*, *Luce* thou hast an-|swer'd him
    well.   690
LUCI = 7*1, 1
    Exeunt. Manet Offic. Adri. Luci. Courtizan   1426
LUCIANA see also *Luc., Luce., Luci.* = 8*1
    Enter Adriana, wife to Antipholis Sereptus, with | Luciana her Sister.   273
    Sure *Luciana* it is two a clocke.   277

LUCIANA cont.

Enter Adriana and Luciana.	504
Enter Adriana and Luciana.	1103
Adr. Ah Luciana, did he tempt thee so?	1104
Adr. Go fetch it Sister: this I wonder at. | Exit Luciana.	1158
Enter Luciana.	1178
Enter Adriana, Luciana, Courtizan, and a Schoole-|master, call'd Pinch.	1321
*They draw. Enter Adriana, Luciana, Courtezan, & others.	1497

LUCKE = *1

*but leane lucke in the match, and yet is she a wondrous | fat marriage.	883

LUNATICKE = 1

And tell his wife, that being Lunaticke,	1276

LUST = 2

By Ruffian Lust should be contaminate?	528
My bloud is mingled with the crime of lust:	536

MACE = 1

with his Mace, then a Moris Pike.	1211

MAD = 21*6

*E.Dro. Why Mistresse, sure my Master is horne mad.	333
Adri. Horne mad, thou villaine?	334
E.Dro. I meane not Cuckold mad, | But sure he is starke mad:	335
Luci. How manie fond fooles serue mad Ielousie? | Exit.	392
My house was at the Phoenix? Wast thou mad,	406
Sleeping or waking, mad or well aduisde:	609
*It would make a man mad as a Bucke to be so bought | and sold.	727
Luc. What are you mad, that you doe reason so?	840
Ant. Not mad, but mated, how I doe not know.	841
Cur. Now out of doubt Antipholus is mad,	1264
The reason that I gather he is mad,	1269
Is a mad tale he told to day at dinner,	1271
*Curt. How say you now? Is not your husband mad?	1328
Anti. Peace doting wizard, peace; I am not mad.	1342
*Ant. Out on thee Villaine, wherefore dost thou mad | mee?	1418
*Dro. Will you be bound for nothing, be mad good | Master, cry the diuell.	1420
*the Mountaine of mad flesh that claimes mariage of me,	1457
Adr. Hold, hurt him not for God sake, he is mad,	1498
Ab. And thereof came it, that the man was mad.	1537
Poisons more deadly then a mad dogges tooth.	1539
To be disturb'd, would mad or man, or beast:	1553
With him his bondman, all as mad as he,	1613
And with his mad attendant and himselfe,	1622
Albeit my wrongs might make one wiser mad.	1694
If he were mad, he would not pleade so coldly:	1749
I thinke you are all mated, or starke mad.	1760

MADE = 11*4

By prosperous voyages I often made	44
Had made prouision for her following me,	51
Made daily motions for our home returne:	63
My Mistris made it one vpon my cheeke:	211
*E.Dro. What patch is made our Porter? my Master | stayes in the street.	658
Why at this time the dores are made against you.	754
A vulgar comment will be made of it;	761
And fetch the chaine, by this I know 'tis made,	776
*my brest had not beene made of faith, and my heart of	934

MADE *cont.*

*steele, she had transform'd me to a Curtull dog, & made | me turne
i'th wheele. 935
Hath almost made me Traitor to my selfe: 952
The chaine vnfinish'd made me stay thus long. 960
Ang. What please your selfe sir: I haue made it for | you. 962
Anti. Made it for me sir, I bespoke it not, 964
Who I made Lord of me, and all I had, 1609
MADLIE = 1
That thus so madlie thou did didst answere me? 407
MADLY = 1
Met vs againe, and madly bent on vs 1624
MADMAN = 1*1
An. How now? a Madman? Why thou peeuish sheep 1082
In this the Madman iustly chargeth them. 1690
MADNESSE = 2
And what's a Feauer, but a fit of madnesse? 1545
A most outragious fit of madnesse tooke him: 1611
MADST = 1
What obseruation mad'st thou in this case? 1108
MAIDE = *1
Anti. Did not her Kitchen maide raile, taunt, and | scorne me? 1360
MAIDS = 1
Beaten the Maids a-row, and bound the Doctor, 1643
MAIST *l.*520 = 1
MAKE = 16*8
Beg thou, or borrow, to make vp the summe, 156
Of whom I hope to make much benefit: 188
And make a Common of my serious howres, 424
When the sunne shines, let foolish gnats make sport, 425
Ant. Ile make you amends next, to giue you nothing 448
S.Dro. Lest it make you chollericke, and purchase me | another drie
basting. 456
*It would make a man mad as a Bucke to be so bought | and sold. 727
Vpon mine hostesse there, good sir make haste: 780
Alas poore women, make vs not beleeue 807
To make it wander in an vnknowne field? 825
*and I know not what vse to put her too, but to make a 887
Therefore make present satisfaction, 986
Dro. Here goe: the deske, the purse, sweet now make | haste. 1136
*as much to say, God make me a light wench: It is writ- | ten, 1237
To make a loathsome abiect scorne of me: 1391
*I am thy prisoner, wilt thou suffer them to make a res- | cue? 1401
Vnquiet meales make ill digestions, 1543
To make of him a formall man againe: 1574
When thou didst make him Master of thy bed, 1635
Mar.Fat. Vnlesse the feare of death doth make me | dote, I see my
sonne *Antipholus* and *Dromio.* 1671
Albeit my wrongs might make one wiser mad. 1694
I see thy age and dangers make thee dote. 1810
I hope I shall haue leisure to make good, 1863
And we shall make full satisfaction. 1889
MAKER = 1
Dro. God and the Rope-maker beare me witnesse, 1378
MAKES = 3*1
Adri. This seruitude makes you to keepe vnwed. 300
Makes me with thy strength to communicate: 570

MAKES . *cont.*
A table full of welcome, makes scarce one dainty dish.	642
Bal. Small cheere and great welcome, makes a mer-|rie feast.	646

MAKING = 3*1
Two shippes from farre, making amaine to vs:	95
To see the making of her Carkanet,	622
Dro. In her forhead, arm'd and reuerted, making | warre against her heire.	914
Stigmaticall in making worse in minde.	1128

MALE = 1
Of such a burthen Male, twins both alike:	59

MALES = 1
Are their males subiects, and at their controules:	293

MALTHORSE = *1
S.Dro. Mome, Malthorse, Capon, Coxcombe, Idi-|ot, Patch,	653

MAN = 37*21
Duk. Nay forward old man, doe not breake off so,	99
Dro. Many a man would take you at your word,	179
A man is Master of his libertie:	281
Man more diuine, the Master of all these,	294
Heere comes your man, now is your husband nie.	317
Where gold and no man that hath a name,	388
S.Dro. Was there euer anie man thus beaten out of	442
S.Dro. There's no time for a man to recouer his haire | that growes bald by nature.	466
S.Dro. Yes, to pay a fine for a perewig, and recouer | the lost haire of another man.	469
Ant. Why, but theres manie a man hath more haire | then wit.	476
S.Dro. Not a man of those but he hath the wit to lose | his haire.	478
Whil'st man and Master laughes my woes to scorne:	601
Enter Antipholus of Ephesus, his man Dromio, Angelo the | Goldsmith, and Balthaser the Merchant.	617
*It would make a man mad as a Bucke to be so bought | and sold.	727
E.Dro. A man may breake a word with your sir, and | words are but winde:	732
S.Dro. Doe you know me sir? Am I *Dromio*? Am I | your man? Am I my selfe?	864
Ant. Thou art *Dromio*, thou art my man, thou art | thy selfe.	866
Dro. I am an asse, I am a womans man, and besides | my selfe.	868
Ant. What womans man? and how besides thy | selfe?	869
Dro. A very reuerent body: I such a one, as a man	881
*so cleane kept: for why? she sweats a man may goe o-|uer-shooes in the grime of it.	894
Dro. As from a Beare a man would run for life,	944
Ang. You are a merry man sir, fare you well. *Exit.*	972
But this I thinke, there's no man is so vaine,	974
I see a man heere needs not liue by shifts,	976
Eph.Ant. A man is well holpe vp that trusts to you,	1005
Adr. Why man, what is the matter?	1150
There's not a man I meete but doth salute me	1184
*a Base-Viole in a case of leather; the man sir, that when	1207
*any man to answer it that breakes his Band: one that	1214
*thinkes a man alwaies going to bed, and saies, God giue | you good rest.	1215
Cur. Your man and you are maruailous merrie sir.	1241
An. Feare me not man, I will not breake away,	1281
Heere comes my Man, I thinke he brings the monie.	1289

MAN *cont.*
Pinch. I charge thee Sathan, hous'd within this man,	1338
Pinch. Mistris, both Man and Master is possest,	1380
Luc. Aye me poore man, how pale and wan he looks.	1399
Pinch. Go binde this man, for he is franticke too.	1405
Hast thou delight to see a wretched man	1407
Adr. I know the man: what is the summe he owes?	1428
Mar. How is the man esteem'd heere in the Citie?	1467
Ab. How long hath this possession held the man.	1511
And much different from the man he was:	1513
Ab. And thereof came it, that the man was mad.	1537
To be disturb'd, would mad or man, or beast:	1553
To make of him a formall man againe:	1574
My Master and his man are both broke loose,	1642
His man with Cizers nickes him like a foole:	1648
Adr. Peace foole, thy Master and his man are here,	1651
A liuing dead man. This pernicious slaue,	1718
There left me and my man, both bound together,	1725
Now am I *Dromio*, and his man, vnbound.	1770
a man denies, you are now bound to beleeue him.	1787
Abbesse. Most mightie Duke, behold a man much | wrong'd.	1813
And so of these, which is the naturall man,	1818
Speake olde *Egeon*, if thou bee'st the man	1827
And *Dromio* my man did bring mee:	1874
I see we still did meete each others man,	1875

MANAGED = 1
Shame hath a bastard fame, well managed,	805

MANET = 2
Exeunt. Manet Offic. Adri. Luci. Courtizan	1426
Exeunt omnes. Manet the two Dromio's and | two Brothers.	1898

MANIE = 2*1
And manie such like liberties of sinne:	268
Luci. How manie fond fooles serue mad Ielousie? | *Exit.*	392
Ant. Why, but theres manie a man hath more haire | then wit.	476

MANNERS = 1
Till that Ile view the manners of the towne,	174

MANY = 1*1
Dro. Many a man would take you at your word,	179
*When one is one too many, goe get thee from the dore.	657

MAR = 10*3

MARBLE = 1
Vnkindnesse blunts it more then marble hard.	369

MARCHANT = 1, 3
Therefore Marchant, Ile limit thee this day	153
Enter Antipholis Erotes, a Marchant, and Dromio.	162
This very day a *Syracusian* Marchant | Is apprehended for a riuall here,	165

MARCHANTS = 1
E.Mar. I am inuited sir to certaine Marchants,	187

MARD = 1
If voluble and sharpe discourse be mar'd,	368

MARFAT = *1

MARIAGE = *1
*the Mountaine of mad flesh that claimes mariage of me,	1457

MARIAN = 1
E.Dro. Maud, Briget, Marian, Cisley, Gillian, Ginn.	652

MARKE = 1*1
*markes I had about mee, as the marke of my shoulder,	931

MARKE *cont.*

Cur. Marke, how he trembles in his extasie.   1334
MARKES = 9*2

Vnlesse a thousand markes be leuied   25
Cannot amount vnto a hundred Markes,   28
Where is the thousand Markes thou hadst of me?   246
E.Dro. I haue some markes of yours vpon my pate: 247
Some of my Mistris markes vpon my shoulders: 248
But not a thousand markes betweene you both.   249
Ant. Thy Mistris markes? what Mistris slaue hast thou?   252
He ask'd me for a hundred markes in gold: 338
Where is the thousand markes I gaue thee villaine?   342
And charg'd him with a thousand markes in gold,   626
*markes I had about mee, as the marke of my shoulder,   931
MARKT = 1

Duke. Haplesse *Egeon* whom the fates haue markt   143
MARRIAGE = 3

Luci. Not this, but troubles of the marriage bed.   301
*but leane lucke in the match, and yet is she a wondrous | fat marriage.   883
Anti. How dost thou meane a fat marriage?   885
MARRIE = *2

Dro. Marrie sir, besides my selfe, I am due to a woman: 872
S.Dro. Marrie he must haue a long spoone that must | eate with the
diuell.   1246
MARRIED = 2

Whose weaknesse married to thy stranger state,   569
What, was I married to her in my dreame?   577
MARRY = 2*6

Luci. Well, I will marry one day but to trie: 316
S.Dro. Marry sir, for this something that you gaue me | for nothing.   446
S.Dro. Marry sir, by a rule as plaine as the plaine bald | pate of Father
time himselfe.   463
S.Dro. Marry and did sir: namely, in no time to re-|couer haire lost
by Nature.   496
E.Ant. I thinke thou art an asse. | *E.Dro.* Marry so it doth appeare   633
Dro. Marry sir, such claime as you would lay to your   876
Dro. Marry sir, she's the Kitchin wench, & al grease,   886
Dro. Marry sir in her buttockes, I found it out by | the bogges.   908
MART = 8*2

Please you, Ile meete with you vpon the Mart,   190
E.Dro. My charge was but to fetch you fro(m) the Mart   239
And from the Mart he's somewhere gone to dinner: 279
I sent him from the Mart? see here he comes.   400
Didst thou deliuer to me on the Mart.   558
He met me on the Mart, and that I beat him,   625
*That you beat me at the Mart I haue your hand to show;   630
If any Barke put forth, come to the Mart,   940
Ile to the Mart, and there for *Dromio* stay,   978
After you first forswore it on the Mart,   1738
MARTS = 1

Nay more, if any borne at *Ephesus* | Be seene at any *Siracusian* Marts
and Fayres: 20
MARUAILOUS = 1

Cur. Your man and you are maruailous merrie sir.   1241
MARUEL = *1

Adr. Patience vnmou'd, no maruel though she pause,   306

MAST = 2
  Had fastned him vnto a small spare Mast,   82
  Fastned our selues at eyther end the mast,   88
MASTER *see also* Mr, Mast. = 30*15
  That in such haste I sent to seeke his Master?   276
  A man is Master of his libertie: 281
  Time is their Master, and when they see time,   282
  Man more diuine, the Master of all these,   294
  Adr. Say, is your tardie master now at hand?   319
  E.Dro. Why Mistresse, sure my Master is horne mad.   333
  E.Dr. Quoth my Master, I know quoth he, no house,   347
  Adri. Hence prating pesant, fetch thy Master home.   357
  That's not my fault, hee's master of my state.   371
  What meanes this iest, I pray you Master tell me?   416
  S.Dro. I am transformed Master, am I not?   590
  S.Dro. Nay Master, both in minde, and in my shape.   592
  Whil'st man and Master laughes my woes to scorne: 601
  Sirra, if any aske you for your Master,   605
  S.Dro. Master, shall I be Porter at the gate?   613
  E.Dro. What patch is made our Porter? my Master | stayes in the
  street.   658
  E.Dro. Let my Master in *Luce*.   682
  Luce. Faith no, hee comes too late, and so tell your | Master.   683
  E.Drom. Master, knocke the doore hard.   700
  E.Dro. If you went in paine Master, this knaue wold | goe sore.   713
  E.Dro. They stand at the doore, Master, bid them | welcome hither.   719
  E.Dro. You would say so Master, if your garments | were thin.   723
  E.Dro. A crow without feather, Master meane you so;   742
  Dro. Master, there's a Barke of *Epidamium*,   1074
  But for their Owner, Master, and your selfe.   1081
  Adr. Where is thy Master *Dromio*? Is he well?   1140
  And bring thy Master home imediately.   1180
  S.Dro. Master, here's the gold you sent me for: what   1196
  Cur. Well met, well met, Master *Antipholus*:   1228
  S.Dro. Master, is this Mistris *Sathan*? | *Ant.* It is the diuell.   1232
  S.Dro. Master, if do expect spoon-meate, or bespeake | a long
  spoone. | *Ant.* Why *Dromio*?   1243
  *but she more couetous, wold haue a chaine: Ma-|ster   1256
  Enter Adriana, Luciana, Courtizan, and a Schoole-|master, call'd Pinch. 1321
  But surely Master not a ragge of Monie.   1374
  Pinch. Mistris, both Man and Master is possest,   1380
  Good Master Doctor see him safe conuey'd   1414
  Dro. Master, I am heere entred in bond for you.   1417
  Dro. Will you be bound for nothing, be mad good | Master, cry the
  diuell.   1420
  S.Dro. Runne master run, for Gods sake take a house,   1501
  When thou didst make him Master of thy bed,   1635
  My Master and his man are both broke loose,   1642
  Adr. Peace foole, thy Master and his man are here,   1651
  S.Drom. Oh my olde Master, who hath bound him | heere?   1823
  S.Dro. Mast.(er) shall I fetch your stuffe from shipbord?   1900
  S.Ant. He speakes to me, I am your master *Dromio*.   1903
MASTERS = 3*1
  Are masters to their females, and their Lords: 298
  For seruants must their Masters mindes fulfill. *Exit*   1102
  Offi. Masters let him go: he is my prisoner, and you | shall not haue
  him.   1403

MASTERS *cont.*
S.Dro. There is a fat friend at your masters house,   1906
MATCH = *1
*but leane lucke in the match, and yet is she a wondrous | fat marriage.   883
MATE = 1
So thou that hast no vnkinde mate to greeue thee,   312
MATED = 2
Ant. Not mad, but mated, how I doe not know.   841
I thinke you are all mated, or starke mad.   1760
MATTER = 2*1
Ant. I will debate this matter at more leisure   1089
Adr. Why man, what is the matter?   1150
*S.Dro. I doe not know the matter, hee is rested on | the case.   1151
MAUD = 1
E.Dro. Maud, *Briget, Marian, Cisley, Gillian, Ginn.*   652
MAW = *1
*Me thinkes your maw, like mine, should be your cooke,   231
MAY *l.*37 100 147 150 468 *639 650 667 *732 764 787 810 *882 *894 *996
   1030 *1218 *1310 1437 1446 1507 *1608 1630 1687 1764 = 17*8
ME *l.*39 41 42 47 51 77 97 121 125 129 142 145 185 186 192 197 198 218
   224 *231 236 238 242 246 256 313 338 350 358 359 360 361 372 382 397
   403 405 407 410 411 413 416 417 420 427 *440 441 445 *446 *456 516
   519 524 529 *542 550 553 558 564 565 570 571 583 596 598 624 625
   *630 663 675 698 *729 737 741 745 755 774 781 782 784 820 826 827
   832 833 847 857 *864 873 *877 *878 *930 935 941 948 952 960 964 989
   991 993 1000 1002 1007 *1031 *1039 1042 1044 1046 1049 *1052 1054
   *1057 1059 1060 1063 1066 1083 1084 1087 1088 1090 1096 1099 1100
   *1111 1117 1123 1153 1160 1161 1184 1186 1187 1188 1189 1190 1191
   *1196 1230 1231 *1236 *1237 1242 *1248 1250 1251 1260 1267 1268
   1281 *1301 *1314 *1319 *1335 1347 1358 1360 *1373 1376 1378 *1383
   1391 1393 1396 *1399 *1400 1410 1412 1424 *1432 1438 *1456 *1457
   1465 1476 1477 1486 1489 1493 1527 1559 1570 1577 1609 *1633 1638
   *1659 1661 *1666 1670 *1671 1674 1675 1678 1679 1680 1686 1695 1697
   1698 1704 1707 1711 1721 1723 1725 1728 1743 1744 1745 *1762 1764
   1771 1775 *1778 1781 1784 1799 1803 1804 1805 1816 1821 1839 1845
   1856 1860 1862 1868 1871 1874 1876 *1903 1907 *1909 = 207*46
MEALES = 1
Vnquiet meales make ill digestions,   1543
MEANE = 9*3
A meane woman was deliuered   58
And goe indeede, hauing so good a meane. | *Exit Dromio.*   180
E.Dro. What meane you sir, for God sake hold your | (hands: 258
E.Dro. I meane not Cuckold mad, | But sure he is starke mad: 335
Thou drunkard thou, what didst thou meane by this?   628
*But though my cates be meane, take them in good part,   649
*E.Dro. A crow without feather, Master meane you so;   742
And in despight of mirth meane to be merrie: 769
There will we dine: this woman that I meane   772
Anti. How dost thou meane a fat marriage?   885
*Ant. What gold is this? What *Adam* do'st thou | meane?   1198
I hope you do not meane to cheate me so?   1260
MEANELY = 1
My wife, not meanely prowd of two such boyes,   62
MEANES = 4
And this it was: (for other meanes was none)   78
What meanes this iest, I pray you Master tell me?   416
He gaines by death, that hath such meanes to die: 838

MEANES *cont.*
Till I haue vs'd the approoued meanes I haue,   1572
MEANING = 2
  Luc. Spake hee so doubtfully, thou couldst not feele | his meaning.   326
  The foulded meaning of your words deceit: 823
MEANST = 1
  Ant. What thou mean'st an officer?   1212
MEANT = *1
  Adr. He meant he did me none: the more my spight   1111
MEASURE = 1*1
  *an Ell and three quarters, will not measure her from hip | to hip.   901
  And therewithall tooke measure of my body.   1192
MEAT = 3*1
  Your meat doth burne, quoth I: my gold quoth he: 340
  S.Dro. No sir, I thinke the meat wants that I haue.   450
  That neuer meat sweet-sauour'd in thy taste,   512
  Bal. Good meat sir is co(m)mon that euery churle affords.   643
MEATE = 3*1
  She is so hot because the meate is colde: 212
  The meate is colde, because you come not home: 213
  S.Dro. Master, if do expect spoon-meate, or bespeake | a long
  spoone. | *Ant*. Why *Dromio*?   1243
  Thou saist his meate was sawc'd with thy vpbraidings,   1542
MEE *l.*320 *575 *669 *929 *931 *1052 *1335 1369 1418 1847 1865
  1895 = 5*9
MEEKE = 1
  They can be meeke, that haue no other cause: 307
MEERE = 1
  A meere Anatomie, a Mountebanke,   1715
MEET = 2
  For ere the ships could meet by twice fiue leagues,   103
  Ang. Ile meet you at that place some houre hence.   783
MEETE = 4*1
  Please you, Ile meete with you vpon the Mart,   190
  S.Dro. Oh yes, if any houre meete a Serieant, a turnes | backe for verie
  feare.   1168
  There's not a man I meete but doth salute me   1184
  Straight after did I meete him with a Chaine.   1436
  I see we still did meete each others man,   1875
MEETES = 1
  When in the streets he meetes such Golden gifts: 977
MELANCHOLLY = 3
  When I am dull with care and melancholly,   183
  Sweet recreation barr'd, what doth ensue | But moodie and dull
  melancholly,   1547
  Comes this way to the melancholly vale;   1589
MEMORIE = 1
  Yet hath my night of life some memorie: 1795
MEN = 7*3
  Such as sea-faring men prouide for stormes: 83
  Or that, or any place that harbours men: 139
  Ant. Why thou didst conclude hairy men plain dea-|lers without wit.   480
  Nay, he's a theefe too: haue you not heard men say,   1174
  *he sir, that takes pittie on decaied men, and giues them   1209
  *they appeare to men like angels of light, light is an   1238
  To walke where any honest men resort.   1492
  A sinne preuailing much in youthfull men,   1519

MEN *cont.*

Duke. One of these men is *genius* to the other: — 1817
Abb. By men of *Epidamium*, he, and I, — 1841
MENAPHON = 1
Duke *Menaphon* your most renowned Vnckle. — 1855
MEND = 2*1
*S.Dro. Thus I mend it: Time himselfe is bald, and — 500
Anti. That's a fault that water will mend. — 896
Will you goe with me, wee'll mend our dinner here? — 1242
MER = 1*2
MERCH = 3
MERCHANT *see also* E.Mar., Mar., Marchant., Mar.Fat., Mer.,
Merch. = 6*2
**Enter the Duke of Ephesus, with the Merchant of Siracusa, | Iaylor, and
other attendants.* — 2
*Duke. Merchant of *Siracusa*, plead no more. — 7
Luc. Perhaps some Merchant hath inuited him, — 278
**Enter Antipholus of Ephesus, his man Dromio, Angelo the | Goldsmith,
and Balthaser the Merchant.* — 617
Enter a Merchant, Goldsmith, and an Officer. — 981
Enter the Merchant and the Goldsmith. — 1463
Gold. Vpon what cause? | *Mar.* To see a reuerent *Siracusian* Merchant, — 1592
Enter the Duke of Ephesus, and the Merchant of Siracuse — 1599
MERCHANTS = 1
To Merchants our well-dealing Countrimen, — 11
MERCILESSE = 1
Worthily tearm'd them mercilesse to vs: — 102
MERCY = 1
Luc. God for thy mercy, they are loose againe. — 1442
MERMAIDE = 1
Oh traine me not sweet Mermaide with thy note, — 832
MERMAIDS = 1
Ile stop mine eares against the Mermaids song. — 954
MERRIE = 8*1
Or I shall breake that merrie sconce of yours — 244
Whil'st I at home starue for a merrie looke: — 364
How now sir, is your merrie humor alter'd? — 402
S.Dro. I am glad to see you in this merrie vaine, — 415
*Bal. Small cheere and great welcome, makes a mer-|rie feast. — 646
And in despight of mirth meane to be merrie: — 769
Gold. Sauing your merrie humor: here's the note — 1010
The ship is in her trim, the merrie winde — 1079
Cur. Your man and you are maruailous merrie sir. — 1241
MERRIER = 1
Reserue them till a merrier houre then this: — 234
MERRILY = 1
Look'd he or red or pale, or sad or merrily? — 1107
MERRY = 2
Lightens my humour with his merry iests: — 184
Ang. You are a merry man sir, fare you well. *Exit.* — 972
MESS = 1
MESSENGER *see also* Mess. = 4
And strike you home without a messenger. — 232
For Gods sake send some other messenger. — 353
And will not lightly trust the Messenger, — 1285
Enter a Messenger. — 1640

MET = 7*1
He met me on the Mart, and that I beat him,	625
And in the instant that I met with you,	990
Cur. Well met, well met, Master *Antipholus*:	1228
Met vs againe, and madly bent on vs	1624
I went to seeke him. In the street I met him,	1702
*By'th'way, we met my wife, her sister, and a rabble more | Of vilde	
Confederates: Along with them	1712
Which accidentally are met together.	1837

METEORS = 1
Oh, his hearts Meteors tilting in his face.	1109

METHINKES see thinkes
METHOD = 1
Or I will beat this method in your sconce.	429

METTALL = 1
As all the mettall in your shop will answer.	1070

MICKLE = 1
The one nere got me credit, the other mickle blame:	675

MIDST = 1
Our helpefull ship was splitted in the midst;	106

MIGHT *l.*132 *710 *1119 *1306 *1373 1471 1694 = 3*4
MIGHTIE = *1
Abbesse. Most mightie Duke, behold a man much | wrong'd.	1813

MIGHTST *l.*1105 = 1
MIGHTY = 1*1
We were encountred by a mighty rocke,	104
Fa. Most mighty Duke, vouchsafe me speak a word:	1762

MILDELY = 1
Luc. She neuer reprehended him but mildely,	1556

MINDE = 6
Darke working Sorcerers that change the minde:	265
Adr. Say, didst thou speake with him? knowst thou | his minde?	322
E.Dro. I, I, he told his minde vpon mine eare,	324
Ant. I thinke thou art in minde, and so am I.	591
S.Dro. Nay Master, both in minde, and in my shape.	592
Stigmaticall in making worse in minde.	1128

MINDES = 2
Did but conuay vnto our fearefull mindes	70
For seruants must their Masters mindes fulfill. *Exit*	1102

MINE *l.*176 197 *231 324 398 *673 780 781 817 828 *850 851 954 1251
1266 *1490 1494 1575 1720 *1736 1792 1816 *1901 = 18*6
MINGLED = 1
My bloud is mingled with the crime of lust:	536

MINION = *3
Anti. Doe you heare you minion, you'll let vs in I | hope?	692
Anti. You'll crie for this minion, if I beat the doore | downe.	702
Anti. You Minion you, are these your Customers?	1344

MINIONS = 1
Adri. His company must do his minions grace,	363

MIRACLE = 1
From whence I thinke you are come by Miracle.	1741

MIRTH = 1
And in despight of mirth meane to be merrie:	769

MISERIE = 1
Thou sham'st to acknowledge me in miserie.	1803

MISFORTUNES = 1
That by misfortunes was my life prolong'd,	122

MISHAP = 1
To beare the extremitie of dire mishap: 144
MISHAPS = 1
To tell sad stories of my owne mishaps.   123
MIST = 1
And in this mist at all aduentures go.   612
MISTRESSE = 7*2
*E.Dro. Why Mistresse, sure my Master is horne mad.   333
My mistresse, sir, quoth I: hang vp thy Mistresse: 344
I know not thy mistresse, out on thy mistresse. | Luci. Quoth who?   345
*no wife, no mistresse: so that my arrant due vnto my   348
Your Mistresse sent to haue me home to dinner?   405
And toldst me of a Mistresse, and a dinner,   413
Some other Mistresse hath thy sweet aspects: 506
MISTRIS = 12*7
My Mistris made it one vpon my cheeke: 211
To pay the Sadler for my Mistris crupper: 221
I from my Mistris come to you in post: 228
My Mistris and her sister staies for you.   241
Some of my Mistris markes vpon my shoulders: 248
*Ant. Thy Mistris markes? what Mistris slaue hast thou?   252
*E.Dro. Your worships wife, my Mistris at the Phoenix;   253
*S.Anti. Sweete Mistris, what your name is else I | know not;   815
*will you send him Mistris redemption, the monie in | his deske.   1156
S.Dro. Master, is this Mistris Sathan? | Ant. It is the diuell.   1232
*S.Dro. Flie pride saies the Pea-cocke, Mistris that | you know. Exit.   1262
*E.Dro. Mistris respice finem, respect your end, or ra-|ther   1325
Pinch. Mistris, both Man and Master is possest,   1380
Oh Mistris, Mistris, shift and saue your selfe,   1641
Mess. Mistris, vpon my life I tel you true,   1653
Harke, harke, I heare him Mistris: flie, be gone.   1658
Adr. Which of you two did dine with me to day? | S.Ant. I, gentle
Mistris.   1856
MODESTIE = 2
Her sober vertue, yeares, and modestie,   751
Adr. As roughly as my modestie would let me.   1527
MOLE = *1
*the Mole in my necke, the great Wart on my left arme,   932
MOME = *1
*S.Dro. Mome, Malthorse, Capon, Coxcombe, Idi-|ot, Patch,   653
MONETHS = 1
From whom my absence was not six moneths olde,   48
MONEY = 6*1
*S.Dro. The one to saue the money that he spends in '   491
And then receiue my money for the chaine.   969
Anti. I pray you sir receiue the money now.   970
I shall receiue the money for the same: 992
Or else you may returne without your money.   1030
Ile giue ere I leaue thee so much money | To warrant thee as I am
rested for.   1282
Anti. But where's the Money?   1292
MONIE = 13*3
There is your monie that I had to keepe.   170
Tell me, and dally not, where is the monie?   224
In what safe place you haue bestow'd my monie;   243
The villaine is ore-wrought of all my monie.   262
I greatly feare my monie is not safe. Exit.   271

MONIE *cont*.

Anti. I am not furnish'd with the present monie:	1017
Gold. The monie that you owe me for the Chaine.	1049
*will you send him Mistris redemption, the monie in | his deske.	1156
Adr. Go *Dromio*, there's the monie, beare it straight,	1179
Some tender monie to me, some inuite me;	1187
Heere comes my Man, I thinke he brings the monie.	1289
E.Dro. Why sir, I gaue the Monie for the Rope.	1293
Adr. Alas, I sent you Monie to redeeme you,	1371
Dro. Monie by me? Heart and good will you might,	1373
But surely Master not a ragge of Monie.	1374
Adr. I sent you monie sir to be your baile	1870

MONSTROUSLY = 1

Which he forswore most monstrously to haue.	1475

MONY = 2*1

Where haue you left the mony that I gaue you.	219
For feare you ne're see chaine, nor mony more.	971
Ant. Why giue it to my wife, and fetch your mony.	1040

MOODE = 2

Abetting him to thwart me in my moode;	564
My wife is in a wayward moode to day,	1284

MOODIE = 1

Sweet recreation barr'd, what doth ensue | But moodie and dull melancholly,	1547

MORE = 20*12

Duke. Merchant of *Siracusa*, plead no more.	7
Nay more, if any borne at *Ephesus* | Be seene at any *Siracusian* Marts and Fayres:	20
My wife, more carefull for the latter borne,	81
But ere they came, oh let me say no more,	97
Was carried with more speed before the winde,	112
Adr. Why should their libertie then ours be more?	284
Man more diuine, the Master of all these,	294
Of more preheminence then fish and fowles,	297
As much, or more, we should our selues complaine:	311
Vnkindnesse blunts it more then marble hard.	369
Ant. Why, but theres manie a man hath more haire | then wit.	476
But wrong not that wrong with a more contempt.	566
Anti. And welcome more common, for thats nothing | but words.	644
Anti. I, to a niggardly Host, and more sparing guest:	648
*Then for her wealths-sake vse her with more kindnesse:	792
Then our earths wonder, more then earth diuine.	819
Farre more, farre more, to you doe I decline:	831
For feare you ne're see chaine, nor mony more.	971
Which doth amount to three odde Duckets more	1013
Gold. You wrong me more sir in denying it.	1054
Ant. I will debate this matter at more leisure	1089
And teach your eares to list me with more heede:	1090
Adr. He meant he did me none: the more my spight	1111
S.Dro. Time is a verie bankerout, and owes more then | he's worth to season.	1172
*suites of durance: he that sets vp his rest to doe more ex-|ploits	1210
*but she more couetous, wold haue a chaine: Ma-|ster	1256
Pinch. More company, the fiend is strong within him	1398
Let's call more helpe to haue them bound againe. | *Runne all out*.	1444
Poisons more deadly then a mad dogges tooth.	1539
Chac'd vs away: till raising of more aide	1625

MORE *cont*.

*By'th'way, we met my wife, her sister, and a rabble more | Of vilde
Confederates: Along with them 1712
MORIS = 1
with his Mace, then a Moris Pike. 1211
MORNING = 1
Duke. Why heere begins his Morning storie right: 1832
MORROW = 1
And that to morrow you will bring it home. 623
MORTALL = 1
For since the mortall and intestine iarres 15
MOSSE = 1
Vsurping Iuie, Brier, or idle Mosse, 572
MOST = 7*6
Home to my house, oh most vnhappy day. 1415
Ant. Oh most vnhappie strumpet. 1416
Though most dishonestly he doth denie it. 1466
Which he forswore most monstrously to haue. 1475
Adr. Iustice most sacred Duke against the Abbesse. 1605
A most outragious fit of madnesse tooke him: 1611
Therefore most gracious Duke with thy command, 1631
E.Ant. Iustice most gracious Duke, oh grant me iu- |(stice, 1666
Fa. Most mighty Duke, vouchsafe me speak a word: 1762
Abbesse. Most mightie Duke, behold a man much | wrong'd. 1813
E.Ant. I came from *Corinth* my most gracious Lord | *E.Dro*. And I
with him. 1851
E.Ant. Brought to this Town by that most famous | Warriour, 1853
Duke *Menaphon* your most renowned Vnckle. 1855
MOTHER = 2
A ioyfull mother of two goodly sonnes: 54
So I, to finde a Mother and a Brother, 203
MOTION = 1
We in your motion turne, and you may moue vs. 810
MOTIONS = 1
Made daily motions for our home returne: 63
MOUE = 1*1
We in your motion turne, and you may moue vs. 810
Luc. With words, that in an honest suit might moue. 1119
MOUES = *1
Ant. To mee shee speakes, shee moues mee for her | theame; 575
MOUNTAINE = *1
*the Mountaine of mad flesh that claimes mariage of me, 1457
MOUNTEBANKE = 1
A meere Anatomie, a Mountebanke, 1715
MOUNTEBANKES = 1
Disguised Cheaters, prating Mountebankes; 267
MOURND = 1
That mourn'd for fashion, ignorant what to feare, 76
MR = 3
Ang. Mr *Antipholus*. | *Anti*. I that's my name. 956
Dro. And gentle Mr I receiu'd no gold: 1386
My Mr preaches patience to him, and the while 1647
MUCH = 10*7
But longer did we not retaine much hope; 68
Of whom I hope to make much benefit: 188
As much, or more, we should our selues complaine: 311
E.Dro. Here's too much out vpon thee, I pray thee let | me in. 737

MUCH *cont.*
 And since I haue not much importun'd you,   983
 *How much your Chaine weighs to the vtmost charect,   1011
 Ant. You gaue me none, you wrong mee much to | say so.   1052
 *as much to say, God make me a light wench: It is writ-|ten,   1237
 For fortie Duckets is too much to loose.   1279
 Ile giue thee ere I leaue thee so much money | To warrant thee as I am rested for.   1282
 Signior *Antipholus*, I wonder much | That you would put me to this shame and trouble,   1477
 And much different from the man he was: 1513
 Ab. Hath he not lost much wealth by wrack of sea,   1516
 A sinne preuailing much in youthfull men,   1519
 He shall not die, so much we tender him.   1604
 Abbesse. Most mightie Duke, behold a man much | wrong'd.   1813
 E.Ant. There take it, and much thanks for my good | cheere.   1881
MUFFLE = 1
 Muffle your false loue with some shew of blindnesse: 794
MURDER *see* murther
MURTHER = *1
 Ant. What will you murther me, thou Iailor thou?   1400
MUSICKE = 1
 That neuer words were musicke to thine eare,   509
MUST = 8*6
 Weeping before for what she saw must come,   74
 But heere must end the story of my life,   140
 If I last in this seruice, you must case me in leather.   361
 Adri. His company must do his minions grace,   363
 *long, I must get a sconce for my head, and Insconce it   432
 E.Anti. Good signior *Angelo* you must excuse vs all,   619
 S.Dro. Nor to day here you must not come againe | when you may.   667
 E.Dro. O Lord I must laugh, haue at you with a Pro-|uerbe,   685
 Thither I must, although against my will: 1101
 For seruants must their Masters mindes fulfill. *Exit*   1102
 S.Dro. Marrie he must haue a long spoone that must | eate with the diuell.   1246
 They must be bound and laide in some darke roome.   1382
 Cur. Sir I must haue that Diamond from you.   1880
MY *l.*4 *30 31 36 37 39 45 47 48 61 62 72 73 81 86 121 122 123 127 140 141 142 146 148 158 184 186 192 193 204 206 211 221 228 230 *239 241 243 247 248 *253 256 259 261 262 271 275 *320 *333 339 340 341 343 344 *347 *348 *349 366 367 371 374 390 406 422 423 424 427 428 *432 *433 514 520 530 531 532 536 545 548 553 559 564 565 568 577 583 592 601 610 620 627 637 *639 *649 651 *658 *665 *671 673 676 682 687 *708 773 779 791 795 812 821 824 847 848 851 852 853 854 856 860 864 *866 868 *872 *893 *931 *932 *934 945 948 952 953 956 969 984 994 999 1000 1019 1020 *1040 1045 1055 1056 1065 1101 *1111 1120 1124 1134 1182 1186 1192 1252 1259 1275 1277 1278 1284 1289 *1311 *1313 *1318 *1323 1337 1339 1346 1348 *1355 *1364 *1403 1409 1415 1434 *1458 1471 1483 1500 1506 1527 1532 1533 1534 1559 1561 *1562 1566 1567 1568 1569 1576 *1578 1584 1586 *1608 *1633 1642 1647 1653 1661 1671 1674 1682 *1684 1685 1691 1694 1708 1711 *1712 1720 1725 1726 1727 *1731 1734 1739 1754 1755 1757 1763 1769 1777 1780 1781 1788 1789 1790 1791 1794 1795 1796 1797 1799 1800 1802 1806 *1823 1844 *1851 1858 1874 *1878 *1881 1891 1892 1893 1897 1908 *1909 1912 = 224*52

MYRE = 1
Great pailes of puddled myre to quench the haire; 1646
MYSELFE *see* selfe
NAILE = *1
S.Dro. Some diuels aske but the parings of ones naile, 1254
NAILES = 1
But with these nailes, Ile plucke out these false eyes, 1392
NAKED = 1
Adr. And come with naked swords, 1443
NAME = 10*6
Reft of his brother, but retain'd his name, 131
Where gold and no man that hath a name, 388
S.Dro. Certaine ones then. | *An.* Name them. 489
And hurle the name of husband in my face, 530
S.Dro. The Porter for this time Sir, and my name is | *Dromio.* 671
E.Dro. O villaine, thou hast stolne both mine office | and my name, 673
*Thou wouldst haue chang'd thy face for a name, or thy | name for an
asse. 677
S.Dro. If thy name be called *Luce, Luce* thou hast an-|swer'd him
well. 690
S.Anti. Sweete Mistris, what your name is else I | know not; 815
Anti. What's her name? | *Dro. Nell* Sir: but her name is three quarters,
that's 899
Ang. Mr *Antipholus.* | *Anti.* I that's my name. 956
Offi. I do, and charge you in the Dukes name to o-|bey me. 1057
And euerie one doth call me by my name: 1186
Fath. Is not your name sir call'd *Antipholus?* 1766
NAMELY = 1*1
S.Dro. Marry and did sir: namely, in no time to re-|couer haire lost
by Nature. 496
Namely, some loue that drew him oft from home. 1523
NAMES = 2
As could not be distinguish'd but by names. 56
Ant. How can she thus then call vs by our names? | Vnlesse it be by
inspiration. 560
NARROW = 1
The passages of allies, creekes, and narrow lands: 1147
NATION = *1
*me thinkes they are such a gentle Nation, that but for 1456
NATIUE = 1
Why thou departedst from thy natiue home? 33
NATIUITIE = 1*1
*Natiuitie to this instant, and haue nothing at his hands 1312
After so long greefe such Natiuitie. 1896
NATIUITY = 1
And you the Kalenders of their Natiuity, 1894
NATURALL = 1
And so of these, which is the naturall man, 1818
NATURE = 2*1
Was wrought by nature, not by vile offence, 38
S.Dro. There's no time for a man to recouer his haire | that growes
bald by nature. 466
S.Dro. Marry and did sir: namely, in no time to re-|couer haire lost
by Nature. 496
NAUGHT *see* nought

NAY = 11*6

Nay more, if any borne at *Ephesus* | Be seene at any *Siracusian* Marts
and Fayres: 20
Duk. Nay forward old man, doe not breake off so,   99
Nay, and you will not sir, Ile take my heeles.   259
*E.Dro. Nay, hee's at too hands with mee, and that my | two eares can
witnesse.   320
*E.Dro. Nay, hee strooke so plainly, I could too well   328
An. Nay not sound I pray you. | *S.Dro*. Sure ones then.   486
An. Nay, not sure in a thing falsing.   488
S.Dro. Nay Master, both in minde, and in my shape.   592
*Gold. Nay come I pray you sir, giue me the Chaine: 1031
A Wolfe, nay worse, a fellow all in buffe: 1145
Nay, he's a theefe too: haue you not heard men say,   1174
S.Dro. Nay, she is worse, she is the diuels dam: 1234
*E.Dro. Nay 'tis for me to be patient, I am in aduer- | sitie.   1301
*E.Dro. Nay, rather perswade him to hold his hands.   1304
**from home, welcom'd home with it when I returne, nay   1317
Adr. And are not you my husband? | *E.Ant*. No, I say nay to that.   1858
E.Dro. Nay then thus: | We came into the world like brother and
brother: 1916

NECKE = 1*2

**the Mole in my necke, the great Wart on my left arme,   932
*Gold. 'Tis so: and that selfe chaine about his necke,   1474
These people saw the Chaine about his necke.   1735

NEED = 1

Be secret false: what need she be acquainted?   801

NEEDE = 1

Duke. It shall not neede, thy father hath his life.   1879

NEEDS = 1*1

*Luce. What needs all that, and a paire of stocks in the | towne?   704
I see a man heere needs not liue by shifts,   976

NEEDY-HOLLOW-EYD-SHARPE-LOOKING-WRETCH = 1

A needy-hollow-ey'd-sharpe-looking-wretch;   1717

NEERE = 3

**effect of fire, and fire will burne: *ergo*, light wenches will | burne, come
not neere her.   1239
*Adr. Oh binde him, binde him, let him not come | neere me.   1396
Good sir draw neere to me, Ile speake to him: 1476

NEITHER = 6*2

Adr. Neither my husband nor the slaue return'd,   275
**season, when in the why and the wherefore, is neither | rime nor
reason. Well sir, I thanke you.   443
*Angelo. Heere is neither cheere sir, nor welcome, we | would faine
haue either.   715
*Baltz. In debating which was best, wee shall part | with neither.   717
But neither Chaine nor Goldsmith came to me: 1007
Ab. Neither: he tooke this place for sanctuary,   1563
Neither disturbed with the effect of Wine,   1692
Ant. Neither. | *Fat. Dromio*, nor thou?   1782

NELL = *1

Anti. What's her name? | **Dro. Nell* Sir: but her name is three quarters,
that's   899

NERE = 6

The one nere got me credit, the other mickle blame: 675
For feare you ne're see chaine, nor mony more.   971
But till this afternoone his passion | Ne're brake into extremity of rage.   1514

NERE *cont.*
 Luc. Nere may I looke on day, nor sleepe on night,   1687
I ne're saw *Siracusa* in my life.   1806
 During which time, he ne're saw *Siracusa*:   1809
NEST = 1
 Farre from her nest the Lapwing cries away;   1133
NETHERLANDS = 1
 Anti. Where stood *Belgia*, the *Netherlands*? | *Dro.* Oh sir, I did not
looke so low. To conclude,   927
NEUER *see also* nere = 19
 Good Sister let vs dine, and neuer fret;   280
That neuer words were musicke to thine eare,   509
That neuer obiect pleasing in thine eye,   510
That neuer touch well welcome to thy hand,   511
That neuer meat sweet-sauour'd in thy taste,   512
S.Dro. I sir? I neuer saw her till this time.   556
S.Dro. I neuer spake with her in all my life.   559
'Tis so, I am an Asse, else it could neuer be,   597
Ant. Consent to pay thee that I neuer had: 1062
Adr. The houres come backe, that did I neuer here.   1167
Else would he neuer so demeane himselfe,   1265
Adr. It may be so, but I did neuer see it.   1437
Ant. I thinke I had, I neuer did deny it.   1487
Luc. She neuer reprehended him but mildely,   1556
And neuer rise vntill my teares and prayers   1584
E.Ant. I neuer came within these Abbey wals,   1742
I neuer saw the Chaine, so helpe me heauen: 1744
E.Ant. I neuer saw you in my life till now.   1777
 Ant. I neuer saw my Father in my life.   1800
NEW = 3
 Dro. Goe backe againe, and be new beaten home?   352
Are you a god? would you create me new?   826
haue you got the picture of old *Adam* new apparel'd?   1197
NEXT = *1
 Ant. Ile make you amends next, to giue you nothing   448
NICKES = 1
 His man with Cizers nickes him like a foole: 1648
NIE = 1
 Heere comes your man, now is your husband nie.   317
NIGGARD = *1
 Ant. Why, is Time such a niggard of haire, being (as   471
NIGGARDLY = *1
 Anti. I, to a niggardly Host, and more sparing guest: 648
NIGHT = 5*4
 Ant. As good to winke sweet loue, as looke on night.   846
I will not harbour in this Towne to night.   939
That time comes stealing on by night and day?   1175
*Is there any ships puts forth to night? may we be gone?   1218
*that the Barke *Expedition* put forth to night, and then   1220
Dro. Faith stay heere this night, they will surely do   1454
Ant. I will not stay to night for all the Towne,   1460
Luc. Nere may I looke on day, nor sleepe on night,   1687
Yet hath my night of life some memorie: 1795
NIMBLE = 1
 As nimble Iuglers that deceiue the eie: 264
NO *l,*7 19 97 157 214 215 236 *306 307 312 *347 *348 388 404 450 *466
*494 *496 498 593 599 606 *683 694 739 828 830 *850 857 *897 *904

NO *cont*.
    *918 974. *1025 1046 1106 1110 1130 1141 1164 *1206 1329 1367 1386
    *1455 1561 1569 *1684 1733 1784 1849 1858 1871 = 40*18
NOAHS = *1
    Dro. No sir, 'tis in graine, *Noahs* flood could not | do it.   897
NOISE = *1
    Adr. Who is that at the doore y keeps all this noise?   707
NONE = 11*2
    And this it was: (for other meanes was none)   78
    Adr. There's none but asses will be bridled so.   288
    S.Dro. If it be sir, I pray you eat none of it. | *Ant*. Your reason?   454
    Adr. I, and let none enter, least I breake your pate.   614
    If euerie one knowes vs, and we know none,   942
    Anti. There's none but Witches do inhabite heere,   946
    Ant. I owe you none, till I receiue the Chaine.   1050
    Ant. You gaue me none, you wrong mee much to | say so.   1052
    Adr. He meant he did me none: the more my spight   1111
    Second to none that liues heere in the Citie: 1470
    Adr. To none of these, except it be the last,   1522
    For certaine Duckets: he with none return'd.   1709
    By *Dromio*, but I thinke he brought it not. | *E.Dro*. No, none by me.   1871
NOR *l*.275 443 507 *667 *715 817 830 857 *965 971 984 1007 1123 1630
    1687 1693 1743 1782 1784 = 16*3
NOSE = 1*1
    Ant. Where *America*, the *Indies*? | *Dro*. Oh sir, vpon her nose, all ore
    embellished with   922
    *to the hot breath of Spaine, who sent whole Ar- | madoes of Carrects to
    be ballast at her nose.   925
NOT *l*.8 *35 38 42 48 53 56 62 68 99 100 101 111 119 145 147 150 167 213
    214 222 223 224 249 251 259 271 301 *326 335 345 371 373 399 *409
    410 435 468 *478 486 488 *492 *498 507 519 524 529 *542 566 586 *588
    590 620 650 *665 *667 734 746 753 795 796 807 815 *818 832 841 *877
    *882 *887 *897 *901 *920 *927 *934 939 964 *965 976 983 984 1009
    1017 *1025 1029 1036 1047 1065 1072 1123 1124 *1151 *1154 1162 1163
    1174 1177 1184 *1200 1205 1231 1239 1253 1260 1281 1285 1307 *1328
    1342 *1343 1354 *1355 1358 1360 1363 1374 *1375 1385 *1396 1403
    *1432 1460 1479 1498 1509 *1516 1517 1525 1530 1532 1533 1558 1561
    1571 *1578 1581 1604 1620 1629 1654 1696 1701 1706 1732 1749 1766
    1767 1774 1781 *1786 1788 1791 1805 1822 1838 1849 *1850 1858 1864
    1867 1869 1871 1879 1908 *1909 1912 *1918 = 131*37
NOTE = 2
    Oh traine me not sweet Mermaide with thy note,   832
    Gold. Sauing your merrie humor: here's the note   1010
NOTHING = 5*7
    There's nothing situate vnder heauens eye,   290
    Ant. Dost thou not know? | *S.Dro*. Nothing sir, but that I am beaten.   435
    S.Dro. Marry sir, for this something that you gaue me | for nothing.   446
    Ant. Ile make you amends next, to giue you nothing   448
    Anti. And welcome more common, for thats nothing | but words.   644
    (Be it for nothing but to spight my wife)   779
    Dro. Swart like my shoo, but her face nothing like   893
    Anti. Thou art sensible in nothing but blowes, and | so is an Asse.   1308
    *Natiuitie to this instant, and haue nothing at his hands   1312
    That I was sent for nothing but a rope.   1379
    Dro. Will you be bound for nothing, be mad good | Master, cry the
    diuell.   1420
    Duke. Come stand by me, feare nothing: guard with | Halberds.   1659

NOTORIOUS = 1
To your notorious shame, I doubt it not. 1072
NOUGHT = 1
Blowes faire from land: they stay for nought at all, 1080
NOW = 36*10
Merch. Oh had the gods done so, I had not now 101
What haue befalne of them and they till now. 126
Now trust me, were it not against our Lawes, 145
My present businesse cals me from you now. 192
What now? How chance thou art return'd so soone. 207
Ant. I am not in᷎ a sportiue humor now: 223
Ant. Now as I am a Christian answer me, 242
Heere comes your man, now is your husband nie. 317
Adr. Say, is your tardie master now at hand? 319
How now sir, is your merrie humor alter'd? 402
E.Ant. Euen now, euen here, not halfe an howre since. 409
S.Dr. Hold sir, for Gods sake, now your iest is earnest, 419
How comes it now, my Husband, oh how comes it, 514
Or sleepe I now, and thinke I heare all this? 578
Now in the stirring passage of the day, 760
Ant. Why how now *Dromio*, where run'st thou so | fast? 862
Anti. I pray you sir receiue the money now. 970
Nor now I had not, but that I am bound | To *Persia*, and want Gilders
for my voyage: 984
Gold. Come, come, you know I gaue it you euen now. 1041
Ant. Fie, now you run this humor out of breath, 1043
An. How now? a Madman? Why thou peeuish sheep 1082
Dro. Here goe: the deske, the purse, sweet now make | haste. 1136
It was two ere I left him, and now the clocke strikes one. 1166
Euen now a tailor cal'd me in his shop, 1190
I see sir you haue found the Gold-smith now: 1229
Cur. Now out of doubt *Antipholus* is mad, 1264
Both one and other he denies me now: 1268
My way is now to hie home to his house, 1275
How now sir? Haue you that I sent you for? 1290
Offi. Good now hold thy tongue. 1303
Curt. How say you now? Is not your husband mad? 1328
Say now, whose suite is he arrested at? 1425
The Ring I saw vpon his finger now, 1435
S.Dro. She that would be your wife, now ran from | you. 1449
This Chaine, which now you weare so openly. 1481
Mar. I am sorry now that I did draw on him. 1510
Euen now we hous'd him in the Abbey heere. 1663
And now he's there, past thought of humane reason. 1664
That then I lost for thee, now grant me iustice. 1670
Now am I *Dromio*, and his man, vnbound. 1770
For lately we were bound as you are now. 1773
E.Ant. I neuer saw you in my life till now. 1777
a man denies, you are now bound to beleeue him. 1787
Though now this grained face of mine be hid 1792
She now shall be my sister, not my wife, 1908
*And now let's go hand in hand, not one before another. | *Exeunt*. 1918
NO-FACE = 1
And with no-face (as 'twere) out-facing me, 1721
NURSE = 1
Adr. I will attend my husband, be his nurse, 1567

NUT = *1
  *a rush, a haire, a drop of blood, a pin, a nut, a cherrie-|stone: 1255
O *l.*673 *685 *1349 *1689 = *4
OATH = 2
  Against my Crowne, my oath, my dignity,   146
  It is a branch and parcell of mine oath,   1575
OATHS = 1
  With circumstance and oaths, so to denie   1480
OBAY = 1
  If we obay them not, this will insue: 586
OBEDIENT = 1
  And floating straight, obedient to the streame,   89
OBEY = 3*1
  Luc. Ere I learne loue, Ile practise to obey.   303
  Offi. I do, and charge you in the Dukes name to o-|bey me.   1057
  Ant. I do obey thee, till I giue thee baile.   1068
  I did obey, and sent my Pesant home   1708
OBEYING = 1
  Before the alwaies winde-obeying deepe   66
OBIECT = 1
  That neuer obiect pleasing in thine eye,   510
OBSCURED = 1
  For what obscured light the heauens did grant,   69
OBSERUATION = 1
  What obseruation mad'st thou in this case?   1108
OCEAN = 1
  That in the Ocean seekes another drop,   200
OCLOCKE *see* clocke
ODDE = 1
  Which doth amount to three odde Duckets more   1013
OF *see also* a' = 184*40
OFF *l.*99 1644 = 4 = 2
OFFENCE = 2
  Was wrought by nature, not by vile offence,   38
  Beheaded publikely for his offence.   1596
OFFENDED = 1
  Disperst those vapours that offended vs,   92
OFFER = 3
  If by strong hand you offer to breake in   759
  Some offer me Commodities to buy.   1189
  Enter three or foure, and offer to binde him: | *Hee striues.*   1394
OFFERD = 1
  That would refuse so faire an offer'd Chaine.   975
OFFI = 3*3
OFFIC = 1, 1
  Exeunt. Manet Offic. Adri. Luci. Courtizan   1426
OFFICE = 2*1
  *E.Dro. O villaine, thou hast stolne both mine office | and my name,   673
  Iulia. And may it be that you haue quite forgot | A husbands office?
  shall *Antipholus*   787
  Diet his sicknesse, for it is my Office,   1568
OFFICER see also Off., Offi., Offic. = 11
  Enter a Merchant, Goldsmith, and an Officer.   981
  Or Ile attach you by this Officer.   987
  If not, Ile leaue him to the Officer.   1047
  Mar. Well Officer, arrest him at my suite.   1056
  Either consent to pay this sum for me, | Or I attach you by this Officer.   1060

OFFICER cont.

Gold. Heere is thy fee, arrest him Officer.	1064
On Officer to prison, till it come. *Exeunt*	1097
Ant. What thou mean'st an officer?	1212
Adr. What wilt thou do, thou peeuish Officer?	1406
He did arrest me with an Officer.	1707
Then fairely I bespoke the Officer	1710

OFFICERS = 1

*bare head, with the Headsman, & other	Officers.*	1600

OFT = 2

Ant. A trustie villaine sir, that very oft,	182
Namely, some loue that drew him oft from home.	1523

OFTEN = 3

By prosperous voyages I often made	44
That others touch, and often touching will,	387
In company I often glanced it:	1535

OFTENTIMES = 1

Hath oftentimes vpbraided me withall:	774

OH *see also* O *l.*97 101 220 287 514 583 584 641 746 832 859 922 *927
1109 *1168 *1343 *1396 1415 1416 1641 *1666 *1778 1788 *1823
1830 = 18*7

OLD = 5

Duk. Nay forward old man, doe not breake off so,	99
In *Ephesus* I am but two houres old,	543
He is deformed, crooked, old, and sere,	1125
haue you got the picture of old *Adam* new apparel'd?	1197
All these old witnesses, I cannot erre.	1798

OLDE = 2*1

From whom my absence was not sixe moneths olde,	48
S.Drom. Oh my olde Master, who hath bound him	heere?	1823
Speake olde *Egeon*, if thou bee'st the man	1827

OMNES = 2

Off. Away, they'l kill vs.	*Exeunt omnes, as fast as may be, frighted.*	1446
*Exeunt omnes. Manet the two Dromio's and	two Brothers.*	1898

ON *see also* a = 34*10

ONCE = 5*1

The time was once, when thou vn-vrg'd wouldst vow,	508
Once this your long experience of your wisedome,	750
Ang. Not once, nor twice, but twentie times you	haue:	965
Duke. Yet once againe proclaime it publikely,	1602
Once did I get him bound, and sent him home,	1617
That hadst a wife once call'd *Aemilia,*	1828

ONE = 19*13

And, which was strange, the one so like the other,	55
To him one of the other twins was bound,	84
My Mistris made it one vpon my cheeke:	211
Luci. Well, I will marry one day but to trie:	316
S.Dro. The one to saue the money that he spends in	491
For if we two be one, and thou play false,	537
Wants wit in all, one word to vnderstand.	546
A table full of welcome, makes scarce one dainty dish.	642
*When one is one too many, goe get thee from the dore.	657
The one nere got me credit, the other mickle blame:	675
*One that claimes me, one that haunts me, one that will	haue me.	873
Dro. A very reuerent body: I such a one, as a man	881
If euerie one knowes vs, and we know none,	942
Luc. Who would be iealous then of such a one?	1129

ONE *cont*.
    *A back friend, a shoulder-clapper, one that counterma(n)ds   1146
    *One that before the Iudgme(n)t carries poore soules to hel.   1149
    *It was two ere I left him, and now the clocke strikes one.   1166
    And euerie one doth call me by my name: 1186
    *any man to answer it that breakes his Band: one that   1214
    Both one and other he denies me now: 1268
    Off. One *Angelo* a Goldsmith, do you know him?   1427
    Each one with irefull passion, with drawne swords   1623
    Albeit my wrongs might make one wiser mad.   1694
    *They brought one *Pinch*, a hungry leane-fac'd Villaine;   1714
    Exit one to the Abbesse.   1761
    Duke. One of these men is *genius* to the other: 1817
    And these two *Dromio's*, one in semblance: 1834
    That by this simpathized one daies error   1887
    *And now let's go hand in hand, not one before another. | *Exeunt*.   1918
ONELY = 1
    In seuen short yeares, that heere my onely sonne   1790
ONES = 3*1
    An. For what reason. | *S.Dro*. For two, and sound ones to.   484
    An. Nay not sound I pray you. | *S.Dro*. Sure ones then.   486
    S.Dro. Certaine ones then. | *An*. Name them.   489
    S.Dro. Some diuels aske but the parings of ones naile,   1254
ONS = 1
    S.Dro. Let him walke from whence he came, lest hee | catch cold on's
    feet.   660
OPE = *1
    Ant. Go fetch me something, Ile break ope the gate.   729
OPEN = 2*1
    E.Ant. Who talks within there? hoa, open the dore.   662
    Lay open to my earthie grosse conceit: 821
    Free from these slanders, and this open shame.   1351
OPENLY = 1
    This Chaine, which now you weare so openly.   1481
OR *l*.139 156 244 261 283 311 *354 381 429 *433 513 522 572 578 587 608
    609 641 *655 *677 793 854 *929 987 1030 1042 1046 1060 1106 1107
    *1243 1252 1259 *1325 1394 1489 1502 1553 1566 1733 1760 1816
    1822 = 44*7
ORATOR = 1
    Be not thy tongue thy owne shames Orator: 796
ORDER = 2
    A charitable dutie of my order,   1576
    Whil'st to take order for the wrongs I went,   1618
ORE = 3
    Spread ore the siluer waues thy golden haires;   835
    Ant. Where *America*, the *Indies*? | *Dro*. Oh sir, vpon her nose, all ore
    embellished with   922
    That's couer'd o're with Turkish Tapistrie,   1093
ORE-WROUGHT = 1
    The villaine is ore-wrought of all my monie.   262
OTHER = 15*2
    *Enter the Duke of Ephesus, with the Merchant of Siracusa, | Iaylor, and
    other attendants.*   2
    And, which was strange, the one so like the other,   55
    And this it was: (for other meanes was none)   78
    To him one of the other twins was bound,   84
    Whil'st I had beene like heedfull of the other.   85

OTHER *cont.*

Ant. Vpon my life by some deuise or other,	261
Adr. How if your husband start some other where?	304
They can be meeke, that haue no other cause:	307
For Gods sake send some other messenger.	353
Dro. And he will blesse y crosse with other beating:	355
*trying: the other, that at dinner they should not drop in | his porrage.	492
Some other Mistresse hath thy sweet aspects:	506
The one nere got me credit, the other mickle blame:	675
Some other giue me thankes for kindnesses;	1188
Both one and other he denies me now:	1268
bare head, with the Headsman, & other | Officers.	1600
Duke. One of these men is *genius* to the other:	1817

OTHERS = 4*1

That others touch, and often touching will,	387
Though others haue the arme, shew vs the sleeue:	809
And yet would herein others eies were worse:	1132
They draw. Enter Adriana, Luciana, Courtezan, & others.	1497
I see we still did meete each others man,	1875

OTHER-WHERE = 1

I know his eye doth homage other-where,	380

OUER-SHOOES = *1

*so cleane kept: for why? she sweats a man may goe o-|uer-shooes in the grime of it.	894

OUER *see* ore

OUGHT = 2

If ought possesse thee from me, it is drosse,	571
Luc. If thou art chang'd to ought, 'tis to an Asse.	595

OUR *l.*8 11 14 18 19 42 43 63 67 70 79 87 88 106 113 145 151 311 560 579 587 *638 *658 819 1008 1076 1242 *1451 1461 1484 1531 1701 1772 1885 = 32*3

OURS = *1

Adr. Why should their libertie then ours be more?	284

OURSELUES *see* selues

OUT *l.*163 167 *233 285 345 397 *442 *669 *735 *737 *905 *908 979 1000 1043 1264 *1316 *1355 1356 1387 1392 *1418 1444 1629 1695 1722 1732 = 17*10

OUTRAGE = 2

Sprung from the rancorous outrage of your Duke,	10
Do outrage and displeasure to himselfe?	1408

OUTRAGIOUS = 1

A most outragious fit of madnesse tooke him:	1611

OUT-FACING = 1

And with no-face (as 'twere) out-facing me,	1721

OWE = 5

Anti. What art thou that keep'st mee out from the | howse I owe?	669
Nor to her bed no homage doe I owe:	830
Gold. Euen iust the sum that I do owe to you,	988
Gold. The monie that you owe me for the Chaine.	1049
Ant. I owe you none, till I receiue the Chaine.	1050

OWES = 1*2

S.Dro. Time is a verie bankerout, and owes more then | he's worth to season.	1172
The debt he owes will be requir'd of me.	1410
Adr. I know the man: what is the summe he owes?	1428

OWLES = 1

We talke with Goblins, Owles and Sprights;	585

OWNE = 9*4

To tell sad stories of my owne mishaps.	123
E.Mar. Sir, I commend you to your owne content. | *Exeunt.*	195
Ant. He that commends me to mine owne content,	197
So great a charge from thine owne custodie.	226
Ant. Thou hast thine owne forme. | *S.Dro.* No, I am an Ape.	593
*Your owne hand-writing would tell you what I thinke.	632
Since mine owne doores refuse to entertaine me,	781
Be not thy tongue thy owne shames Orator:	796
What simple thiefe brags of his owne attaine?	802
Ant. No: it is thy selfe, mine owne selfes better part:	850
*Lampe of her, and run from her by her owne light. I	888
Of his owne doores being shut against his entrance.	1272
Adri. She did betray me to my owne reproofe,	1559

OWNER = 2

That staies but till her Owner comes aboord,	1075
But for their Owner, Master, and your selfe.	1081

OYLE = 1

The Oyle, the *Balsamum*, and Aqua-vitae.	1078

PACKD = 1

That Goldsmith there, were he not pack'd with her,	1696

PACKE = 2

'Tis time I thinke to trudge, packe, and be gone.	943
And art confederate with a damned packe,	1390

PAILES = 1

Great pailes of puddled myre to quench the haire;	1646

PAINE = 1*1

But were we burdned with like waight of paine,	310
E.Dro. If you went in paine Master, this knaue wold | goe sore.	713

PAINES = *1

Abb. Renowned Duke, vouchsafe to take the paines	1883

PAIRE = *1

Luce. What needs all that, and a paire of stocks in the | towne?	704

PALE = 4*1

But, too vnruly Deere, he breakes the pale,	376
Look'd he or red or pale, or sad or merrily?	1107
I know it by their pale and deadly lookes,	1381
Luc. Aye me poore man, how pale and wan he looks.	1399
Of pale distemperatures, and foes to life?	1551

PALME = *1

Dro. I found it by the barrennesse, hard in the palme | of the hand.	911

PARADISE = *1

S.Dro. Not that *Adam* that kept the Paradise: but	1200

PARCELL = 1

It is a branch and parcell of mine oath,	157:

PARCHMENT = *1

*If y skin were parchment, & y blows you gaue were ink,	631

PARDON = 2

For we may pitty, though not pardon thee.	100
I craue your pardon, soone at fiue a clocke,	189

PARENTS = 2

Those, for their parents were exceeding poore,	60
These are the parents to these children,	1836

PARINGS = *1

S.Dro. Some diuels aske but the parings of ones naile,	1254

PARRAT = *1

*the prophesie like the Parrat, beware the ropes end.	1326

PART = 4*3

Her part, poore soule, seeming as burdened   110
That vndiuidable Incorporate | Am better then thy deere selfes better
part.   517
*But though my cates be meane, take them in good part,   649
*Baltz. In debating which was best, wee shall part | with neither.   717
Plead on your part some cause to you vnknowne;   752
*Ant. No: it is thy selfe, mine owne selfes better part: 850
Anti. In what part of her body stands Ireland?   907

PARTED = 2

Who parted with me to go fetch a Chaine,   1698
Thou know'st we parted, but perhaps my sonne,   1802

PARTIALL = 1

I am not partiall to infringe our Lawes;   8

PASSAGE = 1

Now in the stirring passage of the day,   760

PASSAGES = 1

The passages of allies, creekes, and narrow lands: 1147

PASSE = 1*1

I should kicke being kickt, and being at that passe,   636
*Luc. Kneele to the Duke before he passe the Abbey.   1598

PASSED = 1

And passed sentence may not be recal'd   150

PASSION = 2

But till this afternoone his passion | Ne're brake into extremity of rage.   1514
Each one with irefull passion, with drawne swords   1623

PAST = 1

And now he's there, past thought of humane reason.   1664

PATCH = *2

*S.Dro. Mome, Malthorse, Capon, Coxcombe, Idi- |ot, Patch,   653
*E.Dro. What patch is made our Porter? my Master | stayes in the
street.   658

PATE = 5*1

For she will scoure your fault vpon my pate: 230
E.Dro. I haue some markes of yours vpon my pate: 247
*Adri. Backe slaue, or I will breake thy pate a-crosse.   354
*S.Dro. Marry sir, by a rule as plaine as the plaine bald | pate of Father
time himselfe.   463
Adr. I, and let none enter, least I breake your pate.   614
*S.Dro. Breake any breaking here, and Ile breake your | knaues pate.   730

PATIENCE = 6*1

*Adr. Patience vnmou'd, no maruel though she pause,   306
With vrging helpelesse patience would releeue me;   313
This foole-beg'd patience in thee will be left.   315
Balth. Haue patience sir, oh let it not be so,   746
Be rul'd by me, depart in patience,   755
Adr. Did'st speake him faire? | Luc. Haue patience I beseech.   1121
My Mr preaches patience to him, and the while   1647

PATIENT = 4*1

They'll goe or come; if so, be patient Sister.   283
Ant. And to that end sir, I will welcome you. | Offi. Good sir be
patient.   1299
*E.Dro. Nay 'tis for me to be patient, I am in aduer- |sitie.   1301
Ab. Be patient, for I will not let him stirre,   1571
You are not Pinches patient, are you sir?   1774

PATIENTLY = 1

Perchance you will not beare them patiently.   251

PATRON = 1
Haue I bin Patron to *Antipholus*,   1808
PAUSE = *1
   **Adr.* Patience vnmou'd, no maruel though she pause,   306
PAWNE = *1
   **E.Ant.* These Duckets pawne I for my father heere.   1878
PAY = 8*1
To pay the Sadler for my Mistris crupper: 221
If I should pay your worship those againe,   250
   **S.Dro.* Yes, to pay a fine for a perewig, and recouer | the lost haire of
another man.   469
Either consent to pay this sum for me, | Or I attach you by this Officer.   1060
   Ant. Consent to pay thee that I neuer had: 1062
   E.Dro. Here's that I warrant you will pay them all.   1291
And knowing how the debt growes I will pay it.   1413
If any friend will pay the summe for him,   1603
And pay the sum that may deliuer me.   1764
PEACE = 2*1
   Anti. Peace doting wizard, peace; I am not mad.   1342
   **Adr.* Peace foole, thy Master and his man are here,   1651
PEA-COCKE = *1
   **S.Dro.* Flie pride saies the Pea-cocke, Mistris that | you know. *Exit.*   1262
PEEUISH = 1*1
   **An.* How now? a Madman? Why thou peeuish sheep   1082
   Adr. What wilt thou do, thou peeuish Officer?   1406
PENALTY = 1
To quit the penalty, and to ransome him: 26
PENCE = 1
   E.Dro. Oh six pence that I had a wensday last,   220
PENITENT = 1
Are penitent for your default to day.   217
PENTECOST = 1
   Mar. You know since Pentecost the sum is due,   982
PEOPLE = 3
   Ab. Be quiet people, wherefore throng you hither?   1505
Good people enter, and lay hold on him.   1560
These people saw the Chaine about his necke.   1735
PERCEIUE = 1
Might'st thou perceiue austeerely in his eie,   1105
PERCHANCE = 2
Perchance you will not beare them patiently.   251
Perchance I will be there as soone as you.   1022
PERDIE = *1
   **Dro.* Perdie, your doores were lockt, and you shut | out.   1356
PEREWIG = *1
   **S.Dro.* Yes, to pay a fine for a perewig, and recouer | the lost haire of
another man.   469
PERFECT = 1
   Gold. I knew he was not in his perfect wits.   1509
PERFORCE = 2
He rush'd into my house, and tooke perforce   1277
And take perforce my husband from the Abbesse.   1586
PERHAPS = 2
   Luc. Perhaps some Merchant hath inuited him,   278
Thou know'st we parted, but perhaps my sonne,   1802
PERIURD = 1*1
   **Gold.* O periur'd woman! They are both forsworne,   1689

PERIURD *cont*.

There did this periur'd Goldsmith sweare me downe,   1704

PERNICIOUS = 1

A liuing dead man. This pernicious slaue,   1718

PERSEUER = 1

Ile say as they say, and perseuer so: 611

PERSIA = 1

Nor now I had not, but that I am bound | To *Persia*, and want Gilders

for my voyage: 984

PERSON = 3

Haue won his grace to come in person hither,   1585

Anon I'me sure the Duke himselfe in person   1588

To go in person with me to my house.   1711

PERSWADE = *1

E.Dro. Nay, rather perswade him to hold his hands.   1304

PERSWASION = *1

Adr. With what perswasion did he tempt thy loue?   1118

PERUSE = 1

Peruse the traders, gaze vpon the buildings,   175

PESANT = 2

Adri. Hence prating pesant, fetch thy Master home.   357

I did obey, and sent my Pesant home   1708

PHOENIX = 2*1

Home to your house, the *Phoenix* sir, to dinner;   240

E.Dro. Your worships wife, my Mistris at the *Phoenix*;   253

My house was at the *Phoenix*? Wast thou mad,   406

PICTURE = 1

haue you got the picture of old *Adam* new apparel'd?   1197

PIG = 1

The Capon burnes, the Pig fals from the spit;   209

PIGGE = 1

The Pigge quoth I, is burn'd: my gold, quoth he: 343

PIKE = 1

with his Mace, then a Moris Pike.   1211

PIN = *1

*a rush, a haire, a drop of blood, a pin, a nut, a cherrie-|stone: 1255

PINCH = 3*3, 3*1

They'll sucke our breath, or pinch vs blacke and blew.   587

Enter Adriana, Luciana, Courtizan, and a Schoole-|master, call'd Pinch.   1321

Good Doctor *Pinch*, you are a Coniurer,   1330

*They brought one *Pinch*, a hungry leane-fac'd Villaine;   1714

PINCHES = 1

You are not *Pinches* patient, are you sir?   1774

PITTEOUS = 1

And pitteous playnings of the prettie babes   75

PITTIE = *1

*he sir, that takes pittie on decaied men, and giues them   1209

PITTILESSE = 1

A Feind, a Fairie, pittilesse and ruffe: 1144

PITTY = 3

Excludes all pitty from our threatning lookes: 14

For we may pitty, though not pardon thee.   100

Fie on thee wretch, 'tis pitty that thou liu'st   1491

PLACE = 7

Or that, or any place that harbours men: 139

In what safe place you haue bestow'd my monie;   243

If thou hadst beene *Dromio* to day in my place,   676

PLACE *cont.*
  Ang. Ile meet you at that place some houre hence. 783
  Ab. Neither: he tooke this place for sanctuary, 1563
  The place of depth, and sorrie execution, 1590
  And all that are assembled in this place: 1886
PLAIN = *1
  Ant. Why thou didst conclude hairy men plain dea- | lers without wit. 480
PLAINE = *3
  S.Dro. Marry sir, by a rule as plaine as the plaine bald | pate of Father
  time himselfe. 463
  S.Dro. No? why 'tis a plaine case: he that went like 1206
PLAINER = *1
  S.Dro. The plainer dealer, the sooner lost; yet he loo- | seth it in a
  kinde of iollitie. 482
PLAINLY = *1
  E.Dro. Nay, hee strooke so plainly, I could too well 328
PLAY = 2
  For if we two be one, and thou play false, 537
  Come sister, *Dromio* play the Porter well. 607
PLAYNINGS = 1
  And pitteous playnings of the prettie babes 75
PLEAD = 2*2
  Duke. Merchant of *Siracusa*, plead no more. 7
  Antip. Plead you to me faire dame? I know you not: 542
  Plead on your part some cause to you vnknowne; 752
  That he did plead in earnest, yea or no: 1106
PLEADE = 1
  If he were mad, he would not pleade so coldly: 1749
PLEADED = 1
  Luc. Then pleaded I for you. | *Adr.* And what said he? 1115
PLEASE = 5*2
  Please you, Ile meete with you vpon the Mart, 190
  It seemes he hath great care to please his wife. 332
  Since that my beautie cannot please his eie, 390
  Ang. What please your selfe sir: I haue made it for | you. 962
  Go home with it, and please your Wife withall, 967
  And I will please you what you will demand. 1332
  Adr. May it please your Grace, *Antipholus* my husba(n)d, 1608
PLEASETH = 1
  Pleaseth you walke with me downe to his house, 993
PLEASING = 2
  The pleasing punishment that women beare) 50
  That neuer obiect pleasing in thine eye, 510
PLENTIFULL = 1
  it is) so plentifull an excrement? 472
PLUCKE = 1*1
  *If a crow help vs in sirra, wee'll plucke a crow together. 744
  But with these nailes, Ile plucke out these false eyes, 1392
POINTS = 1
  Mar. By this I thinke the Diall points at fiue: 1587
POISON = 1
  I doe digest the poison of thy flesh, 538
POISONS = 1
  Poisons more deadly then a mad dogges tooth. 1539
POLAND = *1
  *a *Poland* Winter: If she liues till doomesday, she'l burne | a weeke
  longer then the whole World. 890

POORE = 7*4

Those, for their parents were exceeding poore,	60
Her part, poore soule, seeming as burdened	110
From my poore cheeke? then he hath wasted it.	366
And feedes from home; poore I am but his stale.	377
Alas poore women, make vs not beleeue	807
*One that before the Iudgme(n)t carries poore soules to hel.	1149
*Adr. Oh that thou wer't not, poore distressed soule.	1343
*Luc. Aye me poore man, how pale and wan he looks.	1399
*Luc. God helpe poore soules, how idlely doe they | talke.	1422
Adr. To fetch my poore distracted husband hence,	1506
Hast thou so crack'd and splitted my poore tongue	1789

PORPENTINE = 4*1

Bring it I pray you to the *Porpentine*,	777
I thought to haue tane you at the *Porpentine*,	959
Your breach of promise to the *Porpentine*,	1035
Promising to bring it to the Porpentine,	1699
*E.Dro. Sir he din'de with her there, at the Porpen-|tine.	1752

PORRAGE = 1

*trying: the other, that at dinner they should not drop in | his porrage.	492

PORTER = 2*2

Come sister, *Dromio* play the Porter well.	607
S.Dro. Master, shall I be Porter at the gate?	613
*E.Dro. What patch is made our Porter? my Master | stayes in the street.	658
*S.Dro. The Porter for this time Sir, and my name is | Dromio.	671

POSSESSE = 1

If ought possesse thee from me, it is drosse,	571

POSSESSION = 3

For euer hows'd, where it gets possession.	767
To yeeld possession to my holie praiers,	1339
Ab. How long hath this possession held the man.	1511

POSSEST = 4

I am possest with an adulterate blot,	535
Possest with such a gentle soueraigne grace,	950
Pinch. Mistris, both Man and Master is possest,	1380
Cries out, I was possest. Then altogether	1722

POST = 3

I from my Mistris come to you in post:	228
If I returne I shall be post indeede.	229
Anti. Go hie thee presently, post to the rode,	937

POUND = 1

Dro. I buy a thousand pound a yeare, I buy a rope. | Exit Dromio	1003

POWER = 1

Some blessed power deliuer vs from hence.	1226

POWRE = 1

Transforme me then, and to your powre Ile yeeld.	827

PRACTISE = 1

Luc. Ere I learne loue, Ile practise to obey.	303

PRAIERS = 1

To yeeld possession to my holie praiers,	1339

PRAIES = 2

And praies that you will hie you home to dinner.	255
My heart praies for him, though my tongue doe curse.	1134

PRAISE = 1

First, he did praise my beautie, then my speech.	1120

PRANKES = 1
And shriue you of a thousand idle prankes: 604
PRATING = 2
Disguised Cheaters, prating Mountebankes; 267
Adri. Hence prating pesant, fetch thy Master home. 357
PRATST = *1
Luc. Why prat'st thou to thy selfe, and answer'st not? 588
PRAY = 13*4
But we that know what 'tis to fast and pray, 216
Ant. Stop in your winde sir, tell me this I pray? 218
E.Dro. I pray you iest sir as you sit at dinner: 227
What meanes this iest, I pray you Master tell me? 416
*to, or else I shall seek my wit in my shoulders, but I pray | sir, why am
I beaten? 433
S.Dro. If it be sir, I pray you eat none of it. | *Ant.* Your reason? 454
An. Nay not sound I pray you. | *S.Dro.* Sure ones then. 486
E.An. Y'are sad signior *Balthazar*, pray God our cheer 638
E.Dro. Here's too much out vpon thee, I pray thee let | me in. 737
Bring it I pray you to the *Porpentine*, 777
Anti. I pray you sir receiue the money now. 970
I pray you see him presently discharg'd, 1015
Gold. Nay come I pray you sir, giue me the Chaine: 1031
Mar. The houre steales on, I pray you sir dispatch. 1038
Come where's the Chaine, I pray you let me see it. 1044
Cur. I pray you sir my Ring, or else the Chaine, 1259
E.Dro. I Sir am *Dromio*, pray let me stay. 1821
PRAYERS = 2
With wholsome sirrups, drugges, and holy prayers 1573
And neuer rise vntill my teares and prayers 1584
PREACHES = 1
My Mr preaches patience to him, and the while 1647
PREHEMINENCE = 1
Of more preheminence then fish and fowles, 297
PRESENCE = 3
Beare a faire presence, though your heart be tainted, 799
Of such inchanting presence and discourse, 951
I promised your presence, and the Chaine, 1006
PRESENT = 6
My present businesse cals me from you now. 192
Therefore make present satisfaction, 986
Anti. I am not furnish'd with the present monie: 1017
Besides this present instance of his rage, 1270
And sure (vnlesse you send some present helpe) 1649
Of you my sonnes, and till this present houre 1891
PRESENTLY = 3
Anti. Go hie thee presently, post to the rode, 937
I pray you see him presently discharg'd, 1015
Against thee presently, if thou dar'st stand: 1495
PRESERUING = 1
In food, in sport, and life-preseruing rest 1552
PREST = 1
Come sister, I am prest downe with conceit: 1181
PRETHEE = 1
Adri. But say, I prethee, is he comming home? 331
PRETTIE = 2
And pitteous playnings of the prettie babes 75
Prettie and wittie; wilde, and yet too gentle; 771

PREUAILD = 1
Anti. You haue preuail'd, I will depart in quiet,   768
PREUAILING = 1
A sinne preuailing much in youthfull men,   1519
PREY = 1
And would haue reft the Fishers of their prey,   118
PRIDE = *1
S.Dro. Flie pride saies the Pea-cocke, Mistris that | you know. *Exit.*   1262
PRIMA *l.*1 616 980 1462 = 4
PRIMUS *l.*1 = 1
PRINCE = *1
E.Ant. Iustice (sweet Prince) against y Woman there: 1673
PRINCES = 2
Which Princes would they may not disanull,   147
And I to thee ingag'd a Princes word,   1634
PRIORIE = 2
This is some Priorie, in, or we are spoyl'd. | *Exeunt to the Priorie.*   1502
PRISON = 1 *1
On Officer to prison, till it come. *Exeunt*   1097
*that *Adam* that keepes the prison; hee that goes in the   1201
PRISONER = 1 *2
*I am thy prisoner, wilt thou suffer them to make a res- |cue?   1401
Offi. Masters let him go: he is my prisoner, and you | shall not haue
him.   1403
Offi. He is my prisoner, if I let him go,   1409
PRIUATE = 1
Ab. Haply in priuate. | *Adr.* And in assemblies too.   1528
PRIUIE = *1
Dromio, swore I was assur'd to her, told me what priuie   930
PRIUILEDGE = 1
And it shall priuiledge him from your hands,   1564
PROCEED = 1
Marchant. | Proceed *Solinus* to procure my fall,   4
PROCLAIME = 1
Duke. Yet once againe proclaime it publikely,   1602
PROCRASTINATE = 1
But to procrastinate his liuelesse end. *Exeunt.*   161
PROCURE = 1
Marchant. | Proceed *Solinus* to procure my fall,   4
PRODIGALL = *1
*calues-skin, that was kil'd for the Prodigall: hee that   1202
PROLONGD = 1
That by misfortunes was my life prolong'd,   122
PROMISD = 4
Sister, you know he promis'd me a chaine,   382
Is that the chaine you promis'd me to day.   1230
Or for my Diamond the Chaine you promis'd,   1252
And for the same he promis'd me a Chaine,   1267
PROMISE = 1
Your breach of promise to the *Porpentine*,   1035
PROMISED = 1
I promised your presence, and the Chaine,   1006
PROMISING = 1
Promising to bring it to the Porpentine,   1699
PROOUE = *1
E.Dro. I am an Asse indeede, you may prooue it by   1310

PROPHESIE = *1
    *the prophesie like the Parrat, beware the ropes end.   1326
PROSPEROUS = 1
    By prosperous voyages I often made   44
PROSTRATE = 1
    Adr. Come go, I will fall prostrate at his feete,   1583
PROTEST = 2
    My wife (but I protest without desert)   773
    But I protest he had the Chaine of me,   1465
PROUD = *1
    An. You would all this time haue prou'd, there is no | time for all
    things.   494
PROUE = 2
    If it proue so, I will be gone the sooner: 269
    Ile proue mine honor, and mine honestie   1494
PROUERBE = *1
    E.Dro. O Lord I must laugh, haue at you with a Pro-|uerbe,   685
PROUIDE = 1
    Such as sea-faring men prouide for stormes: 83
PROUISION = 1
    Had made prouision for her following me,   51
PROUOAKD = 1
    Nor headie-rash prouoak'd with raging ire,   1693
PROWD = 1
    My wife, not meanely prowd of two such boyes,   62
PRUNING = 1
    Who all for want of pruning, with intrusion,   573
PUBLIKELY = 2
    Beheaded publikely for his offence.   1596
    Duke. Yet once againe proclaime it publikely,   1602
PUDDLED = 1
    Great pailes of puddled myre to quench the haire;   1646
PULSE = 2
    Pinch. Giue me your hand, and let mee feele your | pulse.   1335
    And gazing in mine eyes, feeling my pulse,   1720
PUNISHMENT = 1
    The pleasing punishment that women beare)   50
PURCHASE = *1
    S.Dro. Lest it make you chollericke, and purchase me | another drie
    basting.   456
PURE = 1
    Against my soules pure truth, why labour you,   824
PURPOSE = 2
    And told thee to what purpose, and what end.   1086
    On purpose shut the doores against his way: 1274
PURSE = 2*2
    There is a purse of Duckets, let her send it: 1094
    Dro. Here goe: the deske, the purse, sweet now make | haste.   1136
    Ant. Wentst not thou to her for a purse of Duckets.   1375
    S.Ant. This purse of Duckets I receiu'd from you,   1873
PURSUD = 1
    Into this Abbey, whether we pursu'd them,   1627
PUT = 6*2
    To put the finger in the eie and weepe;   600
    *and I know not what vse to put her too, but to make a   887
    If any Barke put forth, come to the Mart,   940
    If any ship put out, then straight away. *Exit*.   979

PUT *cont.*

*that the Barke *Expedition* put forth to night, and then	1220
Signior *Antipholus*, I wonder much	That you would put me to this shame and trouble,	1477
Had hoisted saile, and put to sea to day:	1485
Who put vnluckily into this Bay	1594

PUTS = *1

*Is there any ships puts forth to night? may we be gone?	1218

QUARTER = 1

So he would keepe faire quarter with his bed:	384

QUARTERS = *2

Anti. What's her name? ⌈ *Dro. Nell* Sir: but her name is three quarters, that's	899
*an Ell and three quarters, will not measure her from hip	to hip.	901

QUARTUS *l*.980 = 1

QUENCH = 1

Great pailes of puddled myre to quench the haire;	1646

QUEST = 2

Might beare him company in the quest of him:	132
In quest of them (vnhappie a) loose my selfe.	204

QUESTION = 1

S.Dro. Not I sir, you are my elder.	*E.Dro.* That's a question, how shall we trie it.	1912

QUICKE = 1

How deerely would it touch thee to the quicke,	525

QUIET = 4

We bid be quiet when we heare it crie.	309
Anti. You haue preuail'd, I will depart in quiet,	768
Ab. Be quiet people, wherefore throng you hither?	1505
Ab. Be quiet and depart, thou shalt not haue him.	1581

QUINTUS *l*.1462 = 1

QUIT = 1

To quit the penalty, and to ransome him:	26

QUITE = 1

Iulia. And may it be that you haue quite forgot	A husbands office? shall *Antipholus*	787

QUOTH = 10*2

'Tis dinner time, quoth I: my gold, quoth he:	339
Your meat doth burne, quoth I: my gold quoth he:	340
Will you come, quoth I: my gold, quoth he;	341
The Pigge quoth I, is burn'd: my gold, quoth he:	343
My mistresse, sir, quoth I: hang vp thy Mistresse:	344
I know not thy mistresse, out on thy mistresse.	*Luci.* Quoth who?	345
E.Dr. Quoth my Master, I know quoth he, no house,	347

RABBLE = *1

*By'th'way, we met my wife, her sister, and a rabble more	Of vilde Confederates: Along with them	1712

RAFTE = 1

That floated with thee on the fatall rafte.	1840

RAGE = 6

Besides this present instance of his rage,	1270
Ant. And did not I in rage depart from thence?	1363
That since haue felt the vigor of his rage.	1365
Cur. When as your husband all in rage to day	1433
But till this afternoone his passion	Ne're brake into extremity of rage.	1514
Rings, Iewels, any thing his rage did like.	1616

RAGGE = 1
But surely Master not a ragge of Monie. 1374
RAGGES = *1
*warrant, her ragges and the Tallow in them, will burne 889
RAGING = 2
Thereof the raging fire of feauer bred, 1544
Nor headie-rash prouoak'd with raging ire, 1693
RAILE = *1
*Anti. Did not her Kitchen maide raile, taunt, and | scorne me? 1360
RAILING = 1
It seemes his sleepes were hindred by thy railing, 1540
RAISD = *1
*beating: I am wak'd with it when I sleepe, rais'd with 1315
RAISING = 1
Chac'd vs away: till raising of more aide 1625
RAN = 2*1
*S.Dro. She that would be your wife, now ran from | you. 1449
Ran hether to your Grace, whom I beseech | To giue me ample
satisfaction 1728
Gold. He had my Lord, and when he ran in heere, 1734
RANCOROUS = 1
Sprung from the rancorous outrage of your Duke, 10
RANDONE = 1
And he great care of goods at randone left, 46
RANNE = 1*1
by the salt rheume that ranne betweene *France*, and it. 919
*that I amaz'd ranne from her as a witch. And I thinke, if 933
RANSOME = 1
To quit the penalty, and to ransome him: 26
RAPIER = 1
Enter Antipholus Siracusia with his Rapier drawne, | and Dromio Sirac. 1440
RASH = 1
Nor headie-rash prouoak'd with raging ire, 1693
RATE = 2
Thy substance, valued at the highest rate, 27
E.Dro. Ile serue you sir fiue hundred at the rate. 1295
RATHER = *4
*E.Dro. Return'd so soone, rather approacht too late: 208
*I had rather haue it a head, and you vse these blows 431
*E.Dro. Nay, rather perswade him to hold his hands. 1304
*E.Dro. Mistris *respice finem*, respect your end, or ra-|ther 1325
READ = 2
Let not my sister read it in your eye: 795
And let her read it in thy lookes at boord: 804
REASON = 9*1
*season, when in the why and the wherefore, is neither | rime nor
reason. Well sir, I thanke you. 443
S.Dro. If it be sir, I pray you eat none of it. | Ant. Your reason? 454
An. For what reason. | S.Dro. For two, and sound ones to. 484
*An. But your reason was not substantiall, why there | is no time to
recouer. 498
To know the reason of this strange restraint: 758
Luc. What are you mad, that you doe reason so? 840
*Adri. As if time were in debt: how fondly do'st thou | reason? 1170
Hath he not reason to turne backe an houre in a day? 1177
The reason that I gather he is mad, 1269
And now he's there, past thought of humane reason. 1664

REBUKES = 1
Why beare you these rebukes, and answer not? 1558
RECALD = 1
And passed sentence may not be recal'd 150
RECEIT = 2
Ant. Villaine, thou didst denie the golds receit, 412
Disburse the summe, on the receit thereof, 1021
RECEIUD = 4
You know no *Centaur?* you receiu'd no gold? 404
Dro. And gentle Mr I receiu'd no gold: 1386
That I this day of him receiu'd the Chaine, 1705
S.Ant. This purse of Duckets I receiu'd from you, 1873
RECEIUE = 4
And then receiue my money for the chaine. 969
Anti. I pray you sir receiue the money now. 970
I shall receiue the money for the same: 992
Ant. I owe you none, till I receiue the Chaine. 1050
RECOUER = 1*3
*S.Dro. There's no time for a man to recouer his haire | that growes
bald by nature. 466
*S.Dro. Yes, to pay a fine for a perewig, and recouer | the lost haire of
another man. 469
*S.Dro. Marry and did sir: namely, in no time to re-|couer haire lost
by Nature. 496
*An. But your reason was not substantiall, why there | is no time to
recouer. 498
RECOUERIE = 2
Ant. May he not doe it by fine and recouerie? 468
And beare him home for his recouerie. 1508
RECREATION = 1
Sweet recreation barr'd, what doth ensue | But moodie and dull
melancholly, 1547
RED = 1
Look'd he or red or pale, or sad or merrily? 1107
REDEEME = 2
Who wanting gilders to redeeme their liues, 12
Adr. Alas, I sent you Monie to redeeme you, 1371
REDEMPTION = *1
**will you send him Mistris redemption, the monie in | his deske. 1156
REFT = 2
And would haue reft the Fishers of their prey, 118
Reft of his brother, but retain'd his name, 131
REFUSE = 2
Since mine owne doores refuse to entertaine me, 781
That would refuse so faire an offer'd Chaine. 975
REIOYCE = 1
Embrace thy brother there, reioyce with him. *Exit* 1905
RELEEUE = 1
With vrging helpelesse patience would releeue me; 313
REMAIND = 1
Where would you had remain'd vntill this time, 1350
REMEMBER = 2
Fath. I am sure you both of you remember me. 1771
Dro. Our selues we do remember sir by you: 1772
RENOWNED = 1*1
Duke *Menaphon* your most renowned Vnckle. 1855
*Abb. Renowned Duke, vouchsafe to take the paines 1883

REPAIRE = 1
  A sunnie looke of his, would soone repaire.   375
REPORT = 2
  By computation and mine hosts report.   398
  And that is false thou dost report to vs.   1652
REPREHENDED = 2
  Ab. You should for that haue reprehended him.   1524
  Luc. She neuer reprehended him but mildely,   1556
REPROOFE = 1
  Adri. She did betray me to my owne reproofe,   1559
REPUTATION = 3
  Heerein you warre against your reputation,   747
  Gold. This touches me in reputation.   1059
  Gold. Of very reuerent reputation sir,   1468
REQUIRD = 1
  The debt he owes will be requir'd of me.   1410
RESCUE = *1
  *I am thy prisoner, wilt thou suffer them to make a res-|cue?   1401
RESERUE = 1
  Reserue them till a merrier houre then this: 234
RESORT = 1
  To walke where any honest men resort.   1492
RESPECT = *1
  E.Dro. Mistris *respice finem*, respect your end, or ra-|ther   1325
RESPICE = *1
  E.Dro. Mistris *respice finem*, respect your end, or ra-|ther   1325
REST = 3*1
  *suites of durance: he that sets vp his rest to doe more ex-|ploits   1210
  *thinkes a man alwaies going to bed, and saies, God giue | you good
  rest.   1215
  Ant. Well sir, there rest in your foolerie: 1217
  In food, in sport, and life-preseruing rest   1552
RESTED = 1*2
  S.Dro. I doe not know the matter, hee is rested on | the case.   1151
  *but is in a suite of buffe which rested him, that can I tell,   1155
  Ile giue thee ere I leaue thee so much money | To warrant thee as I am
  rested for.   1282
RESTRAINT = 1
  To know the reason of this strange restraint: 758
RESTS = *1
  *gentlemen are tired giues them a sob, and rests them: 1208
RETAIND = 1
  Reft of his brother, but retain'd his name,   131
RETAINE = 1
  But longer did we not retaine much hope;   68
RETURND = 3*2
  What now? How chance thou art return'd so soone.   207
  E.Dro. Return'd so soone, rather approacht too late: 208
  Adr. Neither my husband nor the slaue return'd,   275
  E.Dro. To a ropes end sir, and to that end am I re-|turn'd.   1297
  For certaine Duckets: he with none return'd.   1709
RETURNE = 5*2
  Made daily motions for our home returne: 63
  And then returne and sleepe within mine Inne,   176
  If I returne I shall be post indeede.   229
  Adr. By thee, and this thou didst returne from him.   551
  Where I will walke till thou returne to me: 941

RETURNE *cont.*

Or else you may returne without your money.	1030
*from home, welcom'd home with it when I returne, nay	1317

REUELL = 1

Reuell and feast it at my house to day,	1346

REUERENCE = *1

*may not speake of, without he say sir reuerence, I haue	882

REUEREND = 1

Duke. She is a vertuous and a reuerend Lady,	1606

REUERENT = 2*1

Dro. A very reuerent body: I such a one, as a man	881
Gold. Of very reuerent reputation sir,	1468
Gold. Vpon what cause? | *Mar.* To see a reuerent *Siracusian* Merchant,	1592

REUERTED = *1

Dro. In her forhead, arm'd and reuerted, making | warre against her heire.	914

REUILD = 1

Dro. Sans Fable, she her selfe reuil'd you there.	1359

REUILE = 1

Anti. And did not she her selfe reuile me there?	1358

RHEUME = 1

by the salt rheume that ranne betweene *France*, and it.	919

RICH = *1

*Rubies, Carbuncles, Saphires, declining their rich As-|pect	924

RIDES = 1

S.Dro. 'Tis true she rides me, and I long for grasse.	596

RIGHT = 3*1

But if thou liue to see like right bereft,	314
S.Dro. Right sir, Ile tell you when, and you'll tell | me wherefore.	663
Luc. First he deni'de you had in him no right.	1110
Duke. Why heere begins his Morning storie right:	1832

RIGOROUS = 1

Haue seal'd his rigorous statutes with their blouds,	13

RIME = 1

*season, when in the why and the wherefore, is neither | rime nor reason. Well sir, I thanke you.	443

RING = 10

And from my false hand cut the wedding ring,	532
A chaine, a chaine, doe you not here it ring.	1163
Cur. Giue me the ring of mine you had at dinner,	1251
Cur. I pray you sir my Ring, or else the Chaine,	1259
A Ring he hath of mine worth fortie Duckets,	1266
My Ring away. This course I fittest choose,	1278
Came to my house, and tooke away my Ring,	1434
The Ring I saw vpon his finger now,	1435
Cur. He did, and from my finger snacht that Ring.	1754
E.Anti. Tis true (my Liege) this Ring I had of her.	1755

RINGS = 1

Rings, Iewels, any thing his rage did like.	1616

RIPE = 1

And left the ship then sinking ripe to vs.	80

RISE = 1

And neuer rise vntill my teares and prayers	1584

RIUALL = 1

This very day a *Syracusian* Marchant | Is apprehended for a riuall here,	165

ROCKE = 1

We were encountred by a mighty rocke,	104

RODE = 1
  Anti. Go hie thee presently, post to the rode,   937
ROMING = 1
  Roming cleane through the bounds of *Asia*,   136
ROOME = 1
  They must be bound and laide in some darke roome.   1382
ROPE = 6
  Buy thou a rope, and bring it home to me.   1002
  Dro. I buy a thousand pound a yeare, I buy a rope. | *Exit Dromio*   1003
  Ant. Thou drunken slaue, I sent thee for a rope,   1085
  E.Dro. Why sir, I gaue the Monie for the Rope.   1293
  Ant. Fiue hundred Duckets villaine for a rope?   1294
  That I was sent for nothing but a rope.   1379
ROPES = 3*2
  And buy a ropes end, that will I bestow   998
  S.Dro. You sent me for a ropes end as soone,   1087
  Enter Dromio Eph. with a ropes end.   1288
  E.Dro. To a ropes end sir, and to that end am I re-|turn'd.   1297
  *the prophesie like the Parrat, beware the ropes end.   1326
ROPE-MAKER = 1
  Dro. God and the Rope-maker beare me witnesse,   1378
ROT = 1
  Euen in the spring of Loue, thy Loue-springs rot?   789
ROUGH *see also* ruffe = 2
  Adr. Why so I did. | *Ab*. I but not rough enough.   1525
  When he demean'd himselfe, rough, rude, and wildly,   1557
ROUGHLY = 1
  Adr. As roughly as my modestie would let me.   1527
ROUND = 1
  Dro. Am I so round with you, as you with me,   358
ROW = 1
  Beaten the Maids a-row, and bound the Doctor,   1643
ROWT = 1
  And that supposed by the common rowt   762
RUBIES = *1
  *Rubies, Carbuncles, Saphires, declining their rich As-|pect   924
RUDE = 2
  When he demean'd himselfe, rough, rude, and wildly,   1557
  But by and by, rude Fishermen of *Corinth*   1843
RUFFE = 1
  A Feind, a Fairie, pittilesse and ruffe: 1144
RUFFIAN = 1
  By Ruffian Lust should be contaminate?   528
RUINATE = 1
  Shall loue in buildings grow so ruinate?   790
RUIND = 1
  By him not ruin'd? Then is he the ground   373
RUINES = 1
  What ruines are in me that can be found,   372
RULD = 1
  Be rul'd by me, depart in patience,   755
RULE = 1*1
  Anti. By what rule sir?   462
  S.Dro. Marry sir, by a rule as plaine as the plaine bald | pate of Father
  time himselfe.   463
RUN = 2*2
  *Lampe of her, and run from her by her owne light. I   888

RUN *cont.*

Dro. As from a Beare a man would run for life,	944
Ant. Fie, now you run this humor out of breath,	1043
*S.Dro. Runne master run, for Gods sake take a house,	1501

RUNNE = 1*1

Let's call more helpe to haue them bound againe. | *Runne all out.*	1444
*S.Dro. Runne master run, for Gods sake take a house,	1501

RUNNING = 1

Luc. How hast thou lost thy breath? | *S.Dro.* By running fast.	1138

RUNS = 1

A hound that runs Counter, and yet draws drifoot well,	1148

RUNST = *1

*Ant. Why how now *Dromio*, where run'st thou so | fast?	862

RUSH = *1

**a rush, a haire, a drop of blood, a pin, a nut, a cherrie-|stone:	1255

RUSHD = 1

He rush'd into my house, and tooke perforce	1277

RUSHING = 1

By rushing in their houses: bearing thence	1615

SACRED = *1

*Adr. Iustice most sacred Duke against the Abbesse.	1605

SAD = 3*1

To tell sad stories of my owne mishaps.	123
*E.An. Y'are sad signior *Balthazar*, pray God our cheer	638
Look'd he or red or pale, or sad or merrily?	1107
Adr. This weeke he hath beene heauie, sower sad,	1512

SADLER = 2

To pay the Sadler for my Mistris crupper:	221
The Sadler had it Sir, I kept it not.	222

SAFE = 6

And soone, and safe, arriued where I was:	52
In what safe place you haue bestow'd my monie;	243
I greatly feare my monie is not safe. *Exit.*	271
Safe at the *Centaur*, and the heedfull slaue	396
Good Master Doctor see him safe conuey'd	1414
I long that we were safe and sound aboord.	1453

SAFETY = 1

The Sailors sought for safety by our boate,	79

SAFFRON = 1

Did this Companion with the saffron face	1345

SAID = 2

Luce. I thought to haue askt you. | *S.Dro.* And you said no.	694
Luc. Then pleaded I for you. | *Adr.* And what said he?	1115

SAIES = *2

**thinkes a man alwaies going to bed, and saies, God giue | you good rest.	1215
*S.Dro. Flie pride saies the Pea-cocke, Mistris that | you know. *Exit.*	1262

SAILD = 1

A league from *Epidamium* had we saild	65

SAILE = 2

Had not their backe beene very slow of saile;	119
Had hoisted saile, and put to sea to day:	1485

SAILORS = 1

The Sailors sought for safety by our boate,	79

SAINT = 1

Teach sinne the carriage of a holy Saint,	800

SAINTS = 1
    I coniure thee by all the Saints in heauen. 1341
SAIST = 1
    Thou saist his meate was sawc'd with thy vpbraidings, 1542
SAKE = 4*4
    Duke. And for the sake of them thou sorrowest for, 124
    E.Dro. What meane you sir, for God sake hold your | (hands: 258
    For Gods sake send some other messenger. 353
    S.Dr. Hold sir, for Gods sake, now your iest is earnest, 419
    Luce. Can you tell for whose sake? 699
    *Then for her wealths-sake vse her with more kindnesse: 792
    Adr. Hold, hurt him not for God sake, he is mad, 1498
    S.Dro. Runne master run, for Gods sake take a house, 1501
SALT = 1
    by the salt rheume that ranne betweene *France*, and it. 919
SALUTE = 1
    There's not a man I meete but doth salute me 1184
SAME = 5
    That very howre, and in the selfe-same Inne, 57
    I shall receiue the money for the same: 992
    And for the same he promis'd me a Chaine, 1267
    Oh if thou bee'st the same *Egeon*, speake: 1830
    And speake vnto the same *Aemilia*. 1831
SANCTUARY = 1
    Ab. Neither: he tooke this place for sanctuary, 1563
SANS = 1
    Dro. *Sans* Fable, she her selfe reuil'd you there. 1359
SANT = 7*1
SANTI = *1
SAP = 1
    Infect thy sap, and liue on thy confusion. 574
SAPHIRES = *1
    *Rubies, Carbuncles, Saphires, declining their rich As-|pect 924
SAP-CONSUMING = 1
    In sap-consuming Winters drizled snow, 1793
SATHAN = 2*1
    Ant. Sathan auoide, I charge thee tempt me not. 1231
    S.Dro. Master, is this Mistris *Sathan*? | *Ant*. It is the diuell. 1232
    Pinch. I charge thee Sathan, hous'd within this man, 1338
SATISFACTION = 3
    Therefore make present satisfaction, 986
    Ran hether to your Grace, whom I beseech | To giue me ample
    satisfaction 1728
    And we shall make full satisfaction. 1889
SAUE = 4*2
    And knowing whom it was their hap to saue, 116
    S.Dro. The one to saue the money that he spends in 491
    Offi. That labour may you saue: See where he comes. 996
    Oh Mistris, Mistris, shift and saue your selfe, 1641
    Deepe scarres to saue thy life; euen for the blood 1669
    Haply I see a friend will saue my life, 1763
SAUING = 1
    Gold. Sauing your merrie humor: here's the note 1010
SAUOURD = 1
    That neuer meat sweet-sauour'd in thy taste, 512
SAW = 10*3
    Weeping before for what she saw must come, 74

SAW *cont.*

S.Dro. I sir? I neuer saw her till this time.	556
Ant. Where *Spaine?* | **Dro.* Faith I saw it not: but I felt it hot in her	
breth.	920
The Ring I saw vpon his finger now,	1435
*vs no harme: you saw they, speake vs faire, giue vs gold:	1455
Which God he knowes, I saw not. For the which,	1706
These people saw the Chaine about his necke.	1735
I neuer saw the Chaine, so helpe me heauen:	1744
E.Ant. I neuer saw you in my life till now.	1777
*Fa. Oh! griefe hath chang'd me since you saw me last,	1778
Ant. I neuer saw my Father in my life.	1800
I ne're saw *Siracusa* in my life.	1806
During which time, he ne're saw *Siracusa*:	1809

SAWCD = 1

Thou saist his meate was sawc'd with thy vpbraidings,	1542

SAWCINESSE = 1

Your sawcinesse will iest vpon my loue,	423

SAWST = 1

Duke. Saw'st thou him enter at the Abbey heere?	1756

SAY = 22*9

Duk. Well *Siracusian*; say in briefe the cause	32
But ere they came, oh let me say no more,	97
They say this towne is full of cosenage:	263
Adr. Say, is your tardie master now at hand?	319
*Adr. Say, didst thou speake with him? knowst thou | his minde?	322
Adri. But say, I prethee, is he comming home?	331
*S.Dro. I sir, and wherefore; for they say, euery why | hath a wherefore.	438
for something. But say sir, is it dinner time?	449
Say he dines forth, and let no creature enter:	606
Ile say as they say, and perseuer so:	611
Say that I lingerd with you at your shop	621
*E.Dro. Say what you wil sir, but I know what I know,	629
*E.Dro. You would say so Master, if your garments | were thin.	723
*may not speake of, without he say sir reuerence, I haue	882
Good sir say, whe'r you'l answer me, or no:	1046
*Ant. You gaue me none, you wrong mee much to | say so.	1052
Adr. Ah but I thinke him better then I say:	1131
Nay, he's a theefe too: haue you not heard men say,	1174
*thereof comes, that the wenches say God dam me, That's	1236
*as much to say, God make me a light wench: It is writ-|ten,	1237
*Curt. How say you now? Is not your husband mad?	1328
Dro. Sir sooth to say, you did not dine at home.	1354
*Ant. Say wherefore didst thou locke me forth to day,	1383
Say now, whose suite is he arrested at?	1425
Off. Two hundred Duckets. | *Adr.* Say, how growes it due.	1429
Duke. A greeuous fault: say woman, didst thou so?	1683
E.Ant. My Liege, I am aduised what I say,	1691
You say he din'd at home, the Goldsmith heere	1750
Denies that saying. Sirra, what say you?	1751
Adr. And are not you my husband? | *E.Ant.* No, I say nay to that.	1858

SAYEST = 1*1

*Anti. Din'd at home? Thou Villaine, what sayest | thou?	1352
Thou sayest his sports were hindred by thy bralles.	1546

SAYING = 1

Denies that saying. Sirra, what say you?	1751

SCAND = 1
Who euery word by all my wit being scan'd,   545
SCANDALL = 1
And not without some scandall to your selfe,   1479
SCANTED = *1
*beasts, and what he hath scanted them in haire, hee hath | giuen them
in wit.   474
SCARCE = 3
Beshrew his hand, I scarce could vnderstand it.   325
*feele his blowes; and withall so doubtfully, that I could | scarce
vnderstand them.   329
A table full of welcome, makes scarce one dainty dish.   642
SCARD = 1
Hath scar'd thy husband from the vse of wits.   1555
SCARRES = 1
Deepe scarres to saue thy life; euen for the blood   1669
SCENA *l.1 616 = 2*
SCHOOLE = 1
Enter Adriana, Luciana, Courtizan, and a Schoole- | master, call'd Pinch. 1321
SCISSORS see cizers
SCOENA *l.980 1462 = 2*
SCONCE = 2*2
Or I shall breake that merrie sconce of yours   244
Or I will beat this method in your sconce.   429
*S.Dro. Sconce call you it? so you would leaue batte- | ring,   430
*long, I must get a sconce for my head, and Insconce it   432
SCORCH = 1
To scorch your face, and to disfigure you: | Cry within.   1656
SCORND = 1
Dro. Certis she did, the kitchin vestall scorn'd you.   1362
SCORNE = 4
Whil'st man and Master laughes my woes to scorne: 601
If he should scorne me so apparantly.   1066
*Anti. Did not her Kitchen maide raile, taunt, and | scorne me?   1360
To make a loathsome abiect scorne of me: 1391
SCOTLAND = 1
Ant. Where Scotland?   910
SCOURE = 1
For she will scoure your fault vpon my pate: 230
SDR = *1
SDRO = 29*44
SDROM = *1
SDROMIO = 2, 1
Enter S.Dromio.   1135
SEA = 4*1
But hath his bound in earth, in sea, in skie.   291
For he is bound to Sea, and stayes but for it.   1016
Had hoisted saile, and put to sea to day: 1485
*Ab. Hath he not lost much wealth by wrack of sea,   1516
Besides her vrging of her wracke at sea,   1835
SEALD = 1
Haue seal'd his rigorous statutes with their blouds,   13
SEAS = 2
The seas waxt calme, and we discouered   94
Lord of the wide world, and wilde watry seas,   295
SEASON = 1*2
*Ant. Come Dromio, come, these iests are out of season,   233

SEASON *cont.*

  *season, when in the why and the wherefore, is neither | rime nor
reason. Well sir, I thanke you.   443
  S.Dro. Time is a verie bankerout, and owes more then | he's worth to
season.   1172

SEA-FARING = 1

  Such as sea-faring men prouide for stormes: 83

SECOND = 2

  for vrging it the second time to me.   441
  Second to none that liues heere in the Citie: 1470

SECRET = 1

  Be secret false: what need she be acquainted?   801

SECUNDUS *l.*272 = 1

SEDITIOUS = 1

  Twixt thy seditious Countrimen and vs,   16

SEE = 33*2

  Whom whil'st I laboured of a loue to see,   133
  Time is their Master, and when they see time,   282
  But if thou liue to see like right bereft,   314
  I see the Iewell best enamaled | Will loose his beautie: yet the gold
bides still   385
  I sent him from the Mart? see here he comes.   400
  S.Dro. I did not see you since you sent me hence   410
  S.Dro. I am glad to see you in this merrie vaine,   415
  I know thou canst, and therefore see thou doe it.   534
  To see the making of her Carkanet,   622
  Ile knocke else-where, to see if they'll disdaine me.   782
  For feare you ne're see chaine, nor mony more.   971
  I see a man heere needs not liue by shifts,   976
  Offi. That labour may you saue: See where he comes.   996
  But soft I see the Goldsmith; get thee gone,   1001
  I pray you see him presently discharg'd,   1015
  Come where's the Chaine, I pray you let me see it.   1044
  I see sir you haue found the Gold-smith now: 1229
  Hast thou delight to see a wretched man   1407
  Good Master Doctor see him safe conuey'd   1414
  Adr. It may be so, but I did neuer see it.   1437
  S.Ant. I see these Witches are affraid of swords.   1448
  Gold. Vpon what cause? | *Mar.* To see a reuerent *Siracusian* Merchant,   1592
  Gold. See where they come, we wil behold his death   1597
  I haue not breath'd almost since I did see it.   1654
  Mar.Fat. Vnlesse the feare of death doth make me | dote, I see my
sonne *Antipholus* and *Dromio.*   1671
  Curt. As sure (my Liege) as I do see your Grace.   1757
  Haply I see a friend will saue my life,   1763
  I see thy age and dangers make thee dote.   1810
  All gather to see them.   1815
  Adr. I see two husbands, or mine eyes deceiue me.   1816
  I, to this fortune that you see mee in.   1847
  If this be not a dreame I see and heare.   1864
  I see we still did meete each others man,   1875
  I see by you, I am a sweet-fac'd youth,   1910
  Will you walke in to see their gossipping?   1911

SEEK = *1

  *to, or else I shall seek my wit in my shoulders, but I pray | sir, why am
I beaten?   433

SEEKE = 6
Forst me to seeke delayes for them and me,	77
To seeke thy helpe by beneficiall helpe,	154
Ile to the Centaur to goe seeke this slaue,	270
That in such haste I sent to seeke his Master?	276
Is wandred forth in care to seeke me out	397
I went to seeke him. In the street I met him,	1702

SEEKES = 1
That in the Ocean seekes another drop,   200

SEEMES = 2*1
It seemes he hath great care to please his wife.	332
*S.Dro. It seemes thou want'st breaking, out vpon thee | hinde.	735
It seemes his sleepes were hindred by thy railing,	1540

SEEMING = 1
Her part, poore soule, seeming as burdened   110

SEENE = 1
Nay more, if any borne at *Ephesus* \| Be seene at any *Siracusian* Marts and Fayres: 20

SEIZD = 1
At length another ship had seiz'd on vs,   115

SELFE = 26*6
Before her selfe (almost at fainting vnder	49
Which though my selfe would gladly haue imbrac'd,	72
Ant. Farewell till then: I will goe loose my selfe,	193
In quest of them (vnhappie a) loose my selfe.	204
That thou art then estranged from thy selfe?	515
Thy selfe I call it, being strange to me:	516
Ah doe not teare away thy selfe from me;	519
As take from me thy selfe, and not me too.	524
Luc. Why prat'st thou to thy selfe, and answer'st not?	588
Knowne vnto these, and to my selfe disguisde:	610
And about euening come your selfe alone,	757
Sing Siren for thy selfe, and I will dote:	834
Ant. No: it is thy selfe, mine owne selfes better part:	850
Ant. Call thy selfe sister sweet, for I am thee:	855
S.Dro. Doe you know me sir? Am I *Dromio*? Am I | your man? Am I my selfe?	864
Ant. Thou art *Dromio*, thou art my man, thou art | thy selfe.	866
Dro. I am an asse, I am a womans man, and besides | my selfe.	868
Ant. What womans man? and how besides thy | selfe?	869
Dro. Marrie sir, besides my selfe, I am due to a woman:	872
Hath almost made me Traitor to my selfe:	952
But least my selfe be guilty to selfe wrong,	953
Ang. What please your selfe sir: I haue made it for | you.	962
Gold. Then you will bring the Chaine to her your | selfe.	1023
But for their Owner, Master, and your selfe.	1081
Anti. And did not she her selfe reuile me there?	1358
Dro. Sans Fable, she her selfe reuil'd you there.	1359
Gold. 'Tis so: and that selfe chaine about his necke,	1474
And not without some scandall to your selfe,	1479
And will haue no atturney but my selfe,	1569
Oh Mistris, Mistris, shift and saue your selfe,	1641
Adr. No my good Lord. My selfe, he, and my sister,	1684

SELFES = 1*1
That vndiuidable Incorporate | Am better then thy deere selfes better part.	517
Ant. No: it is thy selfe, mine owne selfes better part:	850

SELFE-HARMING = 1
   Luci. Selfe-harming Iealousie; fie beat it hence.   378
SELFE-SAME = 1
   That very howre, and in the selfe-same Inne,   57
SELUES = 4
   Both by the *Siracusians* and our selues,   18
   Fastned our selues at eyther end the mast,   88
   As much, or more, we should our selues complaine: 311
   Dro. Our selues we do remember sir by you: 1772
SEMBLANCE = 1
   And these two *Dromio's*, one in semblance: 1834
SENCE = 2
   Indued with intellectuall sence and soules,   296
   Establish him in his true sence againe,   1331
SEND = 6*1
   For Gods sake send some other messenger.   353
   Either send the Chaine, or send me by some token.   1042
   There is a purse of Duckets, let her send it: 1094
   *will you send him Mistris redemption, the monie in | his deske.   1156
   Nor send him forth, that we may beare him hence.   1630
   And sure (vnlesse you send some present helpe)   1649
SENIOR *see* signior
SENSELESSE = 1*1
   Anti. Thou whoreson senselesse Villaine.   1305
   E.Dro. I would I were senselesse sir, that I might   1306
SENSIBLE = *1
   Anti. Thou art sensible in nothing but blowes, and | so is an Asse.   1308
SENT = 15*3
   That in such haste I sent to seeke his Master?   276
   I sent him from the Mart? see here he comes.   400
   Your Mistresse sent to haue me home to dinner?   405
   S.Dro. I did not see you since you sent me hence   410
   She sent for you by *Dromio* home to dinner.   549
   *to the hot breath of Spaine, who sent whole Ar- | madoes of Carrects to
   be ballast at her nose.   925
   S.Dro. A ship you sent me too, to hier waftage.   1084
   Ant. Thou drunken slaue, I sent thee for a rope,   1085
   S.Dro. You sent me for a ropes end as soone,   1087
   You sent me to the Bay sir, for a Barke.   1088
   S.Dro. Master, here's the gold you sent me for: what   1196
   Delay: Here are the angels that you sent for to deliuer | you.   1222
   How now sir? Haue you that I sent you for?   1290
   Adr. Alas, I sent you Monie to redeeme you,   1371
   That I was sent for nothing but a rope.   1379
   Once did I get him bound, and sent him home,   1617
   I did obey, and sent my Pesant home   1708
   Adr. I sent you monie sir to be your baile   1870
SENTENCE = 1
   And passed sentence may not be recal'd   150
SEPARATE = 1
   And ill it doth beseeme your holinesse | To separate the husband and
   the wife.   1579
SEQUELL = 1
   Gather the sequell by that went before.   98
SERE = 1
   He is deformed, crooked, old, and sere,   1125

SEREPTUS = 1
Enter Adriana, wife to Antipholis Sereptus, with | Luciana her Sister.   273
SERIEANT = 1*3
S.Dro. Oh yes, if any houre meete a Serieant, a turnes | backe for verie
feare.   1168
If I be in debt and theft, and a Serieant in the way,   1176
S.Dro. I sir, the Serieant of the Band: he that brings   1213
*were you hindred by the Serieant to tarry for the *Hoy*   1221
SERIOUS = 1
And make a Common of my serious howres,   424
SERUANTS = 2*1
Luc. Dromio, goe bid the seruants spred for dinner.   582
For seruants must their Masters mindes fulfill. *Exit*   1102
Ad. Then let your seruants bring my husband forth   1562
SERUD = *1
Duke. Long since thy husband seru'd me in my wars   1633
SERUE = 3
Adr. Looke when I serue him so, he takes it thus.   286
Luci. How manie fond fooles serue mad Ielousie? | *Exit.*   392
E.Dro. Ile serue you sir fiue hundred at the rate.   1295
SERUED = *1
*my long eares. I haue serued him from the houre of my   1311
SERUICE = 2*1
If I last in this seruice, you must case me in leather.   361
*for my seruice but blowes. When I am cold, he heates   1313
Euen for the seruice that long since I did thee,   1667
SERUITUDE = 1
Adri. This seruitude makes you to keepe vnwed.   300
SET = 2
Dies ere the wearie sunne set in the West: 169
Shall I set in my staffe.   687
SETS = *1
*suites of durance: he that sets vp his rest to doe more ex- | ploits   1210
SEUEN = 2
In seuen short yeares, that heere my onely sonne   1790
Fa. But seuen yeares since, in *Siracusa* boy   1801
SEUERD = 1
Thus haue you heard me seuer'd from my blisse,   121
SHAKE = *1
*be wise, and if you giue it her, the diuell will shake | her Chaine, and
fright vs with it.   1257
SHAL *l.*961 = 1
SHALL *l.*229 244 356 *433 437 613 687 *717 784 787 790 992 1069 1071
 1096 1124 *1319 1403 1564 1604 1863 1879 1889 *1900 1908
 1912 = 22*4
SHALLOW = 1
Smothred in errors, feeble, shallow, weake,   822
SHALT *l.*1581 1679 = 2
SHAME = 7
By falshood and corruption doth it shame: 389
Shame hath a bastard fame, well managed,   805
To your notorious shame, I doubt it not.   1072
Free from these slanders, and this open shame.   1351
Pinch. It is no shame, the fellow finds his vaine,   1367
Signior *Antipholus,* I wonder much | That you would put me to this
shame and trouble,   1477
Beside the charge, the shame, imprisonment,   1482

SHAMEFULL = 1
That would behold in me this shamefull sport.   1393
SHAMELESSE = 1
That she this day hath shamelesse throwne on me.   1678
SHAMES = 2
Be not thy tongue thy owne shames Orator: 796
For these deepe shames, and great indignities.   1730
SHAMST = 1
Thou sham'st to acknowledge me in miserie.   1803
SHAPE = 1
S.Dro. Nay Master, both in minde, and in my shape.   592
SHAPELESSE = 1
Ill-fac'd, worse bodied, shapelesse euery where: 1126
SHARPE = 3
If voluble and sharpe discourse be mar'd,   368
Luc. Alas how fiery, and how sharpe he lookes.   1333
A needy-hollow-ey'd-sharpe-looking-wretch;   1717
SHE = 37*13
SHEE *l.**575 = *2
SHEEP = *1
An. How now? a Madman? Why thou peeuish sheep   1082
SHEL = *1
*a *Poland* Winter: If she liues till doomesday, she'l burne | a weeke
longer then the whole World.   890
SHES = *1
Dro. Marry sir, she's the Kitchin wench, & al grease,   886
SHEW = 2
Muffle your false loue with some shew of blindnesse: 794
Though others haue the arme, shew vs the sleeue: 809
SHIFT = 1
Oh Mistris, Mistris, shift and saue your selfe,   1641
SHIFTS = 1
I see a man heere needs not liue by shifts,   976
SHINES = 1
When the sunne shines, let foolish gnats make sport,   425
SHIP = 7
And left the ship then sinking ripe to vs.   80
Our helpefull ship was splitted in the midst;   106
At length another ship had seiz'd on vs,   115
If any ship put out, then straight away. *Exit.*   979
The ship is in her trim, the merrie winde   1079
What ship of *Epidamium* staies for me.   1083
S.Dro. A ship you sent me too, to hier waftage.   1084
SHIPBORD = *1
S.Dro. Mast.(er) shall I fetch your stuffe from shipbord?   1900
SHIPPES = 1
Two shippes from farre, making amaine to vs: 95
SHIPS = 1*1
For ere the ships could meet by twice fiue leagues,   103
*Is there any ships puts forth to night? may we be gone?   1218
SHIP-WRACKT = 1
Gaue healthfull welcome to their ship-wrackt guests,   117
SHOO = *1
Dro. Swart like my shoo, but her face nothing like   893
SHOOES = *1
*so cleane kept: for why? she sweats a man may goe o-|uer-shooes in
the grime of it.   894

SHOP = 3
Say that I lingerd with you at your shop621
As all the mettall in your shop will answer.1070
Euen now a tailor cal'd me in his shop,1190
SHORE = 1
And if the winde blow any way from shore,938
SHORT = 1
In seuen short yeares, that heere my onely sonne1790
SHOULD *l*.148 *231 250 *284 311 *492 528 598 636 *844 854 973 1036
1048 1066 1160 1286 1524 = 14*4
SHOULDER = *1
*markes I had about mee, as the marke of my shoulder,931
SHOULDERS = 1*3
Some of my Mistris markes vpon my shoulders:248
*tongue, I thanke him, I bare home vpon my shoulders:349
*to, or else I shall seek my wit in my shoulders, but I pray | sir, why am
I beaten?433
*I beare it on my shoulders, as a begger woont her brat:1318
SHOULDER-CLAPPER = *1
*A back friend, a shoulder-clapper, one that counterma(n)ds1146
SHOULDST *l*.526 = 1
SHOW *see also* shew = *2
*That you beat me at the Mart I haue your hand to show;630
*Lesse in your knowledge, and your grace you show not,818
SHOWD = 1
And show'd me Silkes that he had bought for me,1191
SHREW = 1
But like a shrew you first begin to brawle.1037
SHREWISH = 1
My wife is shrewish when I keepe not howres;620
SHRIUE = 1
And shriue you of a thousand idle prankes:604
SHUT = 3*3
Of his owne doores being shut against his entrance.1272
On purpose shut the doores against his way:1274
Whil'st vpon me the guiltie doores were shut,1347
*Ant. Were not my doores lockt vp, and I shut out?1355
*Dro. Perdie, your doores were lockt, and you shut | out.1356
*E.Ant. This day (great Duke) she shut the doores | vpon me,1680
SHUTS = 1
And heere the Abbesse shuts the gates on vs,1628
SICKNESSE = 1
Diet his sicknesse, for it is my Office,1568
SIGHT = 2
And in our sight they three were taken vp113
*Luc. Gaze when you should, and that will cleere | your sight.844
SIGNIOR = 3*3
*E.Anti. Good signior Angelo you must excuse vs all,619
*E.An. Y'are sad signior Balthazar, pray God our cheer638
E.An. Oh signior Balthazar, either at flesh or fish,641
Good Signior take the stranger to my house,1019
Signior Antipholus, I wonder much | That you would put me to this
shame and trouble,1477
*S.Dro. Wee'l draw Cuts for the Signior, till then, | lead thou first.1914
SILKES = 1
And show'd me Silkes that he had bought for me,1191

SILUER = 1
Spread ore the siluer waues thy golden haires;   835
SIMPATHIZED = 1
That by this simpathized one daies error   1887
SIMPLE = 2
What simple thiefe brags of his owne attaine?   802
But she tels to your Highnesse simple truth.   1688
SINCE = 12*4
For since the mortall and intestine iarres   15
Since that my beautie cannot please his eie,   390
I could not speake with *Dromio*, since at first   399
E.Ant. Euen now, euen here, not halfe an howre since.   409
S.Dro. I did not see you since you sent me hence   410
Since mine owne doores refuse to entertaine me,   781
Mar. You know since Pentecost the sum is due,   982
And since I haue not much importun'd you,   983
Gold. You know I gaue it you halfe an houre since.   1051
S.Dro. Why sir, I brought you word an houre since,   1219
That since haue felt the vigor of his rage.   1365
Duke. Long since thy husband seru'd me in my wars   1633
I haue not breath'd almost since I did see it.   1654
Euen for the seruice that long since I did thee,   1667
Fa. Oh! griefe hath chang'd me since you saw me last,   1778
Fa. But seuen yeares since, in *Siracusa* boy   1801
SINDGD = 1
Whose beard they haue sindg'd off with brands of fire,   1644
SING = 1
Sing Siren for thy selfe, and I will dote: 834
SINKE = 1
Let Loue, being light, be drowned if she sinke.   839
SINKING = 1
And left the ship then sinking ripe to vs.   80
SINNE = 3
And manie such like liberties of sinne: 268
Teach sinne the carriage of a holy Saint,   800
A sinne preuailing much in youthfull men,   1519
SINNER = 1
S.Dro. Oh for my beads, I crosse me for a sinner.   583
SIR *l.*182 187 *195 218 222 227 236 *237 240 257 *258 259 344 402 408
   *419 433 435 *438 443 445 *446 449 450 451 453 454 *458 462 *463
   *496 554 556 602 *629 *640 *643 *663 *671 *712 *715 *732 746 753 780
   859 *864 *872 *876 *882 *886 *897 *899 *908 922 *927 958 *962 964
   970 972 *1027 1029 *1031 1038 1046 1054 1067 1071 1076 1088 *1203
   *1207 *1209 *1213 1217 *1219 1229 1241 1253 1259 1290 1293 1295
   *1297 1299 *1306 1354 1387 1464 1468 1476 1488 *1752 1766 1768 1772
   1774 1784 *1786 1820 1821 1849 *1865 1867 1868 1869 1870 1880 *1902
   1912 = 74*40, 2
Enter Dromio. Sir.   1195
Enter the Abbesse with Antipholus Siracusa, | and Dromio Sir.   1811
SIRA = 1
Enter Dromio Sira. from the Bay.   1073
SIRAC = 1
Enter Antipholus Siracusia with his Rapier drawne, | and Dromio Sirac.   1440
SIRACUSA see also S.Ant., S.Anti., S.Dr., S.Dro., S.Drom., S.Dromio.,
   Sir., Sirac. = 4*2
*Enter the Duke of Ephesus, with the Merchant of Siracusa, | Iaylor, and
   other attendants.*   2

SIRACUSA cont.
*Duke. Merchant of *Siracusa*, plead no more.	7
Fa. But seuen yeares since, in *Siracusa* boy	1801
I ne're saw *Siracusa* in my life.	1806
During which time, he ne're saw *Siracusa*:	1809
Enter the Abbesse with Antipholus Siracusa, | and Dromio Sir.	1811

SIRACUSE = 2
Enter the Duke of Ephesus, and the Merchant of Siracuse	1599
S.Ant. No sir, not I, I came from *Siracuse*.	1849

SIRACUSIA = 5
Enter Dromio Siracusia.	401
Enter Iuliana, with Antipholus of Siracusia.	786
Enter Dromio, Siracusia.	861
Enter Antipholus Siracusia.	1183
Enter Antipholus Siracusia with his Rapier drawne, | and Dromio Sirac.	1440

SIRACUSIAN = 6
Nay more, if any borne at *Ephesus* | Be seene at any *Siracusian* Marts and Fayres:	20
Againe, if any *Siracusian* borne | Come to the Bay of *Ephesus*, he dies:	22
Duk. Well *Siracusian*; say in briefe the cause	32
Gold. Vpon what cause? | *Mar*. To see a reuerent *Siracusian* Merchant,	1592
Duke. Speake freely *Siracusian* what thou wilt.	1765
Duke. I tell thee *Siracusian*, twentie yeares	1807

SIRACUSIANS = 1
Both by the *Siracusians* and our selues,	18

SIREN = 1
Sing Siren for thy selfe, and I will dote:	834

SIRRA = 2*1
Sirra, if any aske you for your Master,	605
*If a crow help vs in sirra, wee'll plucke a crow together.	744
Denies that saying. Sirra, what say you?	1751

SIRRAH = 1
But sirrah, you shall buy this sport as deere,	1069

SIRRUPS = 1
With wholsome sirrups, drugges, and holy prayers	1573

SISTER = 24*2
My Mistris and her sister staies for you.	241
Enter Adriana, wife to Antipholis Sereptus, with | Luciana her Sister.	273
Good Sister let vs dine, and neuer fret;	280
They'll goe or come; if so, be patient Sister.	283
Sister, you know he promis'd me a chaine,	382
When were you wont to vse my sister thus?	548
Come sister, *Dromio* play the Porter well.	607
If you did wed my sister for her wealth,	791
Let not my sister read it in your eye:	795
Comfort my sister, cheere her, call her wife;	812
But if that I am I, then well I know, | Your weeping sister is no wife of mine,	828
To drowne me in thy sister floud of teares:	833
Luc. Why call you me loue? Call my sister so.	847
Ant. Thy sisters sister. | *Luc*. That's my sister.	848
Luc. All this my sister is, or else should be.	854
Ant. Call thy selfe sister sweet, for I am thee:	855
Ile fetch my sister to get her good will. *Exit*.	860
Doth for a wife abhorre. But her faire sister	949
Adr. Go fetch it Sister: this I wonder at. | *Exit Luciana*.	1158
Come sister, I am prest downe with conceit:	1181

SISTER *cont.*

Adr. Go beare him hence, sister go you with me:	1424
**Adr.* No my good Lord. My selfe, he, and my sister,	1684
**By'th'way, we met my wife, her sister, and a rabble more | Of vilde	
Confederates: Along with them	1712
And this faire Gentlewoman her sister heere	1861
She now shall be my sister, not my wife,	1908

SISTERS = 1

Ant. Thy sisters sister. | *Luc.* That's my sister.	848

SIT = 1*2

E.Dro. I pray you iest sir as you sit at dinner:	227
*Either get thee from the dore, or sit downe at the hatch:	655
*it when I sit, driuen out of doores with it when I goe	1316

SITUATE = 1

There's nothing situate vnder heauens eye,	290

SIXE = 2

From whom my absence was not sixe moneths olde,	48
E.Dro. Oh sixe pence that I had a wensday last,	220

SKIE = 1

But hath his bound in earth, in sea, in skie.	291

SKIN = 1*2

And teare the stain'd skin of my Harlot brow,	531
*If y skin were parchment, & y blows you gaue were ink,	631
*calues-skin, that was kil'd for the Prodigall: hee that	1202

SLANDER = 1

For slander liues vpon succession:	766

SLANDERS = 1

Free from these slanders, and this open shame.	1351

SLAUE = 7*3

**Ant.* Thy Mistris markes? what Mistris slaue hast thou?	252
Ile to the Centaur to goe seeke this slaue,	270
Adr. Neither my husband nor the slaue return'd,	275
**Adri.* Go back againe, thou slaue, & fetch him home.	351
**Adri.* Backe slaue, or I will breake thy pate a-crosse.	354
Safe at the *Centaur*, and the heedfull slaue	396
To counterfeit thus grosely with your slaue,	563
Ant. Thou drunken slaue, I sent thee for a rope,	1085
And that shall baile me: hie thee slaue, be gone,	1096
A liuing dead man. This pernicious slaue,	1718

SLEEPE = 3*1

And then returne and sleepe within mine Inne,	176
Or sleepe I now, and thinke I heare all this?	578
*beating: I am wak'd with it when I sleepe, rais'd with	1315
Luc. Nere may I looke on day, nor sleepe on night,	1687

SLEEPES = 1

It seemes his sleepes were hindred by thy railing,	1540

SLEEPING = 1

Sleeping or waking, mad or well aduisde:	609

SLEEUE = 2

Come I will fasten on this sleeue of thine:	567
Though others haue the arme, shew vs the sleeue:	809

SLEPT = 1

In bed he slept not for my vrging it,	1532

SLOW = 1

Had not their backe beene very slow of saile;	119

SLUG = 1

Dromio, thou *Dromio*, thou snaile, thou slug, thou sot.	589

SMALL = 1 *1
   Had fastned him vnto a small spare Mast,   82
   Bal. Small cheere and great welcome, makes a mer- | rie feast.   646
SMITH = 1
   I see sir you haue found the Gold-smith now: 1229
SMOTHRED = 1
   Smothred in errors, feeble, shallow, weake,   822
SNACHT = 1
   Cur. He did, and from my finger snacht that Ring.   1754
SNAILE = 1
   Dromio, thou *Dromio*, thou snaile, thou slug, thou sot.   589
SNOW = 1
   In sap-consuming Winters drizled snow,   1793
SO *l*.55 99 101 107 130 180 203 207 *208 212 226 269 283 286 288 312
  *326 *328 *329 *348 358 384 403 407 *430 *460 472 591 597 611 633
  *683 *696 *723 *727 734 *742 746 784 790 840 847 *862 *894 *927 945
  974 975 1052 1066 1104 1224 1260 1265 1282 1308 1437 *1474 1480
  1481 1525 1604 1683 1685 1744 1749 1789 1805 1818 1833 1860
  1896 = 57*16
SOB = *1
   *gentlemen are tired giues them a sob, and rests them: 1208
SOBER = 1
   Her sober vertue, yeares, and modestie,   751
SOFT = 3*1
   An. I knew 'twould be a bald conclusion: but soft, | who wafts vs
   yonder.   502
   But soft, my doore is lockt; goe bid them let vs in.   651
   Luc. Oh soft sir, hold you still: 859
   But soft I see the Goldsmith; get thee gone,   1001
SOFTLY = *1
   Mar. Speake softly, yonder as I thinke he walkes.   1472
SOLD = 1
   *It would make a man mad as a Bucke to be so bought | and sold.   727
SOLE = 1
   My sole earths heauen, and my heauens claime.   853
SOLEMNE = 1
   It hath in solemne Synodes beene decreed,   17
SOLINUS = 1
   Marchant. | Proceed *Solinus* to procure my fall,   4
SOME = 29*2
   E.Dro. I haue some markes of yours vpon my pate: 247
   Some of my Mistris markes vpon my shoulders: 248
   Ant. Vpon my life by some deuise or other,   261
   Luc. Perhaps some Merchant hath inuited him,   278
   Adr. But were you wedded, you wold beare some sway   302
   Adr. How if your husband start some other where?   304
   For Gods sake send some other messenger.   353
   Some other Mistresse hath thy sweet aspects: 506
   Plead on your part some cause to you vnknowne;   752
   Ang. Ile meet you at that place some houre hence.   783
   Anti. Do so, this iest shall cost me some expence. | *Exeunt*.   784
   Muffle your false loue with some shew of blindnesse: 794
   Anti. Then she beares some bredth?   903
   Besides I haue some businesse in the towne,   1018
   Either send the Chaine, or send me by some token.   1042
   Some tender monie to me, some inuite me;   1187
   Some other giue me thankes for kindnesses;   1188

SOME *cont.*

Some offer me Commodities to buy.	1189
Some blessed power deliuer vs from hence.	1226
S.Dro. Some diuels aske but the parings of ones naile,	1254
They must be bound and laide in some darke roome.	1382
And not without some scandall to your selfe,	1479
Some get within him, take his sword away:	1499
This is some Priorie, in, or we are spoyl'd.	*Exeunt to the Priorie.*	1502
Buried some deere friend, hath not else his eye	1517
Namely, some loue that drew him oft from home.	1523
Go some of you, knocke at the Abbey gate,	1637
And sure (vnlesse you send some present helpe)	1649
Yet hath my night of life some memorie:	1795
My wasting lampes some fading glimmer left;	1796

SOMETHING = 1*3

S.Dro. Marry sir, for this something that you gaue me | for nothing.	446
for something. But say sir, is it dinner time?	449
Anti. There is something in the winde, that we can-|not get in.	721
Ant. Go fetch me something, Ile break ope the gate.	729

SOMETIMES = 1

Antiph. Because that I familiarlie sometimes	421

SOMEWHERE = 1

And from the Mart he's somewhere gone to dinner:	279

SOMMERS = 1

Fiue Sommers haue I spent in farthest *Greece,*	135

SONG = 1

Ile stop mine eares against the Mermaids song.	954

SONNE = 8

My woes end likewise with the euening Sonne.	31
At length the sonne gazing vpon the earth,	91
Mar.Fat. Vnlesse the feare of death doth make me | dote, I see my sonne *Antipholus* and *Dromio.*	1671
In seuen short yeares, that heere my onely sonne	1790
Tell me, thou art my sonne *Antipholus.*	1799
Thou know'st we parted, but perhaps my sonne,	1802
If thou art she, tell me, where is that sonne	1839
By force tooke *Dromio,* and my sonne from them,	1844

SONNES = 4

A ioyfull mother of two goodly sonnes:	54
I bought, and brought vp to attend my sonnes.	61
That bore thee at a burthen two faire sonnes?	1829
Of you my sonnes, and till this present houre	1891

SOONE = 9*1

And soone, and safe, arriued where I was:	52
Vnwilling I agreed, alas, too soone wee came aboord.	64
Lest that your goods too soone be confiscate:	164
I craue your pardon, soone at fiue a clocke;	189
What now? How chance thou art return'd so soone.	207
E.Dro. Return'd so soone, rather approacht too late:	208
A sunnie looke of his, would soone repaire.	375
And soone at supper time Ile visit you,	968
Perchance I will be there as soone as you.	1022
S.Dro. You sent me for a ropes end as soone,	1087

SOONER = 1*1

If it proue so, I will be gone the sooner:	269
S.Dro. The plainer dealer, the sooner lost; yet he loo-|seth it in a kinde of iollitie.	482

SOOTH = 2
   Dro. Sir sooth to say, you did not dine at home.   1354
   Adr. Is't good to sooth him in these contraries?   1366
SORCERERS = 2
   Darke working Sorcerers that change the minde: 265
   And lapland Sorcerers inhabite here.   1194
SORCERESSE = 1
   Thou art, as you are all a sorceresse: 1249
SORE = 1
   E.Dro. If you went in paine Master, this knaue wold | goe sore.   713
SORRIE = 1
   The place of depth, and sorrie execution,   1590
SORROW = 2
   Ile vtter what my sorrow giues me ieaue.   39
   What to delight in, what to sorrow for,   109
SORROWES = 1
   Which of these sorrowes is he subiect too?   1521
SORROWEST = 1
   Duke. And for the sake of them thou sorrowest for,   124
SORRY = 2
   Gold. I am sorry Sir that I haue hindred you,   1464
   Mar. I am sorry now that I did draw on him.   1510
SOT = 1
   Dromio, thou *Dromio*, thou snaile, thou slug, thou sot.   589
SOUERAIGNE = 1
   Possest with such a gentle soueraigne grace,   950
SOUGHT = 1
   The Sailors sought for safety by our boate,   79
SOULE = 5*1
   Her part, poore soule, seeming as burdened   110
   My soule should sue as aduocate for thee: 148
   A wretched soule bruis'd with aduersitie,   308
   She that doth call me husband, euen my soule   948
   Adr. Oh that thou wer't not, poore distressed soule.   1343
   To day did dine together: so befall my soule,   1685
SOULES = 2*2
   Indued with intellectuall sence and soules,   296
   Against my soules pure truth, why labour you,   824
   *One that before the Iudgme(n)t carries poore soules to hel.   1149
   Luc. God helpe poore soules, how idlely doe they | talke.   1422
SOULE-KILLING = 1
   Soule-killing Witches, that deforme the bodie: 266
SOUND = 4
   An. For what reason. | *S.Dro.* For two, and sound ones to.   484
   An. Nay not sound I pray you. | *S.Dro.* Sure ones then.   486
   I tell you 'twill sound harshly in her eares.   1287
   I long that we were safe and sound aboord.   1453
SOWER = 1
   Adr. This weeke he hath beene heauie, sower sad,   1512
SPAINE = 1*1
   Ant. Where *Spaine*? | *Dro.* Faith I saw it not: but I felt it hot in her
   breth.   920
   *to the hot breath of Spaine, who sent whole Ar- | madoes of Carrects to
   be ballast at her nose.   925
SPAKE = 3*1
   Luc. Spake hee so doubtfully, thou couldst not feele | his meaning.   326
   S.Dro. What answer sir? when spake I such a word?   408

SPAKE *cont.*

Vnlesse I spake, or look'd, or touch'd, or caru'd to thee.	513
S.Dro. I neuer spake with her in all my life.	559

SPARE = 2

Had fastned him vnto a small spare Mast,	82
I would not spare my brother in this case,	1065

SPARING = *1

Anti. I, to a niggardly Host, and more sparing guest:	648

SPEAK = *1

Fa. Most mighty Duke, vouchsafe me speak a word:	1762

SPEAKE = 10*4

Then I to speake my griefes vnspeakeable:	36
Adr. Say, didst thou speake with him? knowst thou | his minde?	322
I could not speake with *Dromio*, since at first	399
Looke sweet, speake faire, become disloyaltie:	797
Teach me deere creature how to thinke and speake:	820
*may not speake of, without he say sir reuerence, I haue	882
Adr. Did'st speake him faire? | *Luc.* Haue patience I beseech.	1121
*vs no harme: you saw they speake vs faire, giue vs gold:	1455
Mar. Speake softly, yonder as I thinke he walkes.	1472
Good sir draw neere to me, Ile speake to him:	1476
Duke. Speake freely *Siracusian* what thou wilt.	1765
Speake olde *Egeon*, if thou bee'st the man	1827
Oh if thou bee'st the same *Egeon*, speake:	1830
And speake vnto the same *Aemilia*.	1831

SPEAKES = *2

Ant. To mee shee speakes, shee moues mee for her | theame;	575
S.Ant. He speakes to me, I am your master *Dromio*.	1903

SPEAKST = *1

Adr. Dissembling Villain, thou speak'st false in both	1388

SPEECH = 1

First, he did praise my beautie, then my speech.	1120

SPEED = 1

Was carried with more speed before the winde,	112

SPENDS = *1

S.Dro. The one to saue the money that he spends in	491

SPENT = 1

Fiue Sommers haue I spent in farthest *Greece*,	135

SPHERICALL = *1

*to hippe: she is sphericall, like a globe: I could find out | Countries in her.	905

SPIGHT = 2*1

This is the Fairie land, oh spight of spights,	584
(Be it for nothing but to spight my wife)	779
Adr. He meant he did me none: the more my spight	1111

SPIGHTS = 1

This is the Fairie land, oh spight of spights,	584

SPIRIT = 1

And which the spirit? Who deciphers them?	1819

SPIT = 2

The Capon burnes, the Pig fals from the spit;	209
Wouldst thou not spit at me, and spurne at me,	529

SPLITTED = 2

Our helpefull ship was splitted in the midst;	106
Hast thou so crack'd and splitted my poore tongue	1789

SPOONE = 1*1
   S.Dro. Master, if do expect spoon-meate, or bespeake | a long
   spoone. | *Ant*. Why *Dromio*?   1243
   S.Dro. Marrie he must haue a long spoone that must | eate with the
   diuell.   1246
SPOON-MEATE = *1
   S.Dro. Master, if do expect spoon-meate, or bespeake | a long
   spoone. | *Ant*. Why *Dromio*?   1243
SPORT = 5
   When the sunne shines, let foolish gnats make sport,   425
   'Tis holy sport to be a little vaine,   813
   But sirrah, you shall buy this sport as deere,   1069
   That would behold in me this shamefull sport.   1393
   In food, in sport, and life-preseruing rest   1552
SPORTIUE = 1
   Ant. I am not in a sportiue humor now: 223
SPORTS = 1
   Thou sayest his sports were hindred by thy bralles.   1546
SPOUSE = 1
   Drew me from kinde embracements of my spouse;   47
SPOYLD = 1
   This is some Priorie, in, or we are spoyl'd. | *Exeunt to the Priorie*. 1502
SPREAD = 1
   Spread ore the siluer waues thy golden haires;   835
SPRED = 1
   Luc. *Dromio*, goe bid the seruants spred for dinner.   582
SPRIGHTS = 1
   We talke with Goblins, Owles and Sprights;   585
SPRING = 1
   Euen in the spring of Loue, thy Loue-springs rot?   789
SPRINGETH = 1
   Luc. It is a fault that springeth from your eie.   842
SPRINGS = 1
   Euen in the spring of Loue, thy Loue-springs rot?   789
SPRUNG = 1
   Sprung from the rancorous outrage of your Duke,   10
SPURNE = 4
   That like a foot-ball you doe spurne me thus: 359
   You spurne me hence, and he will spurne me hither,   360
   Wouldst thou not spit at me, and spurne at me,   529
STAFFE = 1
   Shall I set in my staffe.   687
STAIES = 3
   My Mistris and her sister staies for you.   241
   That staies but till her Owner comes aboord,   1075
   What ship of *Epidamium* staies for me.   1083
STAIND = 1
   And teare the stain'd skin of my Harlot brow,   531
STALE = 1
   And feedes from home; poore I am but his stale.   377
STAND = 2*4
   E.Dro. They stand at the doore, Master, bid them | welcome hither. 719
   *Your cake here is warme within: you stand here in the | cold. 725
   Then I stand debted to this Gentleman,   1014
   Against thee presently, if thou dar'st stand: 1495
   Duke. Come stand by me, feare nothing: guard with | Halberds. 1659
   Duke. Stay, stand apart, I know not which is which.   1850

STANDS = 3
    That stands on tricks, when I am vndispos'd: 245
    Anti. In what part of her body stands *Ireland*?   907
    Consider how it stands vpon my credit.   1055
STARKE = 2
    E.Dro. I meane not Cuckold mad, | But sure he is starke mad: 335
    I thinke you are all mated, or starke mad.   1760
START = 1
    Adr. How if your husband start some other where?   304
STARUE = 1
    Whil'st I at home starue for a merrie looke: 364
STATE = 3
    That's not my fault, hee's master of my state.   371
    Whose weaknesse married to thy stranger state,   569
    And to thy state of darknesse hie thee straight,   1340
STATUTE = 1
    According to the statute of the towne,   168
STATUTES = 2
    Haue seal'd his rigorous statutes with their blouds,   13
    Against the Lawes and Statutes of this Towne,   1595
STAY = 6*3
    And stay there *Dromio*, till I come to thee;   172
    The chaine vnfinish'd made me stay thus long.   960
    Ile to the Mart, and there for *Dromio* stay,   978
    Blowes faire from land: they stay for nought at all,   1080
    Dro. Faith stay heere this night, they will surely do   1454
    *I could finde in my heart to stay heere still, and turne | Witch.   1458
    Ant. I will not stay to night for all the Towne,   1460
    E.Dro. I Sir am *Dromio*, pray let me stay.   1821
    Duke. Stay, stand apart, I know not which is which.   1850
STAYES = 3
    E.Dro. What patch is made our Porter? my Master | stayes in the
    street.   658
    For he is bound to Sea, and stayes but for it.   1016
    Both winde and tide stayes for this Gentleman,   1032
STAYING = 1
    Who but for staying on our Controuersie,   1484
STEALES = 1
    Mar. The houre steales on, I pray you sir dispatch.   1038
STEALING = 1
    That time comes stealing on by night and day?   1175
STEALTH = 1
    Or if you like else-where doe it by stealth,   793
STEELE = 1*1
    *steele, she had transform'd me to a Curtull dog, & made | me turne
    i'th wheele.   935
    On whose hard heart is button'd vp with steele: 1143
STIFFE = 1
    For with long trauaile I am stiffe and wearie. | Get thee away.   177
STIGMATICALL = 1
    Stigmaticall in making worse in minde.   1128
STILL = 7*1
    Luc. Because their businesse still lies out adore.   285
    I see the Iewell best enamaled | Will loose his beautie: yet the gold
    bides still   385
    Luc. Oh soft sir, hold you still: 859
    Adr. I cannot, nor I will not hold me still.   1123

STILL *cont*.
Anti. Wilt thou still talke? *Beats Dro*.	1327
*I could finde in my heart to stay heere still, and turne | Witch.	1458
Still did I tell him, it was vilde and bad.	1536
I see we still did meete each others man,	1875

STIRRE = 2
Ab. Be patient, for I will not let him stirre,	1571
I will determine this before I stirre.	1639

STIRRING = 1
Now in the stirring passage of the day,	760

STOCKS = *1
Luce. What needs all that, and a paire of stocks in the | towne?	704

STOLNE = *1
E.Dro. O villaine, thou hast stolne both mine office | and my name,	673

STOMACKE = 2
You come not home, because you haue no stomacke:	214
You haue no stomacke, hauing broke your fast:	215

STONE = *1
*a rush, a haire, a drop of blood, a pin, a nut, a cherrie-|stone:	1255

STOOD = 1*1
*no whitenesse in them. But I guesse, it stood in her chin	918
Anti. Where stood *Belgia*, the *Netherlands*? | *Dro*. Oh sir, I did not looke so low. To conclude,	927

STOP = 2
Ant. Stop in your winde sir, tell me this I pray?	218
Ile stop mine eares against the Mermaids song.	954

STORE = *1
*Dost thou coniure for wenches, that y calst for such store,	656

STORIE = 1
Duke. Why heere begins his Morning storie right:	1832

STORIES = 1
To tell sad stories of my owne mishaps.	123

STORMES = 1
Such as sea-faring men prouide for stormes:	83

STORY = 1
But heere must end the story of my life,	140

STRAIGHT = 5*1
And floating straight, obedient to the streame,	89
If any ship put out, then straight away. *Exit*.	979
To *Adriana* Villaine hie thee straight:	1091
Adr. Go *Dromio*, there's the monie, beare it straight,	1179
And to thy state of darknesse hie thee straight,	1340
Straight after did I meete him with a Chaine.	1436

STRANGE = 6*1
And, which was strange, the one so like the other,	55
Adri. I, I, *Antipholus*, looke strange and frowne,	505
Thy selfe I call it, being strange to me:	516
As strange vnto your towne, as to your talke,	544
To know the reason of this strange restraint:	758
Father. Why looke you strange on me? you know | me well.	1775
Haue written strange defeatures in my face:	1780

STRANGER = 3
Whose weaknesse married to thy stranger state,	569
Good Signior take the stranger to my house,	1019
Luc. Then swore he that he was a stranger heere.	1112

STRANGERS = 1
We being strangers here, how dar'st thou trust	225

STRAUNGE = *1
   Duke. Why this is straunge: Go call the Abbesse hi-|ther.   1758
STRAYD = 1
   Stray'd his affection in vnlawfull loue,   1518
STREAME = 1
   And floating straight, obedient to the streame,   89
STREET = 2
   E.Dro. What patch is made our Porter? my Master | stayes in the
   street.   658
   I went to seeke him. In the street I met him,   1702
STREETE = 2
   Tell her, I am arrested in the streete,   1095
   That desp'rately he hurried through the streete,   1612
STREETS = 1
   When in the streets he meetes such Golden gifts: 977
STRENGTH = 2
   Makes me with thy strength to communicate: 570
   Euen in the strength and height of iniurie: 1676
STRIFE = 1
   When the sweet breath of flatterie conquers strife.   814
STRIKE = 1
   And strike you home without a messenger.   232
STRIKES = *1
   *It was two ere I left him, and now the clocke strikes one.   1166
STRIUES = 1
   Enter three or foure, and offer to binde him: | *Hee striues.*   1394
STROAKES = 1
   As you loue stroakes, so iest with me againe: 403
STRONG = 2*1
   If by strong hand you offer to breake in   759
   Pinch. More company, the fiend is strong within him   1398
   Anon I wot not, by what strong escape   1620
STRONGER = 1
   S.Dro. Not on a band, but on a stronger thing: 1162
STROOKE = *2
   E.Dro. Nay, hee strooke so plainly, I could too well   328
   E.Dro. So come helpe, well strooke, there was blow | for blow.   696
STRUCKEN = 1
   The clocke hath strucken twelue vpon the bell: 210
STRUMPET = 1
   Ant. Oh most vnhappie strumpet.   1416
STRUMPETED = 1
   Being strumpeted by thy contagion: 539
STUFFE = 1*3
   Ant. Come to the Centaur, fetch our stuffe from | thence: 1451
   Therefore away, to get our stuffe aboord. *Exeunt*   1461
   S.Dro. Mast.(er) shall I fetch your stuffe from shipbord?   1900
   E.An. Dromio, what stuffe of mine hast thou imbarkt   1901
SUBBORND = *1
   Ant. Thou hast subborn'd the Goldsmith to arrest | mee.   1369
SUBIECT = 2
   Which of these sorrowes is he subiect too?   1521
   Alone, it was the subiect of my Theame: 1534
SUBIECTS = 1
   Are their males subiects, and at their controules: 293
SUBSTANCE = 1
   Thy substance, valued at the highest rate,   27

SUBSTANTIALL = *1
  An. But your reason was not substantiall, why there | is no time to
  recouer.   498
SUCCESSION = 1
  For slander liues vpon succession: 766
SUCH = 13*6
  Of such a burthen Male, twins both alike: 59
  My wife, not meanely prowd of two such boyes,   62
  Such as sea-faring men prouide for stormes: 83
  And manie such like liberties of sinne: 268
  That in such haste I sent to seeke his Master?   276
  Ad. Vnfeeling fools can with such wrongs dispence: 379
  S.Dro. What answer sir? when spake I such a word?   408
  Ant. Why, is Time such a niggard of haire, being (as   471
  *Dost thou coniure for wenches, that y calst for such store,   656
  He gaines by death, that hath such meanes to die: 838
  Dro. Marry sir, such claime as you would lay to your   876
  Dro. A very reuerent body: I such a one, as a man   881
  Possest with such a gentle soueraigne grace,   950
  Of such inchanting presence and discourse,   951
  When in the streets he meetes such Golden gifts: 977
  Luc. Who would be iealous then of such a one?   1129
  *me thinkes they are such a gentle Nation, that but for   1456
  Duke. But had he such a Chaine of thee, or no?   1733
  After so long greefe such Natiuitie.   1896
SUCKE = 1
  They'll sucke our breath, or pinch vs blacke and blew.   587
SUE = 1
  My soule should sue as aduocate for thee: 148
SUFFER = 2*1
  By the wrongs I suffer, and the blowes I beare,   635
  *I am thy prisoner, wilt thou suffer them to make a res- | cue?   1401
  And will not suffer vs to fetch him out,   1629
SUFFERD = 1
  Haue suffer'd wrong. Goe, keepe vs companie,   1888
SUIT = *1
  Luc. With words, that in an honest suit might moue.   1119
SUITE = 4*2
  Mar. Well Officer, arrest him at my suite.   1056
  Offic. I do arrest you sir, you heare the suite.   1067
  Adr. What is he arrested? tell me at whose suite?   1153
  S.Dro. I know not at whose suite he is arested well;   1154
  *but is in a suite of buffe which rested him, that can I tell,   1155
  Say now, whose suite is he arrested at?   1425
SUITES = *1
  *suites of durance: he that sets vp his rest to doe more ex- | ploits   1210
SUM = 4
  Mar. You know since Pentecost the sum is due,   982
  Gold. Euen iust the sum that I do owe to you,   988
  Either consent to pay this sum for me, | Or I attach you by this Officer.   1060
  And pay the sum that may deliuer me.   1764
SUMME = 3*1
  Beg thou, or borrow, to make vp the summe,   156
  Disburse the summe, on the receit thereof,   1021
  Adr. I know the man: what is the summe he owes?   1428
  If any friend will pay the summe for him,   1603

SUMMERS *see* sommers
SUN = *1
  Ant. For gazing on your beames faire sun being by.   843
SUNDER = 1
  Till gnawing with my teeth my bonds in sunder,   1726
SUNNE *see also* sonne = 2
  Dies ere the wearie sunne set in the West: 169
  When the sunne shines, let foolish gnats make sport,   425
SUNNIE = 1
  A sunnie looke of his, would soone repaire.   375
SUPPER = 1
  And soone at supper time Ile visit you,   968
SUPPING = *1
  Ant. Auoid then fiend, what tel'st thou me of sup-|(ping?   1248
SUPPOSED = 1
  And that supposed by the common rowt   762
SUPPOSITION = 1
  And in that glorious supposition thinke,   837
SURE = 11*2
  Sure *Luciana* it is two a clocke.   277
  E.Dro. Why Mistresse, sure my Master is horne mad.   333
  E.Dro. I meane not Cuckold mad, | But sure he is starke mad: 335
  An. Nay not sound I pray you. | *S.Dro.* Sure ones then.   486
  An. Nay, not sure in a thing falsing.   488
  Vntill I know this sure vncertaintie,   580
  Sure these are but imaginarie wiles,   1193
  Anon I'me sure the Duke himselfe in person   1588
  And sure (vnlesse you send some present helpe)   1649
  Curt. As sure (my Liege) as I do see your Grace.   1757
  Fath. I am sure you both of you remember me.   1771
  Dro. No trust me sir, nor I. | *Fa.* I am sure thou dost?   1784
  E.Dromio. I sir, but I am sure I do not, and whatso-|euer   1786
SURELY = 1*1
  But surely Master not a ragge of Monie.   1374
  Dro. Faith stay heere this night, they will surely do   1454
SUSPECT = 1
  And draw within the compasse of suspect   748
SWART = *1
  Dro. Swart like my shoo, but her face nothing like   893
SWAY = *1
  Adr. But were you wedded, you wold bear some sway   302
SWEARE = 1
  There did this periur'd Goldsmith sweare me downe,   1704
SWEATS = *1
  *so cleane kept: for why? she sweats a man may goe o-|uer-shooes in
  the grime of it.   894
SWEET = 7*3
  Some other Mistresse hath thy sweet aspects: 506
  Looke sweet, speake faire, become disloyaltie: 797
  When the sweet breath of flatterie conquers strife.   814
  Oh traine me not sweet Mermaide with thy note,   832
  Ant. As good to winke sweet loue, as looke on night.   846
  My foode, my fortune, and my sweet hopes aime;   852
  Ant. Call thy selfe sister sweet, for I am thee: 855
  Dro. Here goe: the deske, the purse, sweet now make | haste.   1136
  Sweet recreation barr'd, what doth ensue | But moodie and dull
  melancholly,   1547

SWEET *cont.*
   *E.*Ant.* Iustice (sweet Prince) against y Woman there: 1673
SWEETE = *1
   *S.*Anti.* Sweete Mistris, what your name is else I | know not;   815
SWEET-FACD = 1
   I see by you, I am a sweet-fac'd youth,   1910
SWEET-SAUOURD = 1
   That neuer meat sweet-sauour'd in thy taste,   512
SWORD = 3
   Some get within him, take his sword away: 1499
   And thereupon I drew my sword on you: 1739
   Nor euer didst thou draw thy sword on me: 1743
SWORDS = 3
   Adr. And come with naked swords,   1443
   S.Ant. I see these Witches are affraid of swords.   1448
   Each one with irefull passion, with drawne swords 1623
SWORE = 1*2
   **Dromio,* swore I was assur'd to her, told me what priuie 930
   Luc. Then swore he that he was a stranger heere. 1112
   **Adr.* And true he swore, though yet forsworne hee | were. 1113
SWORNE = *1
   **Mar.* Besides, I will be sworne these eares of mine, 1736
SYMPATHIZED *see* simpathized
SYNODES = 1
   It hath in solemne Synodes beene decreed,   17
SYRACUSA = 1
   In *Syracusa* was I borne, and wedde   40
SYRACUSIAN = 1
   This very day a *Syracusian* Marchant | Is apprehended for a riuall here, 165
TABLE = 1
   A table full of welcome, makes scarce one dainty dish. 642
TAILOR = 1
   Euen now a tailor cal'd me in his shop,   1190
TAINTED = 1
   Beare a faire presence, though your heart be tainted, 799
TAKE = 13*5
   Iaylor, take him to thy custodie. | *Iaylor.* I will my Lord. 158
   Dro. Many a man would take you at your word,   179
   Being forbid? There take you that sir knaue.   257
   Nay, and you will not sir, Ile take my heeles.   259
   *Thinkst y I iest? hold, take thou that, & that. *Beats Dro.* 418
   And take vnmingled thence that drop againe | Without addition or
   diminishing,   522
   As take from me thy selfe, and not me too.   524
   *But though my cates be meane, take them in good part, 649
   And as a bud Ile take thee, and there lie: 836
   Good Signior take the stranger to my house,   1019
   And with you take the Chaine, and bid my wife   1020
   Some get within him, take his sword away: 1499
   *S.*Dro.* Runne master run, for Gods sake take a house, 1501
   And take perforce my husband from the Abbesse. 1586
   Whil'st to take order for the wrongs I went,   1618
   He cries for you, and vowes if he can take you,   1655
   *E.*Ant.* There take it, and much thanks for my good | cheere. 1881
   **Abb.* Renowned Duke, vouchsafe to take the paines 1883
TAKEN *see also* tane = 2
   And in our sight they three were taken vp   113

TAKEN *cont.*
And the twin *Dromio*, all were taken vp;   1842
TAKES = 1*1
  Adr. Looke when I serue him so, he takes it thus.   286
  *he sir, that takes pittie on decaied men, and giues them   1209
TALE = 1
  Is a mad tale he told to day at dinner,   1271
TALKE = 4
  As strange vnto your towne, as to your talke,   544
  We talke with Goblins, Owles and Sprights;   585
  Anti. Wilt thou still talke? *Beats Dro.*   1327
  Luc. God helpe poore soules, how idlely doe they | talke. 1422
TALKS = *1
  E.Ant. Who talks within there? hoa, open the dore.   662
TALLOW = *1
  *warrant, her ragges and the Tallow in them, will burne   889
TANE = 2
  I thought to haue tane you at the *Porpentine*,   959
  And I was tane for him, and he for me,   1876
TAPISTRIE = 1
  That's couer'd o're with Turkish Tapistrie,   1093
TARDIE = 1
  Adr. Say, is your tardie master now at hand?   319
TARRY = *1
  *were you hindred by the Serieant to tarry for the *Hoy*   1221
TARTAR = 1
  S.Dro. No, he's in Tartar limbo, worse then hell: 1141
TASKE = *1
  Mer. A heauier taske could not haue beene impos'd,   35
TASTE = 1
  That neuer meat sweet-sauour'd in thy taste,   512
TAUNT = *1
  Anti. Did not her Kitchen maide raile, taunt, and | scorne me? 1360
TEACH = 3
  Teach sinne the carriage of a holy Saint,   800
  Teach me deere creature how to thinke and speake: 820
  And teach your eares to list me with more heede: 1090
TEARE = 2
  Ah doe not teare away thy selfe from me;   519
  And teare the stain'd skin of my Harlot brow,   531
TEARES = 2
  To drowne me in thy sister floud of teares: 833
  And neuer rise vntill my teares and prayers   1584
TEARMD = 1
  Worthily tearm'd them mercilesse to vs: 102
TEETH = 2
  Ant. Yea, dost thou ieere & flowt me in the teeth?   417
  Till gnawing with my teeth my bonds in sunder,   1726
TEL = 1
  Mess. Mistris, vpon my life I tel you true,   1653
TELL = 21*5
  To tell sad stories of my owne mishaps.   123
  Ant. Stop in your winde sir, tell me this I pray?   218
  Tell me, and dally not, where is the monie?   224
  And tell me how thou hast dispos'd thy charge.   238
  What meanes this iest, I pray you Master tell me?   416
  Ant. Shall I tell you why?   437

TELL *cont.*
*Your owne hand-writing would tell you what I thinke. 632
S.Dro. Right sir, Ile tell you when, and you'll tell | me wherefore. 663
Luce. Faith no, hee comes too late, and so tell your | Master. 683
Luce. Haue at you with another, that's when? can | you tell? 688
Luce. Can you tell for whose sake? 699
Ant. What I should thinke of this, I cannot tell: 973
Giue her this key, and tell her in the Deske 1092
Tell her, I am arrested in the streete, 1095
Adr. What is he arrested? tell me at whose suite? 1153
*but is in a suite of buffe which rested him, that can I tell, 1155
Tell me, was he arested on a band? 1161
And tell his wife, that being Lunaticke, 1276
I tell you 'twill sound harshly in her eares. 1287
Still did I tell him, it was vilde and bad. 1536
But tell me yet, dost thou not know my voice? 1781
Tell me, thou art my sonne *Antipholus.* 1799
Duke. I tell thee *Siracusian,* twentie yeares 1807
If thou art she, tell me, where is that sonne 1839
What then became of them, I cannot tell: 1846
TELLER = 1
A thred-bare Iugler, and a Fortune-teller, 1716
TELS = 1
But she tels to your Highnesse simple truth. 1688
TELST = *1
Ant. Auoid then fiend, what tel'st thou me of sup- | (ping? 1248
TEMPT = 2*1
Adr. Ah *Luciana,* did he tempt thee so? 1104
Adr. With what perswasion did he tempt thy loue? 1118
Ant. Sathan auoide, I charge thee tempt me not. 1231
TENDER = 2
Some tender monie to me, some inuite me; 1187
He shall not die, so much we tender him. 1604
TERTIUS *l.*616 = 1
TH *see also* by'th', i'th = 2
Hath homelie age th'alluring beauty tooke 365
Th'vnuiolated honor of your wife. 749
THAN *see* then
THANKE = 4*1
*tongue, I thanke him, I bare home vpon my shoulders: 349
*season, when in the why and the wherefore, is neither | rime nor
reason. Well sir, I thanke you. 443
Ant. Thanke me sir, for what? 445
I will discharge my bond, and thanke you too. 994
But he I thanke him gnaw'd in two my cords, 1769
THANKES = 1
Some other giue me thankes for kindnesses; 1188
THANKS = *1
E.Ant. There take it, and much thanks for my good | cheere. 1881
THAT *see also* y *l.*37 50 57 76 92 96 98 107 122 130 139 164 170 174 182
197 200 216 219 220 244 245 254 255 257 264 265 266 276 307 312 *320
*329 *348 359 372 383 387 388 390 407 *418 421 435 *446 450 451 *460
466 *473 *491 *492 509 510 511 512 515 517 522 527 552 566 621 623
624 625 627 *630 636 *643 *656 *669 *704 *707 *721 762 764 772 778
783 787 808 828 837 838 840 842 *844 *873 *877 *878 896 919 *933 945
947 948 961 975 984 988 990 *996 998 *1005 1049 1062 1075 1096 1098
1106 1112 1117 *1119 *1146 1148 *1149 *1155 1164 1167 1175 1191

THAT *cont.*
   *1200 *1201 *1202 *1206 *1207 *1209 *1210 *1213 *1214 *1220 *1222
1230 *1236 *1246 *1262 1269 1276 1286 1290 1291 *1297 1299 *1306
*1343 1365 1377 1379 1387 1393 *1449 1453 *1456 *1457 1464 1470
*1474 1477 1488 1491 1507 1510 1523 1524 1537 1541 1607 1612 1619
1621 1630 1652 1662 1667 1670 1675 1678 1696 1703 1705 1732 1751
1754 1764 1767 1790 1804 1805 1828 1829 1839 1840 1847 *1853 1858
*1865 1880 1886 1887 *1902 1904 1907 = 154*59

THATS = 6*4
That's not my fault, hee's master of my state.	371
Anti. And welcome more common, for thats nothing | but words.	644
Luce. Haue at you with another, that's when? can | you tell?	688
Ant. Thy sisters sister. | *Luc.* That's my sister.	848
Anti. That's a fault that water will mend.	896
Anti. What's her name? | *Dro. Nell* Sir: but her name is three quarters, that's	899
Ang. Mr *Antipholus.* | *Anti.* I that's my name.	956
That's couer'd o're with Turkish Tapistrie,	1093
*thereof comes, that the wenches say God dam me, That's	1236
S.Dro. Not I sir, you are my elder. | *E.Dro.* That's a question, how shall we trie it.	1912

THE *see also* th', y = 343*95

THEAME = 2
Ant. To mee shee speakes, shee moues mee for her | theame;	575
Alone, it was the subiect of my Theame:	1534

THEE *l.*100 148 152 153 172 177 235 312 315 342 513 525 527 *551 552
571 *655 *657 *735 *737 745 836 855 856 875 937 1001 1062 1068 1085
1086 1091 1096 1104 1205 1231 1250 1282 1296 *1338 1340 1341 1385
1411 *1418 *1490 1491 1495 1496 1607 1634 1667 1668 1670 1733 1807
1810 1829 1840 = 57*9

THEEFE = 1
Nay, he's a theefe too: haue you not heard men say,	1174

THEFT = 1
If I be in debt and theft, and a Serieant in the way,	1176

THEIR *l.*12 13 60 116 117 118 119 120 282 *284 285 293 298 299 370 *924
999 1081 1102 1185 1381 1520 1615 1894 1911 = 25*2

THEM *l.*77 102 124 126 204 234 251 329 474 489 586 *649 651 *719 *889
*918 *1208 *1209 1291 *1401 1444 1500 1626 1627 1650 1690 1712 1815
1819 1844 1846 1874 = 25*9

THEN *l.*36 80 157 176 186 193 234 *284 297 299 366 369 373 *440 453
476 486 489 515 517 540 560 *792 811 819 827 828 890 903 *904 969
979 1014 *1023 1076 1112 1115 1120 1129 1131 1141 *1172 1211 *1220
*1248 1539 1554 *1562 1626 1670 1697 1710 1722 1740 1846 1862 *1914
1916 = 49*10

THENCE = 5
And take vnmingled thence that drop againe | Without addition or diminishing,	522
Ant. And did not I in rage depart from thence?	1363
Ant. Come to the Centaur, fetch our stuffe from | thence:	1451
By rushing in their houses: bearing thence	1615
They fell vpon me, bound me, bore me thence,	1723

THERE *l.*53 170 172 201 257 350 *442 *494 *498 *662 *680 *696 *710
*721 772 780 836 978 1022 1094 1217 *1218 1337 1358 1359 1619 1664
*1673 1696 1704 1725 *1752 *1881 1905 1906 = 23*12

THEREFORE = 13
Therefore by Law thou art condemn'd to die.	29
And therefore homeward did they bend their course.	120

THEREFORE *cont.*

Therefore Marchant, Ile limit thee this day	153
Mer. Therefore giue out you are of *Epidamium,*	163
therefore to the worlds end, will haue bald followers.	501
I know thou canst, and therefore see thou doe it.	534
And therefore 'tis hie time that I were hence:	947
Therefore make present satisfaction,	986
If it were chain'd together: and therefore came not.	1009
Therefore away, to get our stuffe aboord. *Exeunt*	1461
And therefore let me haue him home with me.	1570
Therefore depart, and leaue him heere with me.	1577
Therefore most gracious Duke with thy command,	1631

THEREOF = 4*1

Disburse the summe, on the receit thereof,	1021
*thereof comes, that the wenches say God dam me, That's	1236
Ab. And thereof came it, that the man was mad.	1537
And thereof comes it that his head is light.	1541
Thereof the raging fire of feauer bred,	1544

THERES = 7*4

Adr. There's none but asses will be bridled so.	288
There's nothing situate vnder heauens eye,	290
*Ant. Well sir, learne to iest in good time, there's a | time for all things.	458
*S.Dro. There's no time for a man to recouer his haire | that growes bald by nature.	466
*Ant. Why, but theres manie a man hath more haire | then wit.	476
For there's the house: That chaine will I bestow	778
Anti. There's none but Witches do inhabite heere,	946
But this I thinke, there's no man is so vaine,	974
Dro. Master, there's a Barke of *Epidamium,*	1074
*Adr. Go *Dromio,* there's the monie, beare it straight,	1179
There's not a man I meete but doth salute me	1184

THEREUPON = 2

And thereupon I drew my sword on you:	1739
And thereupon these errors are arose.	1877

THEREWITHALL = 1

And therewithall tooke measure of my body.	1192

THERS = *1

*For a fish without a finne, ther's a fowle without a fether,	743

THESE *l.**233 294 *431 610 1193 *1344 1351 1366 1392 1448 *1490 1521
1522 1558 1730 1735 *1736 1742 1798 1817 1818 1833 1834 1836 1877
*1878 = 23*6

THEY = 19*12

THEYL = 1

Off. Away, they'l kill vs. | *Exeunt omnes, as fast as may be, frighted.*	1446

THEYLL = 3

They'll goe or come; if so, be patient Sister.	283
They'll sucke our breath, or pinch vs blacke and blew.	587
Ile knocke else-where, to see if they'll disdaine me.	782

THIEFE = 1

What simple thiefe brags of his owne attaine?	802

THIN = 1

*E.Dro. You would say so Master, if your garments | were thin.	723

THINE = 5

So great a charge from thine owne custodie.	226
That neuer words were musicke to thine eare,	509
That neuer obiect pleasing in thine eye,	510
Come I will fasten on this sleeue of thine:	567

THINE *cont.*
 Ant. Thou hast thine owne forme. | *S.Dro.* No, I am an Ape.   593
THING = 4
 Commends me to the thing I cannot get: 198
 An. Nay, not sure in a thing falsing.   488
 S.Dro. Not on a band, but on a stronger thing: 1162
 Rings, Iewels, any thing his rage did like.   1616
THINGS = 2
 Ant. Well sir, learne to iest in good time, there's a | time for all things.   458
 An. You would all this time haue prou'd, there is no | time for all
things.   494
THINKE = 19*4
 S.Dro. No sir, I thinke the meat wants that I haue.   450
 Or sleepe I now, and thinke I heare all this?   578
 Ant. I thinke thou art in minde, and so am I.   591
 *Your owne hand-writing would tell you what I thinke.   632
 E.Ant. I thinke thou art an asse. | *E.Dro.* Marry so it doth appeare   633
 Teach me deere creature how to thinke and speake: 820
 And in that glorious supposition thinke,   837
 *that I amaz'd ranne from her as a witch. And I thinke, if   933
 'Tis time I thinke to trudge, packe, and be gone.   943
 Ant. What I should thinke of this, I cannot tell: 973
 But this I thinke, there's no man is so vaine,   974
 Adr. Ah but I thinke him better then I say: 1131
 Heere comes my Man, I thinke he brings the monie.   1289
 *and I thinke when he hath lam'd me, I shall begge with   1319
 Mar. Speake softly, yonder as I thinke he walkes.   1472
 Ant. I thinke I had, I neuer did deny it.   1487
 Mar. By this I thinke the Diall points at fiue: 1587
 From whence I thinke you are come by Miracle.   1741
 I thinke you all haue drunke of *Circes* cup: 1747
 I thinke you are all mated, or starke mad.   1760
 S.Ant. I thinke it be sir, I denie it not.   1867
 Gold. I thinke I did sir, I deny it not.   1869
 By *Dromio*, but I thinke he brought it not. | *E.Dro.* No, none by me.   1871
THINKES = *3
 *Me thinkes your maw, like mine, should be your cooke,   231
 *thinkes a man alwaies going to bed, and saies, God giue | you good
rest.   1215
 *me thinkes they are such a gentle Nation, that but for   1456
THINKS = *1
 E.D. Me thinks you are my glasse, & not my brother: 1909
THINKST = *1
 *Thinkst y I iest? hold, take thou that, & that. *Beats Dro.*   418
THIRTIE = 1
 Thirtie three yeares haue I but gone in trauaile   1890
THIS *I.**30 78 96 107 153 165 173 218 234 263 270 300 301 315 361 415
 416 429 *446 *494 527 *551 554 556 567 578 580 584 586 612 628 *671
 *702 *707 *713 750 754 758 772 776 784 854 *929 939 961 973 974 987
 1014 1032 *1034 1043 1045 1059 1060 1065 1069 1089 1092 1108 1158
 *1198 1232 1270 1278 *1312 *1338 1345 1350 1351 1393 1405 *1454
 1477 1481 1483 1486 1502 1511 1512 1514 1563 1582 1587 1589 1594
 1595 1610 1627 1639 1678 *1680 1686 1690 1695 1704 1705 1718 1740
 1745 1746 1755 *1758 1768 1792 1847 *1853 1861 1864 1868 1873 1886
 1887 1891 1897 = 100*17
THITHER = 2
 Thither I must, although against my will: 1101

THITHER *cont.*

Our dinner done, and he not comming thither,	1701

THOSE *l.*60 92 250 *478 *680 1621 1845 = 5*2

THOU *see also* y *l.*29 33 34 124 149 155 156 157 207 225 238 246 *252 256 312 314 *322 *326 334 *351 406 407 412 414 417 *418 435 *480 508 515 520 526 529 534 537 541 *551 557 558 568 *588 589 591 593 595 628 633 *656 *669 *673 676 *677 *690 698 *735 857 *862 *866 885 941 *997 1002 1063 *1082 1085 1105 1108 1138 *1170 *1198 1212 *1248 1249 1261 1305 *1308 1327 *1343 1352 ⸬1369 *1375 *1383 1384 *1388 1389 *1400 *1401 1406 1407 *1418 *1490 1491 1493 1495 1542 1546 1581 1635 1652 1674 1679 1683 1743 1756 1765 1781 1782 1784 1789 1799 1802 1803 1822 1827 1830 1838 1839 1848 *1901 1914 = 95*37

THOUGH = 9*3

Which though my selfe would gladly haue imbrac'd,	72
For we may pitty, though not pardon thee.	100
But though thou art adiudged to the death,	149
Adr. Patience vnmou'd, no maruel though she pause,	306
*But though my cates be meane, take them in good part,	649
Beare a faire presence, though your heart be tainted,	799
Though others haue the arme, shew vs the sleeue:	809
Adr. And true he swore, though yet forsworne hee | were.	1113
My tongue, though not my heart, shall haue his will.	1124
My heart praies for him, though my tongue doe curse.	1134
Though most dishonestly he doth denie it.	1466
Though now this grained face of mine be hid	1792

THOUGHT = 6

Was carried towards *Corinth*, as we thought.	90
By Fishermen of *Corinth*, as we thought.	114
Luce. I thought to haue askt you. | *S.Dro.* And you said no.	694
I thought to haue tane you at the *Porpentine*,	959
Belike you thought our loue would last too long	1008
And now he's there, past thought of humane reason.	1664

THOUSAND = 7

Vnlesse a thousand markes be leuied	25
Where is the thousand Markes thou hadst of me?	246
But not a thousand markes betweene you both.	249
Where is the thousand markes I gaue thee villaine?	342
And shriue you of a thousand idle prankes:	604
And charg'd him with a thousand markes in gold,	626
Dro. I buy a thousand pound a yeare, I buy a rope. | *Exit Dromio*	1003

THREATNING = 1

Excludes all pitty from our threatning lookes:	14

THRED-BARE = 1

A thred-bare Iugler, and a Fortune-teller,	1716

THREE = 4*2

And in our sight they three were taken vp	113
Anti. What's her name? | *Dro. Nell* Sir: but her name is three quarters, that's	899
*an Ell and three quarters, will not measure her from hip | to hip.	901
Which doth amount to three odde Duckets more	1013
Enter three or foure, and offer to binde him: | *Hee striues.*	1394
Thirtie three yeares haue I but gone in trauaile	1890

THREW = 1

And euer as it blaz'd, they threw on him	1645

THRONG = 1

Ab. Be quiet people, wherefore throng you hither?	1505

THROUGH = 2
    Roming cleane through the bounds of *Asia*,   136
    That desp'rately he hurried through the streete,   1612
THROWNE = 1
    That she this day hath shamelesse throwne on me.   1678
THUS = 13*3
    The children thus dispos'd, my wife and I,   86
    Thus haue you heard me seuer'd from my blisse,   121
    Ant. What wilt thou flout me thus vnto my face   256
    Adr. Looke when I serue him so, he takes it thus.   286
    That like a foot-ball you doe spurne me thus: 359
    That thus so madlie thou did didst answere me?   407
    *S.Dro. Was there euer anie man thus beaten out of   442
    *S.Dro. Thus I mend it: Time himselfe is bald, and   500
    When were you wont to vse my sister thus?   548
    Ant. How can she thus then call vs by our names? | Vnlesse it be by
    inspiration.   560
    To counterfeit thus grosely with your slaue,   563
    The chaine vnfinish'd made me stay thus long.   960
    Thus he vnknowne to me should be in debt: 1160
    Ant. Thou art a Villaine to impeach me thus,   1493
    *Gold. My Lord, in truth, thus far I witnes with him: 1731
    E.Dro. Nay then thus: | We came into the world like brother and
    brother: 1916
THWART = 1
    Abetting him to thwart me in my moode;   564
THY *l*.16 27 33 154 158 238 *252 344 345 *354 357 506 507 511 512 515
    516 517 519 524 538 539 540 569 570 574 *588 *677 *690 789 796 804
    832 833 834 835 848 *850 855 857 866 *869 1064 *1118 1138 1140 1180
    1303 1340 *1401 1442 1540 1542 1546 1554 1555 1631 *1633 1635 *1651
    1669 1743 1810 1879 1905 = 57*12
THYSELFE *see* selfe
TIDE = 1
    Both winde and tide stayes for this Gentleman,   1032
TIGER *see* tyger
TILL = 23*2
    To *Epidamium*, till my factors death,   45
    What haue befalne of them and they till now.   126
    And stay there *Dromio*, till I come to thee;   172
    Till that Ile view the manners of the towne,   174
    And afterward consort you till bed time: 191
    Ant. Farewell till then: I will goe loose my selfe,   193
    Reserue them till a merrier houre then this: 234
    She that doth fast till you come home to dinner: 254
    Luc. Till he come home againe, I would forbeare.   305
    S.Dro. I sir? I neuer saw her till this time.   556
    Luce. Let him knocke till it ake.   701
    *a *Poland* Winter: If she liues till doomesday, she'l burne | a weeke
    longer then the whole World.   890
    Where I will walke till thou returne to me: 941
    Ant. I owe you none, till I receiue the Chaine.   1050
    Ant. I do obey thee, till I giue thee baile.   1068
    That staies but till her Owner comes aboord,   1075
    On Officer to prison, till it come. *Exeunt*   1097
    But till this afternoone his passion | Ne're brake into extremity of rage.   1514
    Till I haue brought him to his wits againe,   1565
    Till I haue vs'd the approoued meanes I haue,   1572

TILL *cont.*
   Chac'd vs away: till raising of more aide   1625
   Till gnawing with my teeth my bonds in sunder,   1726
   E.Ant. I neuer saw you in my life till now.   1777
   Of you my sonnes, and till this present houre   1891
   *S.Dro. Wee'l draw Cuts for the Signior, till then, | lead thou first.   1914
TILTING = 1
   Oh, his hearts Meteors tilting in his face.   1109
TIME = 23*10
   Within this houre it will be dinner time,   173
   And afterward consort you till bed time: 191
   Time is their Master, and when they see time,   282
   'Tis dinner time, quoth I: my gold, quoth he: 339
   for vrging it the second time to me.   441
   for something. But say sir, is it dinner time?   449
   Ant. In good time sir: what's that? | *S.Dro.* Basting.   451
   *Ant. Well sir, learne to iest in good time, there's a | time for all things.   458
   *S.Dro. Marry sir, by a rule as plaine as the plaine bald | pate of Father
   time himselfe.   463
   *S.Dro. There's no time for a man to recouer his haire | that growes
   bald by nature.   466
   *Ant. Why, is Time such a niggard of haire, being (as   471
   *An. You would all this time haue prou'd, there is no | time for all
   things.   494
   *S.Dro. Marry and did sir: namely, in no time to re-|couer haire lost
   by Nature.   496
   *An. But your reason was not substantiall, why there | is no time to
   recouer.   498
   *S.Dro. Thus I mend it: Time himselfe is bald, and   500
   The time was once, when thou vn-vrg'd wouldst vow,   508
   S.Dro. I sir? I neuer saw her till this time.   556
   *S.Dro. The Porter for this time Sir, and my name is | *Dromio.*   671
   Why at this time the dores are made against you.   754
   'Tis time I thinke to trudge, packe, and be gone.   943
   And therefore 'tis hie time that I were hence: 947
   And soone at supper time Ile visit you,   968
   *Anti. No beare it with you, least I come not time e-|nough.   1025
   Adria. What, the chaine? | *S.Dro.* No, no, the bell, 'tis time that I were
   gone: 1164
   *Adri. As if time were in debt: how fondly do'st thou | reason?   1170
   *S.Dro. Time is a verie bankerout, and owes more then | he's worth to
   season.   1172
   That time comes stealing on by night and day?   1175
   Where would you had remain'd vntill this time,   1350
   His word might beare my wealth at any time.   1471
   During which time, he ne're saw *Siracusa*:   1809
TIMELIE = 1
   And happy were I in my timelie death,   141
TIMES = 2*1
   *Ang. Not once, nor twice, but twentie times you | haue: 965
   And carefull houres with times deformed hand,   1779
   Fath. Not know my voice, oh times extremity   1788
TIRED = *1
   *gentlemen are tired giues them a sob, and rests them: 1208
TIS *l.*216 339 595 596 597 776 803 813 *897 943 947 1164 *1206 *1301
  *1474 1491 1755 = 13*4

TO *see also* too = 283*64, 2*1
   *to, or else I shall seek my wit in my shoulders, but I pray | sir, why am
     I beaten? 433
   An. For what reason. | *S.Dro.* For two, and sound ones to. 484
   Luc. Come, come, *Antipholus*, we dine to late. 615
TODAY *see* day
TOGETHER = 5*1
   *If a crow help vs in sirra, wee'll plucke a crow together. 744
   If it were chain'd together: and therefore came not. 1009
   To day did dine together: so befall my soule, 1685
   Where *Balthasar* and I did dine together. 1700
   There left me and my man, both bound together, 1725
   Which accidentally are met together. 1837
TOKEN = 1
   Either send the Chaine, or send me by some token. 1042
TOLD = 4*1
   E.Dro. I, I, he told his minde vpon mine eare, 324
   *Dromio, swore I was assur'd to her, told me what priuie 930
   And told thee to what purpose, and what end. 1086
   Is a mad tale he told to day at dinner, 1271
   Did call me brother. What I told you then, 1862
TOLDST = 1
   And toldst me of a Mistresse, and a dinner, 413
TOMORROW *see* morrow
TONGUE = 5*1
   *tongue, I thanke him, I bare home vpon my shoulders: 349
   Be not thy tongue thy owne shames Orator: 796
   My tongue, though not my heart, shall haue his will. 1124
   My heart praies for him, though my tongue doe curse. 1134
   Offi. Good now hold thy tongue. 1303
   Hast thou so crack'd and splitted my poore tongue 1789
TONIGHT *see* night
TOO *see also* to = 18*7
   Vnwilling I agreed, alas, too soone wee came aboord. 64
   Lest that your goods too soone be confiscate: 164
   **E.Dro.* Return'd so soone, rather approacht too late: 208
   **E.Dro.* Nay, hee's at too hands with mee, and that my | two eares can
     witnesse. 320
   **E.Dro.* Nay, hee strooke so plainly, I could too well 328
   But, too vnruly Deere, he breakes the pale, 376
   As take from me thy selfe, and not me too. 524
   *When one is one too many, goe get thee from the dore. 657
   **Luce.* Faith no, hee comes too late, and so tell your | Master. 683
   **E.Dro.* Here's too much out vpon thee, I pray thee let | me in. 737
   Prettie and wittie; wilde, and yet too gentle; 771
   *and I know not what vse to put her too, but to make a 887
   I will discharge my bond, and thanke you too. 994
   Belike you thought our loue would last too long 1008
   And I too blame haue held him heere too long. 1033
   S.Dro. A ship you sent me too, to hier waftage. 1084
   She is too bigge I hope for me to compasse, 1100
   Nay, he's a theefe too: haue you not heard men say, 1174
   For fortie Duckets is too much to loose. 1279
   Pinch. Go binde this man, for he is franticke too. 1405
   Mar. Yes that you did sir, and forswore it too. 1488
   Binde *Dromio* too, and beare them to my house. 1500
   Which of these sorrowes is he subiect too? 1521

TOO *cont.*

Ab. Haply in priuate. | *Adr.* And in assemblies too.	1528

TOOKE = 9

Hath homelie age th'alluring beauty tooke	365
And therewithall tooke measure of my body.	1192
He rush'd into my house, and tooke perforce	1277
Came to my house, and tooke away my Ring,	1434
Ab. Neither: he tooke this place for sanctuary,	1563
A most outragious fit of madnesse tooke him:	1611
When I bestrid thee in the warres, and tooke	1668
Forsooth tooke on him as a Coniurer:	1719
By force tooke *Dromio*, and my sonne from them,	1844

TOOTH = 1

Poisons more deadly then a mad dogges tooth.	1539

TOUCH = 3

That others touch, and often touching will,	387
That neuer touch well welcome to thy hand,	511
How deerely would it touch thee to the quicke,	525

TOUCHD = 1

Vnlesse I spake, or look'd, or touch'd, or caru'd to thee.	513

TOUCHES = 1

Gold. This touches me in reputation.	1059

TOUCHING = 1

That others touch, and often touching will,	387

TOWARDS = 1

Was carried towards *Corinth*, as we thought.	90

TOWN = *1

E.Ant. Brought to this Town by that most famous | Warriour,	1853

TOWNE = 10*1

According to the statute of the towne,	168
Till that Ile view the manners of the towne,	174
What will you walke with me about the towne,	185
They say this towne is full of cosenage:	263
As strange vnto your towne, as to your talke,	544
Luce. What needs all that, and a paire of stocks in the | towne?	704
S.Dro. By my troth your towne is troubled with vn-|ruly boies.	708
I will not harbour in this Towne to night.	939
Besides I haue some businesse in the towne,	1018
Ant. I will not stay to night for all the Towne,	1460
Against the Lawes and Statutes of this Towne,	1595

TOWNES = 1

To admit no trafficke to our aduerse townes:	19

TRADERS = 1

Peruse the traders, gaze vpon the buildings,	175

TRAFFICKE = 1

To admit no trafficke to our aduerse townes:	19

TRAGICKE = 1

Gaue any Tragicke Instance of our harme:	67

TRAINE = 1

Oh traine me not sweet Mermaide with thy note,	832

TRAITOR = 1

Hath almost made me Traitor to my selfe:	952

TRANSFORMD = *1

*steele, she had transform'd me to a Curtull dog, & made | me turne i'th wheele.	935

TRANSFORME = 1

Transforme me then, and to your powre Ile yeeld.	827

TRANSFORMED = 1
S.Dro. I am transformed Master, am I not? 590
TRAUAILE = 2
For with long trauaile I am stiffe and wearie. | Get thee away. 177
Thirtie three yeares haue I but gone in trauaile 1890
TRAUELLS = 1
Could all my trauells warrant me they liue. 142
TREMBLES = 1
Cur. Marke, how he trembles in his extasie. 1334
TRICKS = 1
That stands on tricks, when I am vndispos'd: 245
TRIE = 2
Luci. Well, I will marry one day but to trie: 316
S.Dro. Not I sir, you are my elder. | *E.Dro.* That's a question, how shall
we trie it. 1912
TRIM = 1
The ship is in her trim, the merrie winde 1079
TROOPE = 1
And at her heeles a huge infectious troope 1550
TROTH = *1
S.Dro. By my troth your towne is troubled with vn-|ruly boies. 708
TROUBLE = 2
And Ile be gone sir, and not trouble you. 1253
Signior *Antipholus*, I wonder much | That you would put me to this
shame and trouble, 1477
TROUBLED = *1
S.Dro. By my troth your towne is troubled with vn-|ruly boies. 708
TROUBLES = 1
Luci. Not this, but troubles of the marriage bed. 301
TRUANT = 1
'Tis double wrong to truant with your bed, 803
TRUCE = 1
Keepe then faire league and truce with thy true bed, 540
TRUDGE = 1
'Tis time I thinke to trudge, packe, and be gone. 943
TRUE = 6*1
Here comes the almanacke of my true date: 206
Keepe then faire league and truce with thy true bed, 540
S.Dro. 'Tis true she rides me, and I long for grasse. 596
Adr. And true he swore, though yet forsworne hee | were. 1113
Establish him in his true sence againe, 1331
Mess. Mistris, vpon my life I tel you true, 1653
E.Anti. Tis true (my Liege) this Ring I had of her. 1755
TRUST = 4
Now trust me, were it not against our Lawes, 145
We being strangers here, how dar'st thou trust 225
And will not lightly trust the Messenger, 1285
Dro. No trust me sir, nor I. | *Fa.* I am sure thou dost? 1784
TRUSTIE = 1
Ant. A trustie villaine sir, that very oft, 182
TRUSTS = *1
Eph.Ant. A man is well holpe vp that trusts to you, 1005
TRUTH = 3*1
Against my soules pure truth, why labour you, 824
I long to know the truth heereof at large. 1439
But she tels to your Highnesse simple truth. 1688
Gold. My Lord, in truth, thus far I witnes with him: 1731

TRY = 1
Try all the friends thou hast in *Ephesus*,   155
TRYING = *1
*trying: the other, that at dinner they should not drop in | his porrage.   492
TURKISH = 1
That's couer'd o're with Turkish Tapistrie,   1093
TURNE = 3*1
We in your motion turne, and you may moue vs.   810
*steele, she had transform'd me to a Curtull dog, & made | me turne
i'th wheele.   935
Hath he not reason to turne backe an houre in a day?   1177
*I could finde in my heart to stay heere still, and turne | Witch.   1458
TURNES = *1
*S.Dro. Oh yes, if any houre meete a Serieant, a turnes | backe for verie
feare.   1168
TWELUE = 1
The clocke hath strucken twelue vpon the bell: 210
TWENTIE = 1*1
*Ang. Not once, nor twice, but twentie times you | haue: 965
Duke. I tell thee *Siracusian*, twentie yeares   1807
TWERE = 1
And with no-face (as 'twere) out-facing me,   1721
TWICE = 1*1
For ere the ships could meet by twice fiue leagues,   103
*Ang. Not once, nor twice, but twentie times you | haue: 965
TWILL = 2
Ant. Well sir, then 'twill be drie.   453
I tell you 'twill sound harshly in her eares.   1287
TWIN = 1
And the twin *Dromio*, all were taken vp;   1842
TWINS = 2
Of such a burthen Male, twins both alike: 59
To him one of the other twins was bound,   84
TWIXT = 1
Twixt thy seditious Countrimen and vs,   16
TWO *see also* too = 18*1
A ioyfull mother of two goodly sonnes: 54
My wife, not meanely prowd of two such boyes,   62
Two shippes from farre, making amaine to vs: 95
Sure *Luciana* it is two a clocke.   277
*E.Dro. Nay, hee's at too hands with mee, and that my | two eares can
witnesse.   320
An. For what reason. | *S.Dro.* For two, and sound ones to.   484
For if we two be one, and thou play false,   537
In *Ephesus* I am but two houres old,   543
*It was two ere I left him, and now the clocke strikes one.   1166
Off. Two hundred Duckets. | *Adr.* Say, how growes it due.   1429
But he I thanke him gnaw'd in two my cords,   1769
Adr. I see two husbands, or mine eyes deceiue me.   1816
That bore thee at a burthen two faire sonnes?   1829
These two *Antipholus*, these two so like,   1833
And these two *Dromio's*, one in semblance: 1834
Adr. Which of you two did dine with me to day? | *S.Ant.* I, gentle
Mistris.   1856
Exeunt omnes. Manet the two Dromio's and | two Brothers.   1898

TWOULD = *1

*An. I knew 'twould be a bald conclusion: but soft, | who wafts vs
yonder.   502
TYGER = 1

And let vs to the Tyger all to dinner,   756
VAINE = 4

S.Dro. I am glad to see you in this merrie vaine,   415
'Tis holy sport to be a little vaine,   813
But this I thinke, there's no man is so vaine,   974
Pinch. It is no shame, the fellow finds his vaine,   1367
VALE = 1

Comes this way to the melancholly vale;   1589
VALUED = 1

Thy substance, valued at the highest rate,   27
VAPOURS = 1

Disperst those vapours that offended vs,   92
VAULT = 1

And in a darke and dankish vault at home   1724
VENOME = 1

The venome clamors of a iealous woman,   1538
VERIE = 2*2

Ant. Villaine thou liest, for euen her verie words,   557
*a beast she would haue me, but that she being a ve-|rie beastly
creature layes claime to me.   878
*S.Dro. Oh yes, if any houre meete a Serieant, a turnes | backe for verie
feare.   1168
*S.Dro. Time is a verie bankerout, and owes more then | he's worth to
season.   1172
VERITIE = *1

*Dro. In veritie you did, my bones beares witnesse,   1364
VERTUE = 1

Her sober vertue, yeares, and modestie,   751
VERTUES = 1

Apparell vice like vertues harbenger: 798
VERTUOUS = 1

Duke. She is a vertuous and a reuerend Lady,   1606
VERY = 5*1

That very howre, and in the selfe-same Inne,   57
Had not their backe beene very slow of saile;   119
This very day a Syracusian Marchant | Is apprehended for a riuall here, 165
Ant. A trustie villaine sir, that very oft,   182
*Dro. A very reuerent body: I such a one, as a man   881
Gold. Of very reuerent reputation sir,   1468
VESTALL = 1

Dro. Certis she did, the kitchin vestall scorn'd you.   1362
VESTMENTS = 1

Doe their gay vestments his affections baite?   370
VICE = 1

Apparell vice like vertues harbenger: 798
VICIOUS = 1

Vicious, vngentle, foolish, blunt, vnkinde,   1127
VIEW = 2

Till that Ile view the manners of the towne,   174
And wander vp and downe to view the Citie.   194
VIGOR = 1

That since haue felt the vigor of his rage.   1365

VILDE = 2
  Still did I tell him, it was vilde and bad.   1536
  *By'th'way, we met my wife, her sister, and a rabble more | Of vilde
  Confederates: Along with them   1712
VILE = 1
  Was wrought by nature, not by vile offence,   38
VILLAIN = *1
  *Adr. Dissembling Villain, thou speak'st false in both   1388
VILLAINE = 12*4
  Ant. A trustie villaine sir, that very oft,   182
  The villaine is ore-wrought of all my monie.   262
  Adri. Horne mad, thou villaine?   334
  Where is the thousand markes I gaue thee villaine?   342
  Ant. Villaine, thou didst denie the golds receit,   412
  Ant. Villaine thou liest, for euen her verie words,   557
  But here's a villaine that would face me downe   624
  *E.Dro. O villaine, thou hast stolne both mine office | and my name,   673
  To Adriana Villaine hie thee straight: 1091
  Ant. Fiue hundred Duckets villaine for a rope?   1294
  Anti. Thou whoreson senselesse Villaine.   1305
  *Anti. Din'd at home? Thou Villaine, what sayest | thou?   1352
  *Ant. Out on thee Villaine, wherefore dost thou mad | mee?   1418
  Ant. Thou art a Villaine to impeach me thus,   1493
  Mar. I dare and do defie thee for a villaine.   1496
  *They brought one Pinch, a hungry leane-fac'd Villaine;   1714
VINE = 1
  Thou art an Elme my husband, I a Vine: 568
VIOLE = *1
  *a Base-Viole in a case of leather; the man sir, that when   1207
VIOLENTLY = 1
  Which being violently borne vp,   105
VISIT = 1
  And soone at supper time Ile visit you,   968
VITAE = 1
  The Oyle, the Balsamum, and Aqua-vitae.   1078
VNBOUND = 1
  Now am I Dromio, and his man, vnbound.   1770
VNCERTAINTIE = 1
  Vntill I know this sure vncertaintie,   580
VNCKLE = 1
  Duke Menaphon your most renowned Vnckle.   1855
VNDER = 2
  Before her selfe (almost at fainting vnder   49
  There's nothing situate vnder heauens eye,   290
VNDERSTAND = 4
  Beshrew his hand, I scarce could vnderstand it.   325
  *feele his blowes; and withall so doubtfully, that I could | scarce
  vnderstand them.   329
  Wants wit in all, one word to vnderstand.   546
  Ant. I vnderstand thee not.   1205
VNDISHONOURED = 1
  I liue distain'd, thou vndishonoured.   541
VNDISPOSD = 1
  That stands on tricks, when I am vndispos'd: 245
VNDIUIDABLE = 1
  That vndiuidable Incorporate | Am better then thy deere selfes better
  part.   517

VNFEELING = *1
Ad. Vnfeeling fools can with such wrongs dispence: 379
VNFINISHD = 1
The chaine vnfinish'd made me stay thus long.   960
VNGALLED = 1
Against your yet vngalled estimation,   763
VNGENTLE = 1
Vicious, vngentle, foolish, blunt, vnkinde,   1127
VNHAPPIE = 2
In quest of them (vnhappie a) loose my selfe.   204
Ant. Oh most vnhappie strumpet.   1416
VNHAPPY = 1
Home to my house, oh most vnhappy day.   1415
VNIUST = 1
So that in this vniust diuorce of vs,   107
VNKINDE = 2
So thou that hast no vnkinde mate to greeue thee,   312
Vicious, vngentle, foolish, blunt, vnkinde,   1127
VNKINDNESSE = 1
Vnkindnesse blunts it more then marble hard.   369
VNKNOWNE = 3
Plead on your part some cause to you vnknowne;   752
To make it wander in an vnknowne field?   825
Thus he vnknowne to me should be in debt: 1160
VNLAWFULL = 1
Stray'd his affection in vnlawfull loue,   1518
VNLESSE = 4*1
Vnlesse a thousand markes be leuied   25
Vnlesse I spake, or look'd, or touch'd, or caru'd to thee. 513
Ant. How can she thus then call vs by our names? | Vnlesse it be by
inspiration.   560
And sure (vnlesse you send some present helpe)   1649
Mar.Fat. Vnlesse the feare of death doth make me | dote, I see my
sonne *Antipholus* and *Dromio*.   1671
VNLUCKILY = 1
Who put vnluckily into this Bay   1594
VNMINGLED = 1
And take vnmingled thence that drop againe | Without addition or
diminishing,   522
VNMOUD = *1
Adr. Patience vnmou'd, no maruel though she pause,   306
VNQUIET = 1
Vnquiet meales make ill digestions,   1543
VNRULY = 1*1
But, too vnruly Deere, he breakes the pale,   376
S.Dro. By my troth your towne is troubled with vn-|ruly boies. 708
VNSEENE = 1
(Vnseene, inquisitiue) confounds himselfe.   202
VNSOUGHT = 1
Hopelesse to finde, yet loth to leaue vnsought   138
VNSPEAKEABLE = 1
Then I to speake my griefes vnspeakeable: 36
VNTILL = 3
Vntill I know this sure vncertaintie,   580
Where would you had remain'd vntill this time,   1350
And neuer rise vntill my teares and prayers   1584

VNTO = 10*1

Cannot amount vnto a hundred Markes,	28
Vnto a woman, happy but for me,	41
Did but conuay vnto our fearefull mindes	70
Had fastned him vnto a small spare Mast,	82
Ant. What wilt thou flout me thus vnto my face	256
*no wife, no mistresse: so that my arrant due vnto my	348
As strange vnto your towne, as to your talke,	544
Knowne vnto these, and to my selfe disguisde:	610
Beare me forthwith vnto his Creditor,	1412
Luc. Complaine vnto the Duke of this indignity.	1582
And speake vnto the same *Aemilia.*	1831

VNTUND = 1

Knowes not my feeble key of vntun'd cares?	1791

VNUIOLATED = 1

Th'vnuiolated honor of your wife.	749

VNWED = 1

Adri. This seruitude makes you to keepe vnwed.	300

VNWILLING = 1

Vnwilling I agreed, alas, too soone wee came aboord.	64

VN-VRGD = 1

The time was once, when thou vn-vrg'd wouldst vow,	508

VOICE = 2

But tell me yet, dost thou not know my voice?	1781
Fath. Not know my voice, oh times extremity	1788

VOLUBLE = 1

If voluble and sharpe discourse be mar'd,	368

VOUCHSAFE = *2

**Fa.* Most mighty Duke, vouchsafe me speak a word:	1762
**Abb.* Renowned Duke, vouchsafe to take the paines	1883

VOW = 2

The time was once, when thou vn-vrg'd wouldst vow,	508
And breake it with a deepe-diuorcing vow?	533

VOWES = 1

He cries for you, and vowes if he can take you,	1655

VOYAGE = 1

Nor now I had not, but that I am bound | To *Persia*, and want Gilders	
for my voyage:	984

VOYAGES = 1

By prosperous voyages I often made	44

VP = 10*3

I bought, and brought vp to attend my sonnes.	61
Which being violently borne vp,	105
And in our sight they three were taken vp	113
Beg thou, or borrow, to make vp the summe,	156
And wander vp and downe to view the Citie.	194
My mistresse, sir, quoth I: hang vp thy Mistresse:	344
Ant. The gold I gaue to *Dromio* is laid vp	395
**Eph.Ant.* A man is well holpe vp that trusts to you,	1005
On whose hard heart is button'd vp with steele:	1143
*suites of durance: he that sets vp his rest to doe more ex-|ploits	1210
**Ant.* Were not my doores lockt vp, and I shut out?	1355
And all the Conduits of my blood froze vp:	1794
And the twin *Dromio*, all were taken vp;	1842

VPBRAIDED = 1

Hath oftentimes vpbraided me withall:	774

VPBRAIDINGS = 1
Thou saist his meate was sawc'd with thy vpbraidings,   1542
VPON = 23*3
At length the sonne gazing vpon the earth,   91
Peruse the traders, gaze vpon the buildings,   175
Please you, Ile meete with you vpon the Mart,   190
The clocke hath strucken twelue vpon the bell: 210
My Mistris made it one vpon my cheeke: 211
For she will scoure your fault vpon my pate: 230
E.Dro. I haue some markes of yours vpon my pate: 247
Some of my Mistris markes vpon my shoulders: 248
Ant. Vpon my life by some deuise or other,   261
E.Dro. I, I, he told his minde vpon mine eare,   324
*tongue, I thanke him, I bare home vpon my shoulders: 349
Vpon what bargaine do you giue it me?   420
Your sawcinesse will iest vpon my loue,   423
*S.Dro. It seemes thou want'st breaking, out vpon thee | hinde.   735
*E.Dro. Here's too much out vpon thee, I pray thee let | me in.   737
And dwell vpon your graue when you are dead;   765
For slander liues vpon succession: 766
Vpon mine hostesse there, good sir make haste: 780
Ant. Where America, the Indies? | Dro. Oh sir, vpon her nose, all ore
   embellished with   922
Consider how it stands vpon my credit.   1055
Whil'st vpon me the guiltie doores were shut,   1347
The Ring I saw vpon his finger now,   1435
Gold. Vpon what cause? | Mar. To see a reuerent Siracusian Merchant,   1592
Mess. Mistris, vpon my life I tel you true,   1653
*E.Ant. This day (great Duke) she shut the doores | vpon me,   1680
They fell vpon me, bound me, bore me thence,   1723
VRGD = 1
The time was once, when thou vn-vrg'd wouldst vow,   508
VRGING = 5
With vrging helpelesse patience would releeue me;   313
for vrging it the second time to me.   441
In bed he slept not for my vrging it,   1532
At boord he fed not for my vrging it: 1533
Besides her vrging of her wracke at sea,   1835
VS l.16 80 92 95 102 107 108 115 280 502 560 587 *619 651 *692 *744 756
   807 808 809 810 942 1226 1257 1261 1446 *1455 1507 1624 1625 1628
   1629 1652 1884 1888 1904 = 33*6
VSD = 1
Till I haue vs'd the approoued meanes I haue,   1572
VSE = 4*4
Doe vse you for my foole, and chat with you,   422
*I had rather haue it a head, and you vse these blows   431
When were you wont to vse my sister thus?   548
*Then for her wealths-sake vse her with more kindnesse: 792
*and I know not what vse to put her too, but to make a   887
*Anti. Good Lord, you vse this dalliance to excuse   1034
Hath scar'd thy husband from the vse of wits.   1555
My dull deafe eares a little vse to heare: 1797
VSURPING = 1
Vsurping Iuie, Brier, or idle Mosse,   572
VTMOST = *1
*How much your Chaine weighs to the vtmost charect,   1011

176

VTTER = 1
Ile vtter what my sorrow giues me leaue.   39
VULGAR = 1
A vulgar comment will be made of it;   761
VEINE *see* vaine
VS *see also* let's
WAFTAGE = 1
S.Dro. A ship you sent me too, to hier waftage.   1084
WAFTS = 1
*An. I knew 'twould be a bald conclusion: but soft, | who wafts vs
yonder.   502
WAIGHT = 2
With lesser waight, but not with lesser woe,   111
But were we burdned with like waight of paine,   310
WAILD = 1
No euill lost is wail'd, when it is gone.   1130
WAKD = *1
*beating: I am wak'd with it when I sleepe, rais'd with   1315
WAKING = 1
Sleeping or waking, mad or well aduisde: 609
WALKE = 5*1
What will you walke with me about the towne,   185
S.Dro. Let him walke from whence he came, lest hee | catch cold on's
feet.   660
Where I will walke till thou returne to me: 941
Pleaseth you walke with me downe to his house,   993
To walke where any honest men resort.   1492
Will you walke in to see their gossipping?   1911
WALKES = *1
Mar. Speake softly, yonder as I thinke he walkes.   1472
WALS = 1
E.Ant. I neuer came within these Abbey wals,   1742
WAN = *1
Luc. Aye me poore man, how pale and wan he looks.   1399
WANDER = 3
And wander vp and downe to view the Citie.   194
To make it wander in an vnknowne field?   825
And here we wander in illusions: 1225
WANDRED = 1
Is wandred forth in care to seeke me out   397
WANT = 2
Who all for want of pruning, with intrusion,   573
Nor now I had not, but that I am bound | To *Persia*, and want Gilders
for my voyage: 984
WANTING = 1
Who wanting gilders to redeeme their liues,   12
WANTS = 2
S.Dro. No sir, I thinke the meat wants that I haue.   450
Wants wit in all, one word to vnderstand.   546
WANTST = *1
S.Dro. It seemes thou want'st breaking, out vpon thee | hinde.   735
WARME = *2
*Your cake here is warme within: you stand here in the | cold.   725
*me with beating: when I am warme, he cooles me with   1314
WARRANT = 4*1
A doubtfull warrant of immediate death,   71
Could all my trauells warrant me they liue.   142

WARRANT *cont.*

*warrant, her ragges and the Tallow in them, will burne	889
Ile giue thee ere I leaue thee so much money | To warrant thee as I am rested for.	1282
E.Dro. Here's that I warrant you will pay them all.	1291

WARRE = 2

Heerein you warre against your reputation,	747
Dro. In her forhead, arm'd and reuerted, making | warre against her heire.	914

WARRES = 1

When I bestrid thee in the warres, and tooke	1668

WARRIOUR = 1

E.Ant. Brought to this Town by that most famous | Warriour,	1853

WARS = *1

Duke. Long since thy husband seru'd me in my wars	1633

WART = *1

*the Mole in my necke, the great Wart on my left arme,	932

WAS = 35*8

WAST *l*.406 = 1

WASTED = 1

From my poore cheeke? then he hath wasted it.	366

WASTING = 1

My wasting lampes some fading glimmer left;	1796

WATER = 3

I to the world am like a drop of water,	199
A drop of water in the breaking gulfe,	521
Anti. That's a fault that water will mend.	896

WATRY = 1

Lord of the wide world, and wilde watry seas,	295

WAUES = 1

Spread ore the siluer waues thy golden haires;	835

WAXT = 1

The seas waxt calme, and we discouered	94

WAY = 5*1

And if the winde blow any way from shore,	938
If I be in debt and theft, and a Serieant in the way,	1176
On purpose shut the doores against his way:	1274
My way is now to hie home to his house,	1275
Comes this way to the melancholly vale;	1589
*By'th'way, we met my wife, her sister, and a rabble more | Of vilde Confederates: Along with them	1712

WAYWARD = 1

My wife is in a wayward moode to day,	1284

WE = 40*5

WEAKE = 1

Smothred in errors, feeble, shallow, weake,	822

WEAKNESSE = 1

Whose weaknesse married to thy stranger state,	569

WEALTH = 3*1

With her I liu'd in ioy, our wealth increast	43
If you did wed my sister for her wealth,	791
His word might beare my wealth at any time.	1471
Ab. Hath he not lost much wealth by wrack of sea,	1516

WEALTHS-SAKE = *1

*Then for her wealths-sake vse her with more kindnesse:	792

WEARE = 1

This Chaine, which now you weare so openly.	1481

WEARIE = 2
Dies ere the wearie sunne set in the West: 169
For with long trauaile I am stiffe and wearie. | Get thee away.   177
WED = 1
If you did wed my sister for her wealth,   791
WEDDE = 1
In *Syracusa* was I borne, and wedde   40
WEDDED = *1
Adr. But were you wedded, you wold bear some sway   302
WEDDING = 1
And from my false hand cut the wedding ring,   532
WEE *l*.64 *717 = 1*1
WEEKE = 2
*a *Poland* Winter: If she liues till doomesday, she'l burne | a weeke
longer then the whole World.   890
Adr. This weeke he hath beene heauie, sower sad,   1512
WEEL = 1*1
Come go with vs, wee'l looke to that anon,   1904
S.Dro. Wee'l draw Cuts for the Signior, till then, | lead thou first.   1914
WEELL = 1*1
*If a crow help vs in sirra, wee'll plucke a crow together.   744
Will you goe with me, wee'll mend our dinner here?   1242
WEEPE = 2
Ile weepe (what's left away) and weeping die.   391
To put the finger in the eie and weepe;   600
WEEPING = 3
Weeping before for what she saw must come,   74
Ile weepe (what's left away) and weeping die.   391
But if that I am I, then well I know, | Your weeping sister is no wife of
mine,   828
WEEPINGS = 1
Yet the incessant weepings of my wife,   73
WEIGHS = *1
*How much your Chaine weighs to the vtmost charect,   1011
WELCOM = *2
*May answer my good will, and your good welcom here.   639
Bal. I hold your dainties cheap sir, & your welcom deer.   640
WELCOMD = *1
*from home, welcom'd home with it when I returne, nay   1317
WELCOME = 5*3
Gaue healthfull welcome to their ship-wrackt guests,   117
That neuer touch well welcome to thy hand,   511
A table full of welcome, makes scarce one dainty dish.   642
Anti. And welcome more common, for thats nothing | but words.   644
Bal. Small cheere and great welcome, makes a mer-|rie feast.   646
Angelo. Heere is neither cheere sir, nor welcome, we | would faine
haue either.   715
E.Dro. They stand at the doore, Master, bid them | welcome hither.   719
Ant. And to that end sir, I will welcome you. | *Offi.* Good sir be
patient.   1299
WELL = 23*7
Duk. Well *Siracusian*; say in briefe the cause   32
Luci. Well, I will marry one day but to trie: 316
E.Dro. Nay, hee strooke so plainly, I could too well   328
*season, when in the why and the wherefore, is neither | rime nor
reason. Well sir, I thanke you.   443
Ant. Well sir, then 'twill be drie.   453

WELL *cont.*

Ant. Well sir, learne to iest in good time, there's a | time for all things. 458
That neuer touch well welcome to thy hand, 511
But I should know her as well as she knowes me. 598
Come sister, *Dromio* play the Porter well. 607
Sleeping or waking, mad or well aduisde: 609
S.Dro. If thy name be called *Luce, Luce* thou hast an-|swer'd him
well. 690
E.Dro. So come helpe, well strooke, there was blow | for blow. 696
Ant. Well, Ile breake in: go borrow me a crow. 741
And doubt not sir, but she will well excuse 753
Shame hath a bastard fame, well managed, 805
But if that I am I, then well I know, | Your weeping sister is no wife of
mine, 828
Ang. I know it well sir, loe here's the chaine, 958
Ang. You are a merry man sir, fare you well. *Exit.* 972
Eph.Ant. A man is well holpe vp that trusts to you, 1005
Gold. Well sir, I will? Haue you the Chaine about | you? 1027
Mar. Well Officer, arrest him at my suite. 1056
Adr. Where is thy Master *Dromio*? Is he well? 1140
A hound that runs Counter, and yet draws drifoot well, 1148
S.Dro. I know not at whose suite he is arested well; 1154
As if I were their well acquainted friend, 1185
Ant. Well sir, there rest in your foolerie: 1217
Cur. Well met, well met, Master *Antipholus*: 1228
And yeelding to him, humors well his frensie. 1368
Father. Why looke you strange on me? you know | me well. 1775
WELL-DEALING = 1
To Merchants our well-dealing Countrimen, 11
WENCH = 1*3
I know a wench of excellent discourse, 770
Dro. Marry sir, she's the Kitchin wench, & al grease, 886
*And here she comes in the habit of a light wench, and 1235
*as much to say, God make me a light wench: It is writ-|ten, 1237
WENCHES = *3
*Dost thou coniure for wenches, that y calst for such store, 656
*thereof comes, that the wenches say God dam me, That's 1236
*effect of fire, and fire will burne: *ergo*, light wenches will | burne, come
not neere her. 1239
WEND = 1
Merch. Hopelesse and helpelesse doth *Egean* wend, 160
WENSDAY = 1
E.Dro. Oh sixe pence that I had a wensday last, 220
WENT = 3*2
Gather the sequell by that went before. 98
E.Dro. If you went in paine Master, this knaue wold | goe sore. 713
S.Dro. No? why 'tis a plaine case: he that went like 1206
Whil'st to take order for the wrongs I went, 1618
I went to seeke him. In the street I met him, 1702
WENTST = *1
Ant. Wentst not thou to her for a purse of Duckets. 1375
WERE *see also* 'twere *l.*60 104 113 141 145 *302 310 *460 509 526 548
*631 723 947 1009 1113 1132 1164 *1170 1185 *1221 *1306 1347 *1355
*1356 1387 1453 1540 1546 1696 1749 1773 1842 = 25*9
WERT *l.**1343 = *1
WEST = 1
Dies ere the wearie sunne set in the West: 169

WHAT *l.*34 39 69 74 76 109 126 152 185 207 216 243 *252 256 *258 372 381 408 416 420 445 462 *474 484 555 577 579 628 *629 *632 *658 *669 *680 *704 801 802 *815 817 840 *869 875 880 *887 892 907 *930 961 *962 973 1048 1083 1086 1108 1115 *1118 1150 1153 1164 *1196 *1198 1212 *1248 1296 1332 *1352 *1400 1406 *1428 1547 1592 1620 1691 1746 1751 1765 1846 1862 *1901 = 58*24

WHATS = 4

Ile weepe (what's left away) and weeping die.	391
Ant. In good time sir: what's that? | *S.Dro.* Basting.	451
Anti. What's her name? | *Dro. Nell* Sir: but her name is three quarters, that's	899
And what's a Feauer, but a fit of madnesse?	1545

WHATSOEUER = *1

E.Dromio. I sir, but I am sure I do not, and whatso- |euer	1786

WHEELE = 1

*steele, she had transform'd me to a Curtull dog, & made | me turne i'th wheele.	935

WHEN *l.*30 183 245 282 286 309 337 408 425 426 *443 508 548 620 *657 *663 667 *688 *739 765 814 *844 977 1130 *1207 *1313 *1314 *1315 *1316 *1317 *1319 1433 1557 1635 1668 1734 = 22*15

WHENCE = 1*1

S.Dro. Let him walke from whence he came, lest hee | catch cold on's feet.	660
From whence I thinke you are come by Miracle.	1741

WHER = 1

Good sir say, whe'r you'l answer me, or no:	1046

WHERE *l.*52 171 219 224 235 246 304 342 380 388 767 782 793 *862 910 913 916 920 922 927 941 *996 1098 1099 1126 1140 1350 1438 1492 *1597 1700 1839 = 29*3

WHEREFORE = 3*6

S.Dro. I sir, and wherefore; for they say, euery why | hath a wherefore.	438
Ant. Why first for flowting me, and then wherefore,	440
*season, when in the why and the wherefore, is neither | rime nor reason. Well sir, I thanke you.	443
S.Dro. Right sir, Ile tell you when, and you'll tell | me wherefore.	663
Ant. Wherefore? for my dinner: I haue not din'd to | day.	665
Ant. Say wherefore didst thou locke me forth to day,	1383
Ant. Out on thee Villaine, wherefore dost thou mad | mee?	1418
Ab. Be quiet people, wherefore throng you hither?	1505

WHERES = 2

Come where's the Chaine, I pray you let me see it.	1044
Anti. But where's the Money?	1292

WHETHER *see also* whe'r = 1

Into this Abbey, whether we pursu'd them,	1627

WHICH *l.*9 55 72 105 147 414 *717 1013 *1155 1475 1481 1521 1706 1809 1818 1819 1837 *1850 1856 *1865 = 17*5

WHILE = 2*1

Ant. While I go to the Goldsmiths house, go thou	997
My Mr preaches patience to him, and the while	1647
While she with Harlots feasted in my house.	1682

WHILST = 6

Whil'st I had beene like heedfull of the other.	85
Whom whil'st I laboured of a loue to see,	133
Whil'st I at home starue for a merrie looke:	364
Whil'st man and Master laughes my woes to scorne:	601
Whil'st vpon me the guiltie doores were shut,	1347
Whil'st to take order for the wrongs I went,	1618

WHITENESSE = *1
    *no whitenesse in them. But I guesse, it stood in her chin   918
WHO *l*.12 201 345 502 545 573 *662 *680 *707 *925 1129 1372 1484 1489
    1520 1594 1609 1698 1819 *1823 1825 = 16*5
WHOEUER *see* euer
WHOLE = 1*1
    *a *Poland* Winter: If she liues till doomesday, she'l burne | a weeke
    longer then the whole World.   890
    *to the hot breath of Spaine, who sent whole Ar- | madoes of Carrects to
    be ballast at her nose.   925
WHOLSOME = 1
    With wholsome sirrups, drugges, and holy prayers   1573
WHOM *l*.48 87 116 133 134 143 188 1674 1728 = 9
WHORESON = 1
    Anti. Thou whoreson senselesse Villaine.   1305
WHOSE = 6*1
    Whose weaknesse married to thy stranger state,   569
    Luce. Can you tell for whose sake?   699
    On whose hard heart is button'd vp with steele: 1143
    Adr. What is he arrested? tell me at whose suite?   1153
    S.Dro. I know not at whose suite he is arested well;   1154
    Say now, whose suite is he arrested at?   1425
    Whose beard they haue sindg'd off with brands of fire,   1644
WHY *l*.33 236 *284 289 *333 433 *471 *476 *480 *498 *588 754 824 847
    *862 *894 *1040 *1082 1150 *1206 *1219 1243 1293 1384 1525 1558
    1746 *1758 *1775 1832 = 15*15, 1*3
    Ant. Shall I tell you why?   437
    S.Dro. I sir, and wherefore; for they say, euery why | hath a wherefore.   438
    Ant. Why first for flowting me, and then wherefore,   440
    *season, when in the why and the wherefore, is neither | rime nor
    reason. Well sir, I thanke you.   443
WIDE = 1
    Lord of the wide world, and wilde watry seas,   295
WIFE = 28*8
    My wife, not meanely prowd of two such boyes,   62
    Yet the incessant weepings of my wife,   73
    My wife, more carefull for the latter borne,   81
    The children thus dispos'd, my wife and I,   86
    E.Dro. Your worships wife, my Mistris at the *Phoenix*;   253
    Enter Adriana, wife to Antipholis Sereptus, with | Luciana her Sister.   273
    It seemes he hath great care to please his wife.   332
    *no wife, no mistresse: so that my arrant due vnto my   348
    I am not *Adriana*, nor thy wife.   507
    Denied my house for his, me for his wife.   553
    My wife is shrewish when I keepe not howres;   620
    And that I did denie my wife and house;   627
    Anti. Are you there Wife? you might haue come | before.   710
    Adri. Your wife sir knaue? go get you from the dore.   712
    Th'vnuiolated honor of your wife.   749
    My wife (but I protest without desert)   773
    (Be it for nothing but to spight my wife)   779
    Comfort my sister, cheere her, call her wife;   812
    But if that I am I, then well I know, | Your weeping sister is no wife of
    mine,   828
    Thou hast no husband yet, nor I no wife: | Giue me thy hand.   857
    So flie I from her that would be my wife. *Exit*   945
    Doth for a wife abhorre. But her faire sister   949

WIFE *cont.*
Go home with it, and please your Wife withall, 967
Among my wife, and their confederates, 999
And with you take the Chaine, and bid my wife 1020
Ant. Why giue it to my wife, and fetch your mony. 1040
Belike his wife acquainted with his fits, 1273
And tell his wife, that being Lunaticke, 1276
My wife is in a wayward moode to day, 1284
Ant. Come goe along, my wife is comming yon-|der. 1323
S.Dro. She that would be your wife, now ran from | you. 1449
And ill it doth beseeme your holinesse | To separate the husband and the wife. 1579
She whom thou gau'st to me to be my wife; 1674
*By'th'way, we met my wife, her sister, and a rabble more | Of vilde
Confederates: Along with them 1712
That hadst a wife once call'd *Aemilia*, 1828
She now shall be my sister, not my wife, 1908
WIL *l.*629 *1597 = *2
WILDE = 2
Lord of the wide world, and wilde watry seas, 295
Prettie and wittie; wilde, and yet too gentle; 771
WILDLY = 1
When he demean'd himselfe, rough, rude, and wildly, 1557
WILES = 1
Sure these are but imaginarie wiles, 1193
WILL *see also* Ile, she'l, they'l, they'll, 'twill, wee'l, wee'll, you'l, you'll
*l.*152 158 173 185 193 230 251 255 259 269 288 315 316 341 *354 *355
360 385 387 423 427 429 501 567 586 599 623 753 761 768 772 775 778
834 *844 856 *873 *889 896 *901 939 941 994 998 1022 *1023 *1027
1070 1089 1123 *1156 *1239 1242 *1257 1281 1285 1291 1299 1332
*1400 1410 1411 1413 *1420 *1454 1460 1567 1569 1571 *1578 1583
1603 1629 1639 1650 *1736 1763 1825 1911 = 64*17, 6*2
Luc. Oh, know he is the bridle of your will. 287
Then let your will attend on their accords. 299
*May answer my good will, and your good welcom here. 639
Ile fetch my sister to get her good will. *Exit.* 860
Anti. What is your will that I shal do with this? 961
Thither I must, although against my will: 1101
My tongue, though not my heart, shall haue his will. 1124
Dro. Monie by me? Heart and good will you might, 1373
WILT *l.*256 1327 *1401 1406 1765 = 4*1
WINDE = 6*1
Was carried with more speed before the winde, 112
Ant. Stop in your winde sir, tell me this I pray? 218
Anti. There is something in the winde, that we can-|not get in. 721
E.Dro. A man may breake a word with your sir, and | words are but
winde: 732
And if the winde blow any way from shore, 938
Both winde and tide stayes for this Gentleman, 1032
The ship is in her trim, the merrie winde 1079
WINDE-OBEYING = 1
Before the alwaies winde-obeying deepe 66
WINE = 1
Neither disturbed with the effect of Wine, 1692
WINGED = 1
The beasts, the fishes, and the winged fowles 292

WINKE = *1
*Ant. As good to winke sweet loue, as looke on night.   846
WINTER = *1
*a *Poland* Winter: If she liues till doomesday, she'l burne | a weeke
longer then the whole World.   890
WINTERS = 1
In sap-consuming Winters drizled snow,   1793
WISE = *1
*be wise, and if you giue it her, the diuell will shake | her Chaine, and
fright vs with it.   1257
WISEDOME = 1
Once this your long experience of your wisedome,   750
WISER = 1
Albeit my wrongs might make one wiser mad.   1694
WISHED = 1
And by the benefit of his wished light   93
WIT = 5*3
Are my discourses dull? Barren my wit,   367
*to, or else I shall seek my wit in my shoulders, but I pray | sir, why am
I beaten?   433
*beasts, and what he hath scanted them in haire, hee hath | giuen them
in wit.   474
*Ant. Why, but theres manie a man hath more haire | then wit.   476
*S.Dro. Not a man of those but he hath the wit to lose | his haire.   478
*Ant. Why thou didst conclude hairy men plain dea-|lers without wit.   480
Who euery word by all my wit being scan'd,   545
Wants wit in all, one word to vnderstand.   546
WITCH = 2*1
*that I amaz'd ranne from her as a witch. And I thinke, if   933
Ant. Auant thou witch: Come *Dromio* let vs go.   1261
*I could finde in my heart to stay heere still, and turne | Witch.   1458
WITCHES = 3
Soule-killing Witches, that deforme the bodie: 266
Anti. There's none but Witches do inhabite heere,   946
S.Ant. I see these Witches are affraid of swords.   1448
WITH = 115*24
WITHALL = *4*1
*feele his blowes; and withall so doubtfully, that I could | scarce
vnderstand them.   329
Hath oftentimes vpbraided me withall: 774
Go home with it, and please your Wife withall,   967
As this is false he burthens me withall.   1686
And this is false you burthen me withall.   1745
WITHIN = 7*4
Within this houre it will be dinner time,   173
And then returne and sleepe within mine Inne,   176
*E.Ant. Who talks within there? hoa, open the dore.   662
*Your cake here is warme within: you stand here in the | cold.   725
And draw within the compasse of suspect   748
*Pinch. I charge thee Sathan, hous'd within this man,   1338
*Pinch. More company, the fiend is strong within him   1398
Some get within him, take his sword away: 1499
To scorch your face, and to disfigure you: | *Cry within.*   1656
E.Ant. I neuer came within these Abbey wals,   1742
E.Dro. Within this houre I was his bondman sir,   1768
WITHOUT = 5*5
And strike you home without a messenger.   232

WITHOUT *cont.*

*Ant. Why thou didst conclude hairy men plain dea-|lers without wit. 480
And take vnmingled thence that drop againe | Without addition or
diminishing, 522
*E.Dro. A crow without feather, Master meane you so; 742
**For a fish without a finne, ther's a fowle without a fether, 743
My wife (but I protest without desert) 773
**may not speake of, without he say sir reuerence, I haue 882
Or else you may returne without your money. 1030
And not without some scandall to your selfe, 1479
WITNES = *1
*Gold. My Lord, in truth, thus far I witnes with him: 1731
WITNESSE = 7*1
Yet that the world may witnesse that my end 37
*E.Dro. Nay, hee's at too hands with mee, and that my | two eares can
witnesse. 320
*Dro. In veritie you did, my bones beares witnesse, 1364
Luci. And I am witnesse with her that she did: 1377
Dro. God and the Rope-maker beare me witnesse, 1378
Adr. Ay me, it is my husband: witnesse you, 1661
Could witnesse it: for he was with me then, 1697
Can witnesse with me that it is not so. 1805
WITNESSES = 1
All these old witnesses, I cannot erre. 1798
WITS = 3
Gold. I knew he was not in his perfect wits. 1509
Hath scar'd thy husband from the vse of wits. 1555
Till I haue brought him to his wits againe, 1565
WITTIE = 1
Prettie and wittie; wilde, and yet too gentle; 771
WIZARD = 1
Anti. Peace doting wizard, peace; I am not mad. 1342
WOE = 2
With lesser waight, but not with lesser woe, 111
Luc. Why, headstrong liberty is lasht with woe: 289
WOES = 2*1
**And by the doome of death end woes and all. 6
My woes end likewise with the euening Sonne. 31
Whil'st man and Master laughes my woes to scorne: 601
WOLD *l.**302 *713 *1256 = *3
WOLFE = 1
A Wolfe, nay worse, a fellow all in buffe: 1145
WOMAN = 6*3
Vnto a woman, happy but for me, 41
A meane woman was deliuered 58
There will we dine: this woman that I meane 772
*Dro. Marrie sir, besides my selfe, I am due to a woman: 872
The venome clamors of a iealous woman, 1538
*E.Ant. Iustice (sweet Prince) against y Woman there: 1673
Duke. A greeuous fault: say woman, didst thou so? 1683
*Gold. O periur'd woman! They are both forsworne, 1689
This woman lock'd me out this day from dinner; 1695
WOMANS = *2
*Dro. I am an asse, I am a womans man, and besides | my selfe. 868
*Ant. What womans man? and how besides thy | selfe? 869
WOMEN = 2
The pleasing punishment that women beare) 50

WOMEN *cont.*
Alas poore women, make vs not beleeue   807
WON = 1
Haue won his grace to come in person hither,   1585
WONDER = 4
Nor by what wonder you do hit of mine: 817
Then our earths wonder, more then earth diuine.   819
Adr. Go fetch it Sister: this I wonder at. | *Exit Luciana.*   1158
Signior *Antipholus*, I wonder much | That you would put me to this
shame and trouble,   1477
WONDROUS = *1
*but leane lucke in the match, and yet is she a wondrous | fat marriage.   883
WONT = 1
When were you wont to vse my sister thus?   548
WOONT = *1
*I beare it on my shoulders, as a begger woont her brat: 1318
WORD = 7*3
Dro. Many a man would take you at your word,   179
S.Dro. What answer sir? when spake I such a word?   408
Who euery word by all my wit being scan'd,   545
Wants wit in all, one word to vnderstand.   546
E.Dro. A man may breake a word with your sir, and | words are but
winde: 732
Ill deeds is doubled with an euill word: 806
S.Dro. Why sir, I brought you word an houre since,   1219
His word might beare my wealth at any time.   1471
And I to thee ingag'd a Princes word,   1634
Fa. Most mighty Duke, vouchsafe me speak a word: 1762
WORDS = 5*2
Mer. Yet this my comfort, when your words are done,   30
That neuer words were musicke to thine eare,   509
Ant. Villaine thou liest, for euen her verie words,   557
Anti. And welcome more common, for thats nothing | but words.   644
E.Dro. A man may breake a word with your sir, and | words are but
winde: 732
The foulded meaning of your words deceit: 823
Luc. With words, that in an honest suit might moue.   1119
WORKING = 1
Darke working Sorcerers that change the minde: 265
WORLD = 5*1
Yet that the world may witnesse that my end   37
I to the world am like a drop of water,   199
Lord of the wide world, and wilde watry seas,   295
Luci. Fie brother, how the world is chang'd with you: 547
*a *Poland* Winter: If she liues till doomesday, she'l burne | a weeke
longer then the whole World.   890
E.Dro. Nay then thus: | We came into the world like brother and
brother: 1916
WORLDS = 1
therefore to the worlds end, will haue bald followers.   501
WORSE = 6
Ill-fac'd, worse bodied, shapelesse euery where: 1126
Stigmaticall in making worse in minde.   1128
And yet would herein others eies were worse: 1132
S.Dro. No, he's in Tartar limbo, worse then hell: 1141
A Wolfe, nay worse, a fellow all in buffe: 1145
S.Dro. Nay, she is worse, she is the diuels dam: 1234

WORSHIP = 1
   If I should pay your worship those againe,   250
WORSHIPS = *1
   E.Dro. Your worships wife, my Mistris at the *Phoenix*;   253
WORTH = 2
   S.Dro. Time is a verie bankerout, and owes more then | he's worth to
   season.   1172
   A Ring he hath of mine worth fortie Duckets,   1266
WORTHILY = 1
   Worthily tearm'd them mercilesse to vs: 102
WOT = 1
   Anon I wot not, by what strong escape   1620
WOULD *see also* 'twould *l.*72 118 147 179 305 313 375 381 383 384 *430
   *494 525 624 *632 637 715 *723 *727 826 *876 *877 *878 944 945 975
   1008 1065 1129 1132 1265 *1306 1350 1393 *1449 1477 1527 1553 1748
   1749 = 31*10
WOULDST *l.*508 529 *677 = 2*1
WRACK = *1
   Ab. Hath he not lost much wealth by wrack of sea,   1516
WRACKE = 1
   Besides her vrging of her wracke at sea,   1835
WRACKT = 1
   Gaue healthfull welcome to their ship-wrackt guests,   117
WRETCH = 2
   Fie on thee wretch, 'tis pitty that thou liu'st   1491
   A needy-hollow-ey'd-sharpe-looking-wretch;   1717
WRETCHED = 2
   A wretched soule bruis'd with aduersitie,   308
   Hast thou delight to see a wretched man   1407
WRITING = *1
   *Your owne hand-writing would tell you what I thinke.   632
WRITTEN = 1*1
   *as much to say, God make me a light wench: It is writ-|ten,   1237
   Haue written strange defeatures in my face: 1780
WRONG = 10*1
   Be it my wrong, you are from me exempt,   565
   But wrong not that wrong with a more contempt.   566
   'Tis double wrong to truant with your bed,   803
   But least my selfe be guilty to selfe wrong,   953
   Ant. You gaue me none, you wrong mee much to | say so.   1052
   Gold. You wrong me more sir in denying it.   1054
   You haue done wrong to this my honest friend,   1483
   It cannot be that she hath done thee wrong.   1607
   Beyond imagination is the wrong   1677
   Haue suffer'd wrong. Goe, keepe vs companie,   1888
WRONGD = 1
   Abbesse. Most mightie Duke, behold a man much | wrong'd.   1813
WRONGS = 3*1
   Ad. Vnfeeling fools can with such wrongs dispence: 379
   By the wrongs I suffer, and the blowes I beare,   635
   Whil'st to take order for the wrongs I went,   1618
   Albeit my wrongs might make one wiser mad.   1694
WROUGHT = 2
   Was wrought by nature, not by vile offence,   38
   The villaine is ore-wrought of all my monie.   262
Y = *7
   Dro. And he will blesse y crosse with other beating: 355

Y *cont.*

    *Thinkst y I iest? hold, take thou that, & that. *Beats Dro.*   418
    *If y skin were parchment, & y blows you gaue were ink,   631
    *Dost thou coniure for wenches, that y calst for such store,   656
    **Adr.* Who is that at the doore y keeps all this noise?   707
    **E.Ant.* Iustice (sweet Prince) against y Woman there: 1673

YARE = *1
    **E.An.* Y'are sad signior *Balthazar*, pray God our cheer   638

YEA = 2
    Ant. Yea, dost thou ieere & flowt me in the teeth?   417
    That he did plead in earnest, yea or no: 1106

YEARE = 1
    Dro. I buy a thousand pound a yeare, I buy a rope. | *Exit Dromio*   1003

YEARES = 5
    Her sober vertue, yeares, and modestie,   751
    In seuen short yeares, that heere my onely sonne   1790
    Fa. But seuen yeares since, in *Siracusa* boy   1801
    Duke. I tell thee *Siracusian*, twentie yeares   1807
    Thirtie three yeares haue I but gone in trauaile   1890

YEELD = 2
    Transforme me then, and to your powre Ile yeeld.   827
    To yeeld possession to my holie praiers,   1339

YEELDING = 1
    And yeelding to him, humors well his frensie.   1368

YEERES = 1
    At eighteene yeeres became inquisitiue   128

YEILD *see* yeeld
YEILDING *see* yeelding

YES = 1*2
    **S.Dro.* Yes, to pay a fine for a perewig, and recouer | the lost haire of
    another man.   469
    **S.Dro.* Oh yes, if any houre meete a Serieant, a turnes | backe for verie
    feare.   1168
    Mar. Yes that you did sir, and forswore it too.   1488

YET = 15*4
    **Mer.* Yet this my comfort, when your words are done,   30
    Yet that the world may witnesse that my end   37
    Yet the incessant weepings of my wife,   73
    Merch. My yongest boy, and yet my eldest care,   127
    Hopelesse to finde, yet loth to leaue vnsought   138
    Yet will I fauour thee in what I can;   152
    I see the Iewell best enamaled | Will loose his beautie: yet the gold
    bides still   385
    **S.Dro.* The plainer dealer, the sooner lost; yet he loo-|seth it in a
    kinde of iollitie.   482
    Against your yet vngalled estimation,   763
    Prettie and wittie; wilde, and yet too gentle;   771
    Thou hast no husband yet, nor I no wife: | Giue me thy hand.   857
    *but leane lucke in the match, and yet is she a wondrous | fat marriage.   883
    **Adr.* And true he swore, though yet forsworne hee | were.   1113
    And yet would herein others eies were worse: 1132
    A hound that runs Counter, and yet draws drifoot well,   1148
    Duke. Yet once againe proclaime it publikely,   1602
    But tell me yet, dost thou not know my voice?   1781
    Yet hath my night of life some memorie: 1795
    S.Ant. And so do I, yet did she call me so: 1860

YONDER = 1*2
   An. I knew 'twould be a bald conclusion: but soft, | who wafts vs
   yonder. 502
   Ant. Come goe along, my wife is comming yon-|der. 1323
   Mar. Speake softly, yonder as I thinke he walkes. 1472
YONGEST = 1
   Merch. My yongest boy, and yet my eldest care, 127
YOU *see also* y'are = 222*78
YOUL = 1
   Good sir say, whe'r you'l answer me, or no: 1046
YOULL = *3
   S.Dro. Right sir, Ile tell you when, and you'll tell | me wherefore. 663
   Anti. Doe you heare you minion, you'll let vs in I | hope? 692
   Anti. You'll crie for this minion, if I beat the doore | downe. 702
YOUR *l*.10 *30 164 170 179 189 *195 215 217 218 230 *231 *237 240 250
   *253 *258 287 299 304 317 319 340 362 402 405 *419 423 428 429 454
   *498 544 555 562 563 605 614 621 *630 *632 *639 *640 *683 *708 *712
   *723 *725 *730 *732 734 747 749 750 752 757 763 765 794 795 799 803
   810 *815 *818 823 827 828 842 *843 844 864 *876 961 *962 967 1006
   1010 *1011 *1023 1030 1035 *1040 1070 1072 1081 1090 *1203 1217
   1241 1307 *1325 *1328 *1335 1337 *1344 1356 1431 1433 *1449 1479
   *1562 1564 1579 *1608 1610 1641 1656 1688 1728 1757 1766 1767 1855
   1870 *1900 *1902 *1903 1906 = 83*43
YOURS = 2
   Or I shall breake that merrie sconce of yours 244
   E.Dro. I haue some markes of yours vpon my pate: 247
YOURSELFE *see* selfe
YOUTH = 1
   I see by you, I am a sweet-fac'd youth, 1910
YOUTHFULL = 1
   A sinne preuailing much in youthfull men, 1519
& *l*.*351 417 *418 *631 *640 *886 *935 *1497 1600 *1909 = 2*8